Filmmakers Series
edited by
Anthony Slide

1. *James Whale,* by James Curtis. 1982
2. *Cinema Stylists,* by John Belton. 1983
3. *Harry Langdon,* by William Schelly. 1982
4. *William A. Wellman,* by Frank Thompson. 1983
5. *Stanley Donen,* by Joseph Casper. 1983
6. *Brian DePalma,* by Michael Bliss. 1983
7. *J. Stuart Blackton,* by Marian Blackton Trimble. 1985
8. *Martin Scorsese and Michael Cimino,* by Michael Bliss. 1985
9. *Franklin J. Schaffner,* by Erwin Kim. 1985
10. *D. W. Griffith at Biograph,* by Cooper C. Graham et al. 1985
11. *Some Day We'll Laugh: An Autobiography,* by Esther Ralston. 1985
12. *The Memoirs of Alice Guy Blaché,* trans. by Roberta and Simone Blaché. 1986
13. *Leni Riefenstahl and Olympia,* by Cooper C. Graham. 1986
14. *Robert Florey,* by Brian Taves. 1987
15. *Henry King's America,* by Walter Coppedge. 1986
16. *Aldous Huxley and Film,* by Virginia M. Clark. 1987
17. *Five American Cinematographers,* by Scott Eyman. 1987
18. *Cinematographers on the Art and Craft of Cinematography,* by Anna Kate Sterling. 1987
19. *Stars of the Silents,* by Edward Wagenknecht. 1987
20. *Twentieth Century-Fox,* by Aubrey Solomon. 1988
21. *Highlights and Shadows: The Memoirs of a Hollywood Cameraman,* by Charles G. Clarke. 1989
22. *I Went That-a-Way: The Memoirs of a Western Film Director,* by Harry L. Fraser; edited by Wheeler Winston Dixon and Audrey Brown Fraser. 1990
23. *Order in the Universe: The Films of John Carpenter,* by Robert C. Cumbow. 1990
24. *The Films of Freddie Francis,* by Wheeler Winston Dixon. 1991
25. *Hollywood Be Thy Name,* by William Bakewell. 1991
26. *The Charm of Evil: The Life and Films of Terence Fisher,* by Wheeler Winston Dixon. 1991

27. *Lionheart in Hollywood: The Autobiography of Henry Wilcoxon*, with Katherine Orrison. 1991
28. *William Desmond Taylor: A Dossier*, by Bruce Long. 1991
29. *The Films of Leni Riefenstahl*, 2nd ed., by David B. Hinton. 1991
30. *Hollywood Holyland: The Filming and Scoring of "The Greatest Story Ever Told,"* by Ken Darby. 1992
31. *The Films of Reginald LeBorg: Interviews, Essays, and Filmography*, by Wheeler Winston Dixon. 1992
32. *Memoirs of a Professional Cad*, by George Sanders, with Tony Thomas. 1992
33. *The Holocaust in French Film*, by André Pierre Colombat. 1993
34. *Robert Goldstein and "The Spirit of '76,"* edited and compiled by Anthony Slide. 1993
35. *Those Were the Days, My Friend: My Life in Hollywood with David O. Selznick and Others*, by Paul Macnamara. 1993
36. *The Creative Producer*, by David Lewis; edited by James Curtis. 1993
37. *Reinventing Reality: The Art and Life of Rouben Mamoulian*, by Mark Spergel. 1993
38. *Malcolm St. Clair: His Films, 1915–1948*, by Ruth Anne Dwyer. 1997
39. *Beyond Hollywood's Grasp: American Filmmakers Abroad, 1914–1945*, by Harry Waldman. 1994
40. *A Steady Digression to a Fixed Point*, by Rose Hobart. 1994
41. *Radical Juxtaposition: The Films of Yvonne Rainer*, by Shelley Green. 1994
42. *Company of Heroes: My Life as an Actor in the John Ford Stock Company*, by Harry Carey, Jr. 1994
43. *Strangers in Hollywood: A History of Scandinavian Actors in American Films from 1910 to World War II*, by Hans J. Wollstein. 1994
44. *Charlie Chaplin: Intimate Close-Ups*, by Georgia Hale, edited with an introduction and notes by Heather Kiernan. 1995
45. *The Word Made Flesh: Catholicism and Conflict in the Films of Martin Scorsese*, by Michael Bliss. 1995
46. *W. S. Van Dyke's Journal: White Shadows in the South Seas (1927–1928) and other Van Dyke on Van Dyke*, edited and annotated by Rudy Behlmer. 1996
47. *Music from the House of Hammer: Music in the Hammer Horror Films, 1950–1980*, by Randall D. Larson. 1996
48. *Directing: Learn from the Masters*, by Tay Garnett. 1996
49. *Featured Player: An Oral Autobiography of Mae Clarke*, edited with an introduction by James Curtis. 1996

50. *A Great Lady: A Life of the Screenwriter Sonya Levien*, by Larry Ceplair. 1996
51. *A History of Horrors: The Rise and Fall of the House of Hammer*, by Denis Meikle. 1996
52. *The Films of Michael Powell and the Archers*, by Scott Salwolke. 1997
53. *From Oz to E. T.: Wally Worsley's Half-Century in Hollywood—A Memoir in Collaboration with Sue Dwiggins Worsley*, edited by Charles Ziarko. 1997
54. *Thorold Dickinson and the British Cinema*, by Jeffrey Richards. 1997

Thorold Dickinson and the British Cinema

Jeffrey Richards

Filmmakers Series, No. 54

The Scarecrow Press, Inc.
Lanham, Md., & London
1997

SCARECROW PRESS, INC.

Published in the United States of America
by Scarecrow Press, Inc.
4720 Boston Way
Lanham, Maryland 20706

4 Pleydell Gardens, Folkestone
Kent CT20 2DN, England

Copyright © 1997 by Jeffrey Richards

First published as *Thorold Dickinson: The Man and His Films*,
London, Croom Helm 1986

All rights reserved. No part of this publication may be reproduced, stored in a retrieval system, or transmitted in any form or by any means, electronic, mechanical, photocopying, recording, or otherwise, without the prior permission of the publisher.

British Library Cataloguing in Publication Information Available

Library of Congress Cataloging-in-Publication Data

Richards. Jeffrey.
    Thorold Dickinson and the British cinema / Jeffrey Richards.
        p.   cm.—(Filmmakers series : no. 54)
    Rev. ed. of: Thorold Dickinson. c1986.
    Filmography: p.
    Includes bibliographical references and indexes.
    ISBN 0-8108-3279-8 (cloth : alk. paper)
    1. Dickinson, Thorold—Criticism and interpretation.
I. Richards, Jeffrey. Thorold Dickinson. II. Title. III. Series.
PN1998.3.D485R53   1997
791.43'0233'092—dc21   97-3065
                                                                CIP

ISBN 0-8108-3279-8 (cloth: alk. paper)

∞™ The paper used in this publication meets the minimum requirements of American National Standard for Information Sciences—Permanence of Paper for Printed Library Materials, ANSI Z39.48-1984.
Manufactured in the United States of America.

In memory of

Thorold and Joanna
Dickinson

CONTENTS

Introduction to the U.S. Edition		xi
Preface to the First British Edition		xiii
1	Dickinson's Philosophy of Film and Method of Work	1
2	Early Years and Influences	22
3	First Features: *The High Command, Spanish ABC,* and *The Arsenal Stadium Mystery*	39
4	Victorian Values: *Gaslight*	60
5	Tracts for the Times: *The Prime Minister* and *The Next of Kin*	75
6	Emergent Africa: *Men of Two Worlds*	97
7	Machiavellians and Mephistophelians: *The Queen of Spades*	122
8	'Films of Value to Humanity': *Secret People, Hill 24 Doesn't Answer, Power among Men*	135
9	Dickinson and Film Education	159
Conclusion		169
Filmography		177
Select Bibliography		181
Index of Film Titles		185
General Index		189
About the Author		195

Introduction to the U.S. Edition

The British cinema has always operated in the shadow of Hollywood. 'The entire earth is being unconsciously Americanized by the American movie picture. . . . America is swamping the world' was not written yesterday, though it might well have been. It was said in 1924 by the *Morning Post* and is a measure of the problem that has perennially bedevilled the cinema industry in Britain—how to cope with the overwhelming popularity of American films and how to create a distinctively British national cinema.

In a stimulating recent book, *Waving the Flag* (Clarendon Press, 1995), Andrew Higson has identified the options open to British filmmakers in the cinema's heyday. He describes five different strategies, all of which have been adopted, several of them simultaneously over the years. The first is the collusion strategy, which means throwing in the towel, accepting that the public wants American films, and making money by distributing and exhibiting them. This line has consistently been taken by the section of the British cinema industry involved in distribution and exhibition, and it has brought it into regular conflict with the producers of British films and the government, which in the past, though not now, saw film as a vital means of national projection and self-promotion. The second strategy was government protection for the film industry. This has taken a variety of forms, from the introduction of a compulsory quota for British films on British screens, through subsidies and tax incentives, to the freezing of American film company funds to encourage Hollywood to produce more films in Britain. All of these initiatives have worked up to a point and helped to produce the conditions under which a viable British film industry was possible. But none of them has been continued for long enough to ensure permanent health for the industry. A wider strategy of European cooperation to compete with Hollywood, which has seen the 'Film Europa' movement of the late 1920s and the EEC initiative to produce a common audiovisual policy, has not been possible for much of this century due to two world wars, the rise of fascism, and the Cold War.

When it comes to film production, Higson sees two alternatives: direct competition with an emulation of Hollywood on the one hand, and a policy of product differentiation—making films that Hollywood either would not or could not—on the other. Both have been tried.

Gaumont British in the 1930s and Rank in the 1940s and 1950s went in for big-budget pictures, sometimes with imported American stars, aimed at an international market. The policy foundered on the companies' inability to get wide American showings, due to U.S. protectionism and the fact that often, though not always, the British films were just not as good as their Hollywood counterparts.

Higson sees three main areas of product differentiation. There are cheap and cheerful British comedies, rooted in the music hall tradition such as Gracie Fields's *Sing As We Go*. There is the 'heritage' film, with location shooting, period authenticity and an upper-class setting, such as *Comin' through the Rye*. Finally, there is the British documentary tradition with its emphasis on realism rather than escapism, education rather than entertainment. It became accessible to the general public when fused with the melodrama of everyday life, notably in a succession of wartime films like *Millions Like Us* and *This Happy Breed*.

Dickinson worked in all three areas of British filmmaking. He edited *Sing As We Go*. He made his 'heritage film', *The Prime Minister*, about the life of Benjamin Disraeli. He worked both in documentary and in documentary-melodrama (*The Next of Kin, Men of Two Worlds*). But he also sought to promote a fourth option: a British art house cinema which would explore serious, often ethical issues, in a European style (*Gaslight, Queen of Spades, Secret People*). It was the eventual failure of this option that led him to abandon his directorial career.

The struggle to create a native British cinema goes on, and many of the strategies identified by Higson are still being pursued. Filmmakers are pressing the government still for aid and assistance. What people recognize as British cinema is still represented by 'heritage' films (*Room with a View, Remains of the Day*), small-scale, documentary-style realistic dramas (*My Beautiful Laundrette, Letter to Brezhnev*), and international epics seeking—usually unsuccessfully—to emulate Hollywood (*Revolution, Memphis Belle*). No one, however, has yet taken up Dickinson's European art house option, and while Britain continues to be of two minds about its membership in the European Union, that is unlikely to change.

Preface to the First British Edition

'Forgotten film director dies', said one newspaper announcing the death of Thorold Dickinson in 1984. This gave me pause for thought. It was not literally true, for he had remained up until the end an honoured and respected figure. But it was perhaps figuratively true, in the sense that his directorial career had ended in 1953; the department of Film Studies he had founded at University College, London, had been closed down; and the cause of film education to which he had committed so much of his energy had suffered savage blows from changes in government education policy. Furthermore, no one had yet succeeded in locating Dickinson securely in the story of the British film industry and British film culture. I had undertaken a week of interviews with Dickinson on his career and beliefs during the course of a very pleasurable stay with him and his wife Joanna at their cottage near Lambourn in 1976. This was part of a research project that for various reasons I subsequently laid aside. I decided to resuscitate it and to pursue the search for Dickinson and his place in the history of the British cinema. I have endeavoured wherever possible to let Dickinson speak for himself, and so I have supplemented my interviews with other interviews Dickinson gave over the years, notably a long one published in *Film Dope*, with his articles and his book *A Discovery of Cinema*. Dr. K. R. M. Short kindly loaned me the tape of an unpublished interview he had conducted with Dickinson in 1981. Sidney Cole, Lindsay Anderson, and James Leahy generously spared the time to talk to me at length about Dickinson, and Raymond Durgnat wrote to me illuminatingly about the experience of being taught by Dickinson. Frances Thorpe kindly wrote to me about the work of the Slade Film History register and helped me with the Dickinson Papers, which were still in the process of being sorted. Anthony Aldgate, Michael Todd, Elaine Burrows, Pat Robinson, and Stephen Constantine provided valuable advice and assistance of various sorts. Barry Salt, Charles Barr, and James Leahy read earlier drafts of some of the material included here, and I benefitted from their perceptive comments and criticisms. Extracts from Thorold Dickinson's *A Discovery of Cinema* (1971) appear by permission of Oxford University Press. Film stills appear by courtesy of the Stills Division of the British Film Institute. I hope that what follows will serve to negate the headline that inspired me to take up my pen.

ONE

Dickinson's Philosophy of Film and Method of Work

Addressing a British Film Institute summer school in Bangor in August 1944, Thorold Dickinson declared, 'Fictional film production is one long struggle between commerce and art, and the director is the member of the production team who sits on the fence between the two camps. His legs dangle first on one side and then the other'.[1] Throughout his career Dickinson was in the forefront of this struggle, but his ultimate objective was not so much to reconcile the two as to subject commerce to art. He was constantly seeking alternative systems to the one in which he was forced to work. He was truly like the central figure in one of his major works, a man of two worlds. This was true in a number of respects. He was an artist forced to work in a world of commerce. He was an intellectual at large in a world of entrepreneurs. But he was also at war within himself. A born teacher, he sought constantly to educate; to raise levels of perception and appreciation of ideas, culture, and film; to promote reason, logic, argument, and analysis. But he was at the same time a romantic, drawn to storytelling as an art, to the irrational and the fantastic, to visual splendour and emotional intensity. He was drawn instinctively, on the one hand, to the atmospheric, studio-created romanticism of Marcel Carné and, on the other hand, to the unpolished, 'life in the raw' vision of the Italian neorealists. This in part explains the switchback of his career from *Spanish ABC* to *Gaslight*, from *Men of Two Worlds* to *The Queen of Spades*, from *Secret People* to *Hill 24 Doesn't Answer*. It explains both his strengths and his weaknesses, his successes and his failures. Ironically, it is the films that he took on at short notice and worked on at high intensity, relying on his instinct and emotional commitment to see him through (*Gaslight, The Queen of Spades, Hill 24*), that are among his most successful, and the films on which he laboured for years, constantly revising and rethinking and allowing his intellect full control, that are amongst his least successful (*Secret People, Men of Two Worlds*).

It is undoubtedly this inner conflict that caused him to be drawn consistently to the theme of 'secret people', something of which he himself was not consciously aware. 'Hidden in each of us is a secret person brought out by circumstances', says the preface to *Secret People*, and this could be the motto that binds together his work into a coherent *oeuvre*. In his early thrillers, it is at the level of the motivation of the whodunnit and why. But as his films became more psychologically mature and complex, they explored the working out of this 'coming out' process, something that led almost always to death or madness (*Gaslight, The Queen of Spades, Secret People,* and *Hill 24*). Only the hero of *Men of Two Worlds* escapes this fate, and even he has by the end passed through madness and faced death.

Dickinson's view of his life and his art is lucidly summarized in *A Discovery of Cinema* (1971), in which he subsumed material from many of the articles he had written over the years, incorporated his reflections on cinema's history and development, and provided a magisterial overview of the whole film culture, past, present, and future.

He made a fundamental distinction between the *movie* and the *film*:

> The *movie* is for popular entertainment. It is the product of an industry dominated by the producer in which there is no individual film-maker but a team or unit under the producer's control. The producer hires one or more writers who complete the bulk of their work before the director is engaged to work on their script. On this the rubber stamp *final* is more than a formality: the script is not to be tampered with. The director's work is done when the shooting is finished. . . . [T]he producer and editor are responsible for the final version and the director has no means of redress if he finds his intention distorted in the outcome. With their habitual precision, the French describe this kind of director (who is an interpreter like an orchestral conductor) as a *metteur-en-scène*, a term borrowed from the theatre. The movie is the journalism of cinema during its first sixty years. . . . But it survived only by lapping up the new ideas for which every showman has to look if he is not to be left behind. These new ideas were and are being tested by the pioneers and non-conformists, the film-makers (in French *réalisateurs*), whose work adorns the higher reaches of cinema and is described as *film*, the personal statement of an author who is his own producer and director. The *movie* is explicit and complete in itself. Its audience is passive. The *film* is not com-

plete: it poses implications which stimulate the audience. It involves the audience. . . . The *film* which makes demands without compromise is an acquired taste, difficult for those accustomed to stimulation by the word rather than the picture. Such a film is normally the personal statement of an artist, a film-maker, a *réalisateur*. If he is not the original author, but like Shakespeare he transmutes the ideas of another and makes them his own, he deserves to be named the author.[2]

This passage contains the essence of the Dickinsonian worldview and both explicitly and implicitly locates his intellectual position precisely. Dickinson rejects the dream-factory conveyor belt of the Hollywood tradition, as he interpreted it, with its strict producer control, its overriding aim of maximising profit, its commitment to undemanding, time-filling entertainment. His contempt for this outlook was crystallized by the fate of *Citizen Kane*: 'the only stylish and influential American film of that period', which was 'seen . . . and rejected by the mass audience'.[3] This model of filmmaking, he concluded, had predominated in the British cinema, where he found himself, a *film* man, trapped in a *movie* world. He sought liberation for himself and the British cinema in the continental tradition of art cinema, making films of ideas for discriminating audiences. It was something he sought singlemindedly to infiltrate into the British cinema, a bid that ended in the effective extinction of his career in the commercial feature filmmaking industry after the box office disaster of *Secret People*.

The admiration for nonconformists, the steeping in French critical theory, the reference to musical form, the strong commitment to the ideal of directorial control—all of them ideas present in the preceding passage—also reflect his own life and experience. He would recount with pride Patrick Hamilton's comment on *Gaslight* that it was 'a French film made in English'. To him that was the highest form of praise. His stance was, of course, profoundly and unashamedly elitist. For it centred on a dismissal of the 'passive', undiscriminating mass audience and the unimaginative hacks pandering to them. But this is an almost inevitable concomitant of embracing the high culture as opposed to the popular culture.

Historically, he saw the development of cinema as hinging on four structural factors, whose interplay signalled the advances made in cinema: the sociopolitical climate, the creativity of the filmmakers, technological innovation, and the capacity of the audience to appreciate the result. He divided film history into three phases: silent (1895-1927), early sound (1928-late 1950s), and modern sound (since the late 1950's). 'The leading participants in these three phases were all non-conformists who refused to accept conventions deriving from existing forms of entertainment'.[4] His heroes and for him the significant figures in silent film history were precisely those who were nonconformists, innovators, and searchers after universal truths: Griffith, Eisenstein, Stroheim, Flaherty, and Chaplin. He saw himself as sharing these qualities.

Dickinson was not one of those, however, who regarded silent films as the height of film art. 'The range of silent film was wide but shallow. . . . There was no depth because there was no speech, and in most cases without speech there can be no characterization except in the limited field of mime. The silent film had mastered space but it took the sound film another thirty years to conquer time, and only by the combination of these two could human character be established in depth on the screen'.[5]

Nevertheless, the visual dynamism of the Russian silent cinema, particularly the work of Eisenstein, had a profound influence on Dickinson. The second great influence was the French cinema of the thirties. But here his ambivalence becomes clear. He was a life-long admirer of Renoir: 'He wanted his films to be lifelike and few of them have the balance of the well-made film which was the norm of that time. . . . He rejected the formulae of well-made, well-balanced artifice, of theatre, of fragmentation'.[6] But at the same time Dickinson was also greatly affected by the films of Marcel Carné. In 1971 he was to reject Carné's style totally: 'Under the influence of the theatre during the late 1930's we were convinced by the films of Marcel Carné. . . . Thirty years later they carry little conviction, seem theatrical, artificial period pieces in the context of today'.[7] But this was written after the impact of neorealism and under the influence of the rejection of studio shooting, which reached its peak in the 1970s.

There has now been a return to the virtues of studio shooting, artifice, and a total reevaluation of filmmakers like Michael Powell, David Lean, and Marcel Carné, who epitomize the imaginative and creative use of the studio to project their visions of the world. The Dickinson films most valued by present-day cineastes (*Gaslight* and *The Queen of Spades*) are precisely the most 'artificial'. Carné's description of his own style as 'an invented realism, created out of nothing', is echoed in Dickinson's claim in the 1940s to be seeking 'a paraphrase of reality which will contain the essence of the real'.[8] Carné, romantic, fatalist, left-of-centre, influenced by German Expressionist cinema, the poet of doomed loves, differs from Dickinson, however, in the last resort. For Dickinson was ultimately an English moralist, and the animating passions in his films were almost never sexual passions but rather greed or political idealism. Love in Dickinson's work was usually that very English sexless quality that typified British cinema and was in Dickinson's case perhaps reinforced by his Anglican upbringing. Love was almost never the motivating factor of his films, as it was almost always of Carné's.

Dickinson was next most radically affected by the revelation after the war of Italian neorealism:

> The importance of neo-realism lies in its attitude, a new way of thinking which had evolved logically. The conventional theatricality of cinema lies in the artificiality of plot, contrived design necessitating the use of studios, and dialogue demanding experienced actors who when they achieve stardom are marketed as personalities. In neo-realism the aim is behaviour, disarmingly natural, by unknown, unrecognizable persons in front of a camera that happens to be turning at the time. They killed the formality of the theatrical film, they showed that art could exist without obvious artifice so long as the subject-matter was strong enough to hold the work together. A trivial subject cannot work in this kind of cinema.[9]

He particularly admired the description applied to them by Cesare Zavattini as 'films of value to humanity'. So Antonioni, Fellini, and Rosi, who grew out of this movement, entered his pantheon of heroes. So too did Bresson, an indication that he came increasingly to regard uncompromising intellectual integrity and visual and stylistic austerity as the ideal. 'Since he makes no concessions, one has to be in the mood to go out and meet him; he is never an entertainer. His clarity pierces and can hurt'.[10]

This led him almost inevitably to a preference for black and white over colour:

> Serious film-makers have been reluctant to use colour until their choice of subjects challenges them to do so. Their avoidance has been instinctive as much as reasoned. Superficially speaking colour is a step towards reality and certainly its judicious use is essential if you want to study surfaces. It adds a necessary dimension to factual films about people, places and processes. But this dimension exerts such a magnetic attraction for a spectator that critical perception of meanings can be seriously impaired. As in the case of music, colour should be an essential ingredient in the drama for it to be stimulating. . . . Colour is an asset to a *movie* but it can be a liability in the *film*.[11]

In technological change, he saw the film reaching its final goal, with wide screen and depth of focus permitting action to be staged in a single shot. 'Fragmentation of the image was no longer justified except in the eyes of commerce, and the deceptive, imperceptible joint of shot to shot had become a concession to inadequacy rather than an accepted convenience'.[12]

Antonioni was one of the great exponents of this new creative use of cinema's flexibility.

> He began to renounce the incident, to minimize the action which had been the chief asset and to develop introspection, reflecting the depths of his own character and experience. He is one of those rare filmmakers of whom it is true to say that before studying his films it is rewarding to study his life. It is only then, for example, that one can appreciate his sturdy balance, courage and sense of humour and look for them in his work.[13]

Dickinson had now, after years of meditating on the nature of film, argued himself into an impossible position. Why should spectators have to know something of directors' lives to appreciate their films? That is the business of the professional critic, certainly not of the moviegoer, or even the intelligent filmgoer. Here intellect is triumphing over instinct, elitism over common sense. For, as Umberto Eco has said, comprehensibility is a moral duty for the academic. It is equally true of the artist. If artists cannot communicate, they might as well give up displaying their work. There is a point at which Dickinson's much vaunted individualism and nonconformity becomes self-indulgence. Where then is the intellectual rigour?

'The New Wave', particularly the work of Godard, Malle, and Resnais, attracted his approbation, and he concluded:

> During the 1960's, the situation of cinema sharply divided the mean-minded from the generous. For the mean, it was a time when attendance at circuit cinemas and consequently the number of cinemas continued to decline. For the generous, it was the time when the art house and ciné-club movements spread all over the world and when the numbers of non-conformist film-makers proliferated to a degree unforeseen before the technical innovations of Phase Three began to become available. For the mean, Hollywood, and therefore the film in general, declined with the closing of studios and the brash intrusion of television, while for the generous the film was developing beyond

the need for artifice of studios and into the possibility of working in surroundings formerly inaccessible. For the mean, the commerce of cinema was becoming more exacting, demanding higher standards of intelligence and education than the old brigade possess. For the generous, the cinema was coming of age, a challenge no longer beneath the dignity of the fine and performing arts which are older by so many thousands of years.[14]

So only when it ceased to be a mass medium could cinema become what Dickinson wanted: an art form for the elite.

But films cost money, and Dickinson faced always the threat that the cinema would become merely the tool of television. He rejected both the free market and totalitarianism:

Under capitalism all ideas on film (talking commercially) are filtered through a minuscule caucus of business men, the establishment which controls distribution and in countries like Britain exhibition as well, and whose aim is to make money. Under Communism and Maoism a caucus always functions with the additional filter of a political censorship.[15]

At this point he pulled back from the extreme position he seemed to be advancing earlier and returned once again to the question of the audience:

The audience is the key to the possibility of the expansion of range open to the artist. Imaginative comprehension of what is on the screen gives continuing life to a creative work. A completed film can be said to exist only when it is on the screen, and non-comprehension of its ideas is as deadly to those ideas as a bullet is to a body. Artists can transmute the world for us, but the audience is the catalyst with the power to recognize their worth, and only if there is recognition of good work in this young medium will there be continuing employment of those whose work is shown. Where talent is not used and appreciated it withers away. The catalyst receives in its collective mind provocative additions to the understanding of something new or of new thoughts on old problems, a myriad repercussions. And if this adds up to exploratory thinking, it must, to have any results, be followed by action. But film criticism is rarely achieved. Just as knowledge and understanding of the long established arts is an element in education (an enrichment of our lives), so should the advantage of knowing something about and understanding cinema (and television) be included in our upbringing.[16]

It was then the traditional liberal answer, as advanced in *Spanish ABC* and *Men of Two Worlds*—education. Dickinson advocated the introduction of film education in primary schools, the promotion of an intelligent and literate film culture through the preservation, study, and discussion of films.

In conversation, Dickinson stressed that it was essential for a filmmaker to know his or her audience:

> There's an awful lot to learn about the film audience. In France, a bigger proportion of the film audience is in the Paris neighbourhood than in England is in the London neighbourhood. So whereas you can take so many more risks in France because so much of your money is coming back from an educated, cultivated audience in Paris than from all the scattered people in the countryside, here in England a bigger proportion of the public have nothing to do with London and are much less well educated and much less sophisticated.[17]

Once the filmmaker knows the audience, he or she must seek to communicate with them by appealing to their experience of life: 'the only way to make an audience not "screen conscious" is that they have sufficient experience of life to appreciate your experience of life. Those people who make films which don't take that into account are called *avant garde*. But they are not communicating'.

Dickinson recalled that he first became aware of the effect of film on an audience during the showing when he visited Birmingham during the run there of the Gracie Fields film *Sing As We Go*, which he had edited. He entered the cinema where it was showing:

> In the middle of the afternoon performance, we stood at the entrance to the circle. Gracie was just going to come in and give one of her numbers and at the moment of her entry as the music went into her song, the whole audience, up till then sitting back in their seats, suddenly went forward in their seats as one. Right through the song they sat like that and when she finished, the whole audience sat back again and relaxed, began lighting cigarettes etc. This is film stardom. This is what the distributor wants, a unanimous reaction from the audience. Because they go home and say to everyone 'You must see it'.

In his book, Dickinson revived an idea he had long been advancing, that audiences should themselves become the collective patrons of filmmakers. For he believed that the greatest problem in cinema was the promotion and exploitation of films:

> This business about promoting and making one film and then how to sell it is an awful problem. Nowadays the *avant garde* in America particularly are trying to make up cooperatives to distribute their own stuff because the ordinary distributor doesn't understand these films. Because he doesn't understand, he has no way to put any zingo into the sale. People say, 'Why don't the cinemas show them?' but there's no one to get behind them. It's like a publisher—a publisher can't sell a book he doesn't understand.

Once again, he took his model from France where Renoir's *La Marseillaise* (1938) had been financed by trade unions and Maurice Cloche's *Monsieur Vincent* (1947) by Roman Catholic social clubs. Dickinson suggested that federations of film societies commission films with subscribers paying for their tickets in advance. It was an idea that he had first canvassed in 1938 when he had seen it as a crucial expression of audience power:

> Subscribers would doubtless insist first on tabulating their dislikes and would find much ground therein for mutual agreement, as the replies to questionnaires on the subject so often indicate. Few of them would approve of the indiscriminate use of music to fill pauses in the sound track or to bolster an otherwise boring scene; they would insist on a scene being designed in an entertaining manner or the matter being put over in a different, maybe an entirely new, way. They would also demand of their experts that they study the methods which Hollywood adopts to avoid the class snobbery that is so prevalent in British films. . . . A good deal more plain-speaking would clear the ground for a statement of what the articulate filmgoer really does want.[18]

But failing this, Dickinson's final idea was for state subsidy for film production, recognizing it as an art form like opera and theatre. In proposing this, he was accepting the failure of the traditional promoters of film.

> One can talk until one is blue in the face about filmmaking as an art and so on. But somewhere along the line there has got to be a promoter, an impresario to take the burden off the filmmaker and also to take the exploitation in hand. It's these people who are missing. The problem with most promoters is that they choose to distribute only

the pictures they understand and that they feel will appeal to the audiences they represent. The only answer is to educate the distributors. This is what has been happening in America. University graduates have been going into production, distribution and exhibition. This is what ought to happen here. I remember in 1968 when I went over to the American Film Institute and I went to see the Goldwyn Studios. The studio manager received us—he was a graduate of something like Harvard, a most knowledgeable, interesting chap to talk to. Here, what do you find? These self-made chaps, awfully nice but they can hardly spell, half of them.

Dickinson reckoned it was this lack of general cultural awareness on the part of British promoters that prevented him from making more films. He tended to be looked on with some suspicion as a pillar of the 'highbrow' Film Society. He pointed to Sam Goldwyn as the sort of producer British films lacked. 'There was nothing cheap about a Goldwyn film—because he loved quality'. This love of quality was manifested in Goldwyn's choice of top-quality artists and technicians, and then leaving them to get on with the job. Dickinson felt that someone like that was needed in Britain, but no one ever quite came up to that standard.

Dickinson had been happiest working with Filippo del Giudice, head of Two Cities Films: 'Del Giudice was a very good influence. His failing was that he was not a trained film impresario. He just had the feeling for it, and he used to leave a tremendous amount to the filmmakers. But at least he gave them protection'. Del Giudice had also believed in the value of good scripts and set up a brains trust to report on all scripts submitted to Two Cities. It included Dickinson, Rebecca West, Laurence Olivier, Earl St. John, and Compton Mackenzie and was presided over by Kenneth Pickthorn. It met monthly, and Dickinson recalled that among the projects they considered was Winston Churchill's story treatment for a biographical film about his ancestor the Duke of Marlborough.

The other two potential impresarios Dickinson could point to were Michael Balcon, with whom he worked twice ('Balcon had this quality to a certain extent, but he had to be very much more careful with his money'), and Alexander Korda, for whom Dickinson never worked but with whom he had been associated in the setting up of the British Film Academy. Korda had the same concern for quality as Goldwyn, and Dickinson particularly admired *The Private Life of Henry VIII*, but he found flaws in Korda. He thought his films somehow cold, lifeless, and lacking in emotion for all their superb technical credits. He thought Korda employed too many foreigners at a time when many promising British technicians were unemployed, that he interfered far too much and preferred to surround himself with deferential figures rather than people who would stand up to him. All of this, Dickinson believed, combined to explain the lifelessness of his films.

In the absence of suitable private impresarios, Dickinson therefore concluded that the state should take on the role. He pointed to Sweden as the ideal, a country that sponsored all the developments he sought: a national film school; subsidies for filmmakers; the promotion of a film culture by archives, research, and educational study; festivals, lecture tours, and so forth; and films made relatively cheaply and aimed at intelligent audiences.

He was, of course, speaking out of his experience of ten years of film teaching at the Slade School of Fine Art (University College, London) and of his deep involvement with the film society movement. But his proposal also reflected another area of personal experience. The one period of his career in which he was working with the cultural grain rather than against it was the Second World War, which he described as

> the finest hour of British cinema . . . when an enlightened group of enthusiasts in the temporary Ministry of Information harnessed the resources of the film industry to further the war effort, ranging in output from public entertainment of an escapist or patriotic nature to private instruction on every conceivable topic. . . . [The Ministry's argument was] that while the propaganda film is invaluable, the skilful film of entertainment has the double advantage of diverting the native and impressing the foreigner as evidence of British morale. The film division was given control of all negative film which was made available to producers only after approval of each script. This veto, intelligently applied, raised the quality of the British product without removing the element of competition from the lack of which a nationalized output is liable to suffer.[19]

Like so much of Dickinson's book, this argument bristles with paradox. The man who makes *The Queen of Spades*, a film of which he is very proud and which is the quintessence of studio artifice, soundly rejects that whole mode of filming in favour of an austere realism. The man who dismissed Hollywood for its producer-dominated conveyer belt of mindless movies praises Samuel Goldwyn as the ideal impresario. The man who rejects a state-run Communist-type film industry because of political censorship and centralization advocates it in a modified form in a liberal democracy. In all these matters, heart and head, instinct and intellect are in conflict. But it was out of that conflict that his art was born.

Dickinson never ceased to hanker for the Ministry of Information even after the war, and this concept clearly lay behind his ideas when he approached Group 3, the body set up to use money from the new British Film Production Fund for training new technicians and feature directors and promoting the strength of the native industry. He wrote to John Baxter, managing director of Group 3, in 1953, outlining his plans for a proper story and research department to prepare and package ideas:

> My opinion is to tackle the problem as we tackled similar problems during the war. A certain amount of order and discipline is needed. It is useless to wait for subjects to turn up. Film makers have got to live and cannot be expected to spend time and other assets on looking for a particular kind of subject of which only a few examples can be accepted. . . . If Group 3 were to develop an idea that goes beyond the scope of its physique, it would be possible to sell the proposition to a studio of appropriate size and resources. But the main policy should be to develop less conventional subjects on a scale modest enough to give them a chance to pay their way. They should not be modest imitations of films that are better made elsewhere. They should be refreshingly different. And they should be conceived and developed with this policy in view.[20]

The sort of projects that Dickinson had in mind are revealing and instructive:

> Few people realize that quite a proportion of the British Empire was reluctantly acquired and administered as a direct result of the humane desire to abolish slavery. To keep out the slavers, the British had to step in. This is a subject that has never been tackled in England. Yet abroad our Imperialism is invariably regarded as the result of greed. Regarding modern subjects, I suggest you approach the public relations officers of ministries, professions, industries and firms which organize export trade and the import of raw materials to put you in touch with key personalities who have the imagination to recount anecdotes and experiences as well as to give information about current enterprises. Regarding theatre and ballet there was a scheme to do a film about the Old Vic with Dame Edith Evans as Lillian Baylis. Could this be taken over? Has research been done into dramatizing the achievements of Dame Ninette de Valois or Margot Fonteyn?[21]

Baxter replied to the effect that they could not afford to set up such a department but that they would be happy to consider any definite proposal Dickinson might wish to put forward.[22] Dickinson seems not to have pursued the matter. However, he lived long enough to see the emergence of Channel 4 as just such a patron of intelligent films for discriminating audiences as he had envisaged.

It is clear that Dickinson viewed cinema in terms of a progressive upwards curve from theatricality to realism, from studio to location shooting, from narrative to nonnarrative structures, from the mass audience to a selective audience. The attainment of these goals was the ideal. They were regarded as absolute virtues when he was teaching and writing. But since his retirement, the pendulum has swung back again, and a new generation of filmmakers, raised on the products of the 'Golden Age of Hollywood' and the British cinema's 'finest hour' (the 1940s), has returned to the freedom to create that studio artifice gives, eschewing documentary realism, *cinema verité*, and a non narrative approach, something that Dickinson would surely have viewed as perverse.

Nevertheless, Dickinson was an early exponent of the concept of the 'director's cinema', believing firmly in the director as the shaping intelligence of the film. He expounded his ideas at length in *Sight and Sound* in which he coined the term *filmwright* to apply to the creative director, a term overtaken by the French *auteur*. In the article, he castigated the Hollywood cinema in which producer and writer had a greater influence than the director, and he downgraded the role of the writer:

> The creative writer seldom has the patience to master the elements of cinema to the full. But if he has any experience in writing dialogue, he can ensure that his intentions are carried out by failing to render his story in visuals and by taking the easier course of telling the story in dialogue only. Here he is enthusiastically supported by the narrow-minded among the economists. It takes far longer and costs far more to visualize a story on the screen than to grind it out in endless talk. There is no doubt that a writer is more interested in the speaking of his dialogue which is a direct expression of his talent, than he is in any interpretation which the director may give to his descriptions of visual action.[23]

He explained the decline in quality in Carné's postwar films over his prewar films by suggesting that the director had become subordinate to his writer, Jacques Prévert, and lost his creative freedom. For Dickinson the true creator was always the director, the filmwright:

> The art of the sound film lies in creating a performance which the articulate audience is satisfied can exist in no other medium. Firstly, the story clearly and simply carried, in the main, through visuals, beautiful or ugly as the drama demands, apt movement or action within each shot, progress through sharp rhythmic conflict from shot to shot, visuals that are more than moving pictures, visuals that convey meanings and that stir emotions by the significant selection of acting, use of background, use of light and shade, visuals in two dimensions but consciously contrived to suggest a third dimension. Secondly, the story pointed and commented on by a harmonious contrast of sound, all manner of sounds on which the filmwright rings the changes as his imagination dictates. Principally, there is dialogue to reveal character by conversation which often can be quite effectively irrelevant to the direct progress of the story. There is a place for the witty, the finely composed and for the apparently ineffective. Stupid words and a halting delivery can convey a peak of tragedy on the screen. In a sound film the way the words are spoken is as important as the words themselves.[24]

The article provoked a reply from the eminent Hollywood screenwriter Howard Koch, who stoutly affirmed the creative role of the writer:

> It seems incontrovertible to me that the writer is the primary creative source. He puts down on paper the significant symbol, visual as well as auditory, through which character is revealed in a progressive series of definitive tensions. It is the writer's imagination that first previews . . . the substance of what eventually appears on the screen.[25]

Koch pointed to William Wyler as his ideal type of creative director:

> Besides his sensitive appraisal of dramatic values and his abundant technical resources, he displays an unswerving allegiance to the true line of every story he is putting on film. . . . In the preparation period he never tells a writer what to write—he has too much respect for the creative process—but he is relentless in pushing the writer to a fuller realisation of the story he set out to tell. Once on the set Wyler further enriches the action that was preconceived in the script by his meticulous attention to every detail of the production.[26]

Koch clearly sees the director as sympathetic interpreter rather than primary creator. Dickinson replied in brief in the letter columns of

Sight and Sound, but he was championed elsewhere by two of the young lions of the new generation of cineastes.[27] Lindsay Anderson in *Sequence*, while conceding that the role of the screenwriter was generally undervalued, came down firmly on Dickinson's side of the argument:

> When it comes . . . to talking in general terms, Mr. Dickinson shows himself truly and firstly a man of the cinema. His emphasis on the expressive potentialities of film technique is the result of a proper realisation that what a film says should be inseparable from the way it says it. This striving towards integrity in the creative process is the reverse of Mr. Koch's attitude, who is more concerned to preserve the integrity of his script than to see it assembled into a new thing, an original film.[28]

The same view was endorsed by Karel Reisz, in his seminal work *The Technique of Film Editing* (1953):

> Whatever the precise nature of the producer-director-writer-editor relationship which obtains on any film, the essential condition would seem to be that the ultimately controlling mind should conceive and execute the continuity in primarily visual terms, in terms of the choreography and editing of visually telling strips of film. In practice this means that the director should normally be in charge. It is he who is responsible for planning the visual continuity during shooting and he is therefore in the best position to exercise a unifying control over the whole production.[29]

Not surprisingly, Anderson and Reisz were to become leading practitioners of the 'director's cinema' during the 1960s.

Dickinson expounded his ideas about directorial control in a six-part radio series *A Film Is Made* that he cowrote with Roger Manvell and in which he took the part of the director.[30] The film project was a typical Dickinson choice, a short novel by Turgenev, *The Torrents of Spring*, which Dickinson insisted should be preserved against unnecessary rewriting and should retain its unhappy ending. It was to be filmed with an Anglo-Italian cast, using continental locations and studio work in England. Once again Dickinson made clear the director's ultimate responsibility for the script: 'It is the director who steers the pictures and sounds to link together into a satisfactory continuity. . . . The actual writing of the shooting script is always done under the director's control, if not by the director himself'.[31]

During his career, Dickinson came as close as possible to being the complete *auteur* or filmwright of his theory. For he worked on the scripts of almost all his films, directed, controlled casting, supervised editing, and worked closely with art directors, cinematographers, and composers to achieve the effects he envisaged.

As he told the BFI Summer School in 1944:

> I am one of those who believe that the true function of the director begins with or immediately after the choice of subject and ends only with the delivery of the first positive copy of the film to the public cinema. Nor should a director allow a subject to be thrust upon him. . . . A good script is one which edits the subject before production. A good deal of nonsense is talked about the editing or mounting of sound films. This nonsense is a hangover from the silent film. The bulk of directors of silent films worked from quite a rough script. They did not predetermine the balance of their dramatic values. They shot their action in many different ways and only in the cutting room did they determine the dramatic form of their film. To my mind it is unwise to predetermine on paper the exact visual composition of a film, whether sound or silent. But you can, in a sound film, determine in their proper order the dramatic values you want to express, and you can exactly set out the bulk of dialogue and sound effects . . . In the early days of the production the vital element begins to develop. Sometimes it startles you. You make an experiment in tempo—and how important timing is!—you work out some deliberate movement of the camera to bring out a value in a melodramatic scene, which emphasizes the story point and avoids the danger of over-dramatizing. The art of selection does not stop with the completion of the script. Far from it. Selection and emphasis are the two great assets of the positive use of the camera, particularly in the true film which does not rely on dialogue to make its every point. Selection, emphasis and timing count heavily in the direction of the players. So many of them are accustomed to the technique of the stage, where they project their personalities out through the full width of the proscenium arch into the furthest limits of the gallery. Who is their audience in the film studio? Their director, who is to them the living representative of the camera lens. All other elements in the studio, human and mechanical, must in the moments of creative work subordinate themselves to that one personality. Pity the director who falters, who is unsure. The whole structure totters. The director controls the player's performance, keeping it in check, throttled down almost to an unbearable extent unless the players are highly disciplined and utterly trusting—until the climaxes come, one by one, more and

more intensely as the story proceeds. In those climaxes the director relaxes the restraint to build the tension before the fade out. . . . Close collaborator with the director at this stage is the editor, who assembles the material shot in rough order and shows it to the director as a guide to the future evolution of the film. Another close collaborator is the art director who works ahead of the unit, providing the backgrounds within which the drama is played. . . . Through all the turmoil of such a production, someone must be in control. Someone must keep in mind through a period of considerable mental and physical strain a precise image of the balance of dramatic values, necessary to make every story point clear on the screen. When intentions fail to materialize, someone must be there to substitute an alternative means of presenting an idea. That person should work from a plan of his own and should control the editing of the production. That is the film director.[32]

It all began with the script, and Dickinson worked with or without credit on the scripts of all his films except *The Prime Minister*. In almost all of the films, he would also improvise on the set and alter plot and dialogue where necessary to accommodate bits of business thought up on the spot or, in the case of location shooting, to fit the action to the place he was working in. For instance, the final landing and battle in *The Next of Kin* were worked out on location in Mevagissey in conferences with the army liaison officer, the production manager, and officers of the regiment loaned by the War Office to play the attacking force. The only occasion when he eschewed the freedom to improvise was during *Gaslight*. His plan for this film was to work out an absolutely precise shooting plan, which would not be deviated from and which would allow the built-in nervosity of the subject and the tension of the actors to play off against the perfectly regulated shooting.

He would also call in the cinematographer, art director, and composer as early as possible. He liked to have the cinematographer in to discuss his plans for the lighting and for any elaborate visual devices. In *Gaslight*, for instance, he wanted to have the dimming of the gaslight done in long shot to get the effect of the room darkening. But cinematographer Bernard Knowles proclaimed this impossible and so Dickinson had to have an insert of the lamp dimming each time it happened. His most rewarding relationship was, he felt, with Otto Heller, who photographed *The High Command* and *The Queen of Spades*. He had a special rapport with Heller, who instinctively grasped what he wanted, and together they worked out the dazzling visual effects of *Queen of Spades*.

NOTES

1. British Film Institute (BFI), *Film Appreciation and Visual Education*: (London: BFI, 1944) p. 3.
2. Thorold Dickinson, *A Discovery of Cinema* (London: Oxford University Press, 1971), pp. 3-5.
3. Ibid., p. 75.
4. Ibid., p. 8.
5. Ibid., p. 35.
6. Ibid., p. 69.
7. Ibid., p. 6.
8. A Two Cities Films publicity handout, BFI Thorold Dickinson microfiche.
9. Dickinson, *A Discovery of Cinema*, p. 80.
10. Ibid., p. 84.
11. Ibid., p. 108.
12. Ibid., p. 109.
13. Ibid., p. 111-112.
14. Ibid., p. 121.
15. Ibid., p. 135.
16. Ibid., p. 137.
17. This and all subsequent unattributed quotes are from interviews conducted with Thorold Dickinson by the author, April 8-12, 1976.
18. Thorold Dickinson, 'Why Not a National Film Society?', *Sight and Sound* (Summer 1938), pp. 75-77.
19. Dickinson, *A Discovery of Cinema*, p. 77.
20. Letter from Thorold Dickinson to John Baxter, June 15, 1953, Dickinson Papers.
21. Ibid.
22. Letter from John Baxter to Thorold Dickinson, June 23, 1953, Dickinson Papers.
23. Thorold Dickinson, 'The Filmwright and the Audience', *Sight and Sound* (March 1950), p. 21. The same ideas are also explored in Thorold Dickinson, 'The Third Eye', ed., John Sutro, *Diversions* (London: Max Parrish, 1950), pp. 170-77.
24. Dickinson, 'The Filmwright and the Audience', p. 25.
25. Howard Koch, 'A playwright looks at the "filmwright"', *Sight and Sound* (July 1950), p. 211.
26. Ibid.
27. *Sight and Sound* (November 1950), p. 303.

28. Lindsay Anderson, 'The Director's Cinema', *Sequence* 12 (Autumn 1950), p. 11.
29. Karel Reisz, *The Technique of Film Editing* (London: Focal Press, 1958), p. 58.
30. Thorold Dickinson and Roger Manvell, 'A Film Is Made', ed., R. Manvell and R. K. Neilson Baxter, *The Cinema 1951* (Harmondsworth: Penguin, 1951), pp. 9-56.
31. Ibid., pp. 22-23.
32. BFI, *Film Appreciation and Visual Education* pp. 4, 6, 9-10, 14.
33. Sir Arthur Bliss, *As I Remember* (London: Faber, 1970) p. 168.

TWO

Early Years and Influences

Thorold Dickinson was born on November 16, 1903, the son of the Archdeacon of Bristol, the Venerable Charles Henry Dickinson, and Beatrice Vindhya (née Thorold). He claimed descent both from Lady Godiva and Thorold the dwarf of the Bayeux Tapestry. He was educated at Clifton College, Bristol, and at Keble College, Oxford, where he studied history. But he devoted more time to college theatricals and to his burgeoning interest in film than to his academic work. He became resolved to work in films after seeing the German Expressionist classic *The Last Laugh* at Oxford, and he achieved his ambition sooner than he had anticipated, for, although due to take his finals in 1925, he was held back for a year for spending too much time producing college plays.

One of his friends at Keble was Malcolm Pearson, son of George Pearson, one of the leading British filmmakers of the day, and through Malcolm, Dickinson got to know George. George Pearson, forced by financial problems to close his English studio, had set up a production in France, a comedy *Mr. Preedy and the Countess*, which was to be shot with a largely British cast at the Eclair Studios in Epinay near Paris and in the Abel Gance Studios at Billancourt. George Pearson invited Dickinson to join the unit as interpreter and jack-of-all-trades. He began eagerly to pick up the rudiments of filmmaking, learning everything that Pearson had to teach. He recalled later that Pearson was 'a born and generous teacher. Until Film Schools were invented you could not have had a better guide than George Pearson. His gentleness, his firmness, his abiding sense of humour—I could go on for hours'.[1] It is clear that Pearson had an enormous influence on Dickinson, not only in the technical side of filmmaking but in his attitude to teaching. Dickinson's description of Pearson anticipates Sidney Cole's description of Dickinson as teacher and guide to him.

Dickinson was also fascinated to watch the films being shot alongside Pearson's comedy at Billancourt. They were Abel Gance's *Napoleon* and Viatcheslav Tourjansky's *Michael Strogoff*, two of the most memorable products of French cinema in those years. For his part, Pearson, impressed by Dickinson's 'deep interest and understanding of the film medium', invited the young man to join him on his next project.[2] This was to be a vehicle for the Brazilian actress Mona Maris, star of *Mr. Preedy* and protégée of the wireless pioneer Guglielmo Marconi, who was willing to finance a film starring her. Pearson rapidly abandoned the 'appalling novel' that he had originally intended filming and set out with Dickinson to write an original screenplay about a family of travelling puppeteers, called *The Little People*. As Dickinson recalled:

> We visited an old puppet theatre in Milan and studied behind the scenes. We wrote together and separately, and before the script was finished George had to go back to London and I went to Paris, each of us to go on organizing the production at the same time. There was no international telephone and we corresponded by cable. In a week or two George lined up the cast and the unit and the costumes, writing all the time. My great coup was to assemble the puppeteers and persuade André Derain to lend us his priceless collection of eighteenth century puppets. The art directors were to be Alberto Cavalcanti and Erik Aes. But they could not begin work immediately, so I designed or rather dictated to the studio art department the first set, a cottage interior which had to have a revolving ceiling for the sequence where Frank Stanmore as the old puppeteer got plastered. I went on writing minor scenes for the script. I also functioned (as before) as French interpreter to the entire unit. There were no trade unions in those days and hours were long. The whole film including exteriors on the French Riviera was made for around £8,000. Alas! It was a resounding flop because it was unprecedented, as a British film; there was no art house movement in those days.[3]

After this heady experience of filmmaking, Dickinson returned to Oxford, received his B.A., and started looking for work in the film industry. But film production in Britain was at a low ebb. His family, who did not approve of his filmic interests, wanted him to work in Kenya. But Leslie Banks, who as a former Keble College student had taken an interest in the college plays and had got to know Dickinson, arranged for him to get a job as stage manager with the Lena Ashwell players at Notting Hill Gate. Then the passing of the Cinematograph Films Act in 1927, with its compulsory quota for British films, dramatically revived film production, and Dickinson went to work again for George Pearson, who was now producing for his Welch-Pearson Company at the Stoll Studios, Cricklewood. He was assistant director on Pearson's production of John Buchan's *Huntingtower* and then was asked to edit a Spanish story, *Love's Option*. 'I made a terrible hash of my first job . . . and George with his habitual courtesy and patience recut the whole film at night while preparing his next production'.[4]

At this point the British film industry was overtaken by another of its major upheavals—the arrival of sound—and it plunged Dickinson into another of what were to become regular experiences for him of film salvage. Pearson had produced a silent film, *Auld Lang Syne* (1928), with Harry Lauder. But Paramount said that they would only take the film if it was converted to a part-talkie and Lauder sang his own songs. This presented Dickinson and Pearson with a major problem:

> Originally the songs were supposed to be accompanied by the cinema orchestra, and with sub-titles. . . . And so with a viewing machine and the gramophone records, we synchronized all the songs. Took us weeks and weeks because when these scenes were shot, the camera had been hand-cranked which, of course, is not as regular as electrically motivated camerawork. What we did was to take an optical print and on the edge of each shot I put dots in red ink to show how many times the frame was to be photographed again. Normally, you did one frame with one dot on it, the next frame with two, and this stretched it to sound speed. But because it had been hand-cranked, sometimes you had to put three dots, sometimes you had to leave a frame out to make it stay in sync. I laboriously did the handwork on about 2,000 feet of optical print, which was a hell of a job. George took the film to Paramount in Hollywood and they walked into the screening, saying it was impossible and by the time the show was over, they'd bought the rights. . . . It's probably the only film to have been synchronized in that way.[5]

In 1929, Dickinson found himself out of work again, as the studios wired for sound. Pearson was forced to travel to Hollywood to produce *Journey's End*, the smash-hit R. C. Sherriff play, to which he and his partner Tommy Welch had bought the rights. Pearson could not afford to take Dickinson with him but gave him letters of introduction to film people in New York. Dickinson spent September-November 1929 studying sound techniques and audience reactions to sound, and on his return to England, again with a recommendation from Pearson, he got a job in the cutting rooms at Herbert Wilcox's British and Dominion Studios, Elstree, where he worked with and learned from Duncan Mansfield, the chief editor at Elstree, and earned £12 a week, £4 more than he had been getting with Welch-Pearson. He recalled the excitement of being in on the birth of the new techniques:

> In those days, they lined up four cameras side by side, loaded with 1,000 feet of negative film and one sound recorder also with 1,000 feet of sound negative. And this constituted the sound of one reel of the film. It was never edited and re-recording was unknown. When we got the rush prints the next morning, we just matched the positive image with the sound, cutting from camera strip to camera strip. Nobody dared to put scissors into the sound track. The result was known as a canned play. Then they imported from Hollywood this strange idea about overlaying tracks and mixing them, re-recording them together. I was the editor assigned to what are called tenant pictures, made by people who hired the studio. Wilcox had all the cream of the talent of the studio and the tenants had people like me! So when this apparatus came in, where you turned over one camera as in a silent film and each shot had its own soundtrack, they decided to try it out on an unsuspecting tenant. I remember getting all this stuff and instead of having these great rolls, you had little rolls, synchronized with numbers on the edge . . . and I thought, well, what fun, this is much better, you can alter the timing and everything now . . . got entirely immersed in this and I looked up suddenly and there was the whole staff of the cutting room and some of the management, all standing round watching. So, of course, we were able to mix six other sounds onto the soundtrack and the real sound film began. That was early in 1930.[6]

While he was at Elstree, Dickinson edited Maurice Elvey's *The School for Scandal* (1930), Victor Saville's *The Sport of Kings* (1931), Sidney Morgan's *Contraband Love* (1931), and two Carmine Gallone musicals, *Going Gay* and *For Love of You*, made, respectively, in 1930 and 1931 but not released until 1933. But then he parted company with Elstree: 'I was fired for being satirical about somebody on the staff'.

He returned to Stoll Studios at Cricklewood, where Sinclair Hill was in charge of production, and there edited Hill's productions *Other*

People's Sins (1931) and *The Great Gay Road* (1931) and an eight-episode British-made Universal serial *Lloyd of the C.I.D.* (1931). It was at Stoll that Dickinson first met Sidney Cole, who was to become a close friend and associate and received his cinematic education from Dickinson, whom he described as 'a very kindly person . . . a born teacher'. Five years younger than Dickinson, he had joined the film industry in October 1930 at Stoll Studios, as a reader in the story department, later became a second assistant, and then joined Dickinson in the cutting rooms. The atmosphere at Stoll seems to have been creative and sympathetic, and when the studio closed in 1938, Cole penned an affectionate obituary in *Ciné-Technician*:

> I would like to pay tribute to its method of working in those days when Sinclair Hill was director of productions. Before a picture went on the floor they had a script conference. This too often merely means four or five people agreeing as hard as they can with the producer. And nowadays having any script conference at all seems to be an obsolete custom. All the more honour to the Stoll units of those days who had *real* script conferences.
>
> The complete script was read through by the scenario editor (Leslie Howard Gordon) to the entire unit. The technicians affected by any special scene could discuss its exact details with the director and with each other in advance, and everybody went on the floor, knowing exactly what the picture was about. . . . But perhaps even more important, these circumstances meant that the unit went on the floor as a unit, as a team, with a sense of working together to produce as good a picture as they collectively could make.[7]

When Hill moved to the Tobis Studio, Wembley, to direct an independent production, *The First Mrs. Fraser*, in 1932, Dickinson went with him to edit it, and he also edited Himansu Rai's *Karma* (1932), the first sound film recorded in Urdu and produced by a British company set up to tap the vast cinema potential of the Indian subcontinent.

After this, Dickinson was called in by Captain Hon. Richard Norton, head of United Artists' British productions, to perform yet another rescue job on the expensive romantic drama *Perfect Understanding*, which was to be Gloria Swanson's comeback film, starring and produced by her and costing £150,000. Shooting had begun under the experienced director Rowland V. Lee on the Riviera, with the leading male role, Swanson's husband, being played by her real-life spouse Michael Farmer. But Farmer had not proved a good enough actor to sustain the part and so production was halted, as Swanson had the script rewritten, recast Farmer in a supporting role, and signed Laurence Olivier, who was returning to England from Hollywood after his screen career failed to take off there. Swanson and Lee quarrelled, and he left the production to be replaced by the inexperienced Cyril Gardner, who, Norton recalled, 'turned out to be so frightfully high strung, with some nervous digestive trouble, that he would collapse in a corner of the studio after almost every take'.[8] Half the cast was struck down by a virulent form of flu, expensively prolonging shooting, and eventually money ran out before the end of the production. Dickinson was faced with the task of retrieving what he could from the footage already shot. This involved a speedboat race, which in the original version the husband won but which he now had to lose ('I went to work on this. It was the sort of thing I enjoyed enormously, and putting in a "scene missing" caption occasionally for close-ups and so on, I managed to make an unknown character win the race'.) He also dubbed new dialogue over close-ups of Swanson to bridge gaps in the story.

The finished film was a box office flop. But it had been filmed as an independent production at Ealing Studios, and Reg Baker, the joint managing director of Ealing, was so impressed with Dickinson's rescue job that he invited him to join the editorial staff at Ealing, where he remained until 1936 working on productions for Associated Talking Pictures (ATP), who owned the studio, and tenant productions leasing facilities there.

Many of the films Dickinson worked on in the 1930s epitomize what was wrong with British cinema in those years and explain why mass audiences stayed away from them in droves. But they all provided valuable experience for Dickinson to master the technical side of his work and sometimes to experiment. Bowled over by Eisenstein's montage effects, which he had seen at Film Society showings, he sought to emulate them in some of the films he worked on. 'I loved it', he recalled. 'I used to put elements of that into British films.' In particular, he sought to liven up the films of Basil Dean, 'who knew nothing about cinema and directed films like theatre. In those days the editorial relief was the montage sequence which we used to introduce after a long dialogue scene for visual relief. A montage sequence was like a cadenza in a concerto. I used to enjoy making them'.[9] He certainly deserved some relief from the diet of tosh he was having to work on.

The First Mrs. Fraser (1932) was a tiresome, interminable screen version of St. John Ervine's celebrated stage play, about the marital and extramarital problems of the leisured upper class, displaying a smart, cynical attitude to sex and divorce. It starred an ageing, stagey Henry Ainley and a young Joan Barry, overacting grotesquely. Despite a few outdoor location scenes and a lavish, saucily engaging but largely irrelevant nightclub sequence featuring Billy Cotton and his band, Frances Day, and Naunton Wayne, *The First Mrs. Fraser* was essentially a static piece of 'canned theatre', notable only for ham-fisted direction and stilted acting. But the nightclub sequence set Dickinson some problems, as Sidney Cole, who was an assistant on the picture, remembered:

> In those days, you didn't have playback and you didn't have the prerecording or dubbing process which we subsequently had. Consequently in the cabaret sequence in *The First Mrs. Fraser*, Thorold had to work out as the editor with the director how long each scene that was being filmed during the music took, so that you could know which piece of music would actually be played during the recording of that dialogue scene. Then of course you had to work out what other shots could be taken, that you could cut away to, to bridge any places where that didn't quite work, so that you could lay a few frames of picture over the bars that weren't right in direct recording.[10]

Perfect Understanding found Dickinson in similar territory, dealing with adulterous high jinks among the idle rich in Mayfair, the Home Counties, and the Riviera. Here the inventive McKnight Kauffer titles, Dickinson's tight editing, and a charismatic appearance by Laurence Olivier fail to compensate for the unremarkable script, the obtrusive score, and the anonymous direction. But the rescue job that Dickinson performed on the speedboat race footage proved adequate recompense in terms of challenge.

Typical of the products of Dean's regime at Ealing were *The Impassive Footman* (1931) and *Loyalties* (1933). Both were based on stage plays, the former by 'Sapper' and the latter by John Galsworthy, and were shot by Dean as straight theatrical transcriptions. In the former, however, Dickinson experimented with the effect that he had seen in Alexeieff's short film *Night on a Bare Mountain*, the visual effect produced by a 'screen of movable pinheads, in which visual compositions melt insensibly into each other'. In *Loyalties*, he filmed the climactic suicide of Captain Dancy, who throws himself from the window of his Park Lane flat after he has lost the criminal libel case that he has brought against the Jew who accused him of theft on a country weekend. Dickinson had the outside of the window and the side of the house built on an endless roller. He had a man tied to a trapeze and photographed him being dropped, as the side of the building revolved. Then he took a second unit to Park Lane, tied an Eyemo camera to a steel rope, and dropped it from the roof, to capture the falling man's whirling view of Park Lane as he fell. The two sequences were then intercut, and Dickinson's reward was the gasp of astonishment from 1,200 people at the trade show at the Cambridge Theatre.

Java Head, which Dickinson edited, he had also to complete when the American director J. Walter Ruben fell ill and returned to Hollywood. He shot the ending, a few inserts, and montages. The result was nevertheless appalling, a very bad adaptation of Joseph Hergesheimer's novel about rival sailing ship dynasties. Cheaply done, on a handful of cramped and threadbare sets, it had no feel of the sea, utilizing merely a couple of studio deck sets to represent the great sailing ships. A usually reliable cast (Edmund Gwenn, Ralph Richardson, John Loder, etc.) could make no headway against a stilted, cliché-ridden screenplay and flat, static direction, and the film was wholly lacking in epic sweep, dramatic tension, and period feel.

More satisfying artistically were the films that Dickinson edited for Phoenix Films, a company formed to produce low-budget quality films with a particular emphasis on first-class photography. Their first film, *Death at Broadcasting House* (1934), which Dickinson did not edit, cost only £16,000 and won critical plaudits for its ingenious story, unique settings, and excellent cinematography.

The company rented facilities at Ealing, and Dickinson was assigned to edit their next two productions. Both films were directed, as was *Death at Broadcasting House*, by Reginald Denham, who Dickinson described as 'an unpretentious, disciplined and efficient director'. The same might be said of the two films Dickinson edited for him. *The Silent Passenger* (1935) was a Lord Peter Wimsey detective story, admirably photographed by Jan Stallich and including atmospheric location shooting at Liverpool St. Station and the LNER [London North-Eastern Railway] Engineering Works at Stratford. *Calling the Tune* (1936) was a rather thin story about skullduggery in the gramophone record industry, chiefly remarkable for its behind-the-scenes glimpses of the famous (George Robey, Sir Henry Wood, Sir Cedric Hardwicke, etc.) making their recordings.[11]

Perhaps Dickinson's greatest success as an editor was *Sing As We Go* (1934), the Gracie Fields musical that Basil Dean had shot partly on location in Blackpool. Dickinson was handed the cans of film and asked to have it ready for showing in forty-two days. He worked from 9 A.M. to 11 P.M. every day for five weeks, eventually moving into the studio, sleeping in the viewing theatre, and not leaving its confines for the last two weeks. The result was Gracie Fields's best film, which Dickinson improved by speeding up a fairground chase sequence, and adding an inventive travel montage and a sharply cut montage of the cotton mills at work.

For all the worthlessness of most of the films he worked on during these years, Dickinson learned his editing craft and set himself high standards. What he learned in the cutting rooms as he laboured on these largely forgettable productions he never forgot. He had wax-pencilled on his cutting room walls some warnings for overoptimistic film directors:

> It can't be done optically.
> The music won't improve it.
> It won't look better on the big screen.

All were excuses he had heard over the years for bad directorial technique. Sidney Cole recalled, 'He couldn't tolerate anything except devotion to the job in hand and integrity in doing it'. But his attitude to editing was in part influenced by his life-long passion for music. His reference to montage as a 'cadenza' indicates the importance of musical form to his filmic thinking, Sidney Cole remembered:

> He once defined editing, the putting together of pieces of film, as being like the way in which the basic steps are put together in classical ballet to achieve something new, a different story, a different mood, and so on. Although the steps are all basic, they are put together in different combinations to achieve different results.[12]

In examining other directors' films at close quarters Dickinson learned lessons that stood him in good stead when he came to make his own directorial debut. First, there was his desire to keep exposition to a minimum, not to overload a film with 'matter'. In retrospect, he felt that his first feature *The High Command* had 'too much matter', story threads raised and dropped (Carson's inheritance, Heverill's mess funds deficit, Mrs. Cloam's extramarital relationships, etc.). On the other hand, *Gaslight* had none of this excess matter.

> There is no point in *Gaslight* where one is feeding the audience with information that is not essentially dramatic. Whereas *The Queen of Spades* has all these sequences at the beginning. You've got to know these things before the film can get airborne. I always used to talk about a film getting airborne and I think that *Gaslight* got airborne

from the opening shot. It took straight off. Whereas *The Queen of Spades* went hopping along the ground for several reels until finally you could say 'Thank God, we can take off'. Another thing, you have to watch carefully in the construction of a film is that you don't have to refuel the plane before you finish— take on new information to get you through to the end.

Again, *The High Command* was guilty of this. Dickinson was quite clear that a story must be told with a limited amount of 'matter': 'I've always thought that a long short story was the ideal shape for a film— the novella—what the French call a "'nouvelle'".

This concentration on the narrative thread was to influence Dickinson's visual style. He was above all anxious that the audience should not become 'screen conscious', aware that they were watching a film. So he would refrain from inserting too many close-ups. He would do conversations in medium shot with the two people speaking in the shot; it was, he says, 'more natural, richer'. It allowed the audience to absorb what they were saying without distraction. It recalls John Ford's advice: 'Give them a scene, then give them scenery', but don't mix up the two. Dickinson kept the close-ups for the dramatically intense moments. For instance, he was very proud of the enormous close-up at the end of *Gaslight*, in which Anton Walbrook goes mad. It is the emotional climax of the film and lasts a minute. Dickinson begins it in silence, lets it run on until he thinks the impact is made on the audience, then brings in the music and carries on the shot to its full length, providing the audience with a double jolt.

Blending in with the technical training of the cutting rooms, there was the creative and aesthetic influence of the Film Society.[13] The Film Society had been founded in 1925 to promote a serious interest in the art of film, and it showed uncut imported prints of German, Russian, French, and experimental films. The films were free of censorship, were regularly reviewed in the newspapers, and were distributed to other societies by a non-profit-making releasing organization set up by the Society. The list of its founding members gives a good idea of its place in the intellectual life of the period, including Lord David Cecil, Roger Fry, John Maynard Keynes, J. B. S. Haldane, Julian Huxley, Augustus John, E. McKnight Kauffer, George Bernard Shaw, John Strachey, Ellen Terry, and H. G. Wells. It had originally a governing council of six, consisting of Ivor Montagu, Hugh Miller, Frank Dobson, Iris Barry, Sidney Bernstein, and Walter C. Mycroft.

Dickinson joined the Society while still at Oxford and in 1930 took over technical presentation of the programmes, selecting and titling prints and supervising projection. He remained in charge until 1939 when, on the outbreak of war, it was Dickinson who closed the Society down, because the import of continental films was now impossible. Dickinson brought in fellow editors Sidney Cole and Ray Pitt to help in the technical work, and in 1932 he joined the governing council, which was expanded over the years to include Anthony Asquith, Ellen Wilkinson, John Grierson, Sidney Cole, Robert Herring, Basil Wright, and Elsie Cohen. Dickinson became very friendly with Professor Jack Isaacs of King's College, London, another Council member who wrote the programme notes and to whom Dickinson supplied technical data.

Dickinson, working by day as a humble editor, became at weekends one of this glittering circle of intellectual luminaries, 'a curious double existence', he called it. But he happily immersed himself in the continental classics being imported by the Society: German Expressionist works like *The Cabinet of Dr. Caligari, Raskolnikov, Joyless Street,* and *Nosferatu* and the great Russian silents such as *Battleship Potemkin, October, Mother, Earth,* and *Storm over Asia,* for instance. Films like these were to leave their imprint on the visual style of *The Queen of Spades,* and in 1948 Dickinson was to collaborate with Catherine de la Roche on the book *Soviet Cinema.* He contributed the section on silent film.

Many experimental films, the so-called 'absolute' films, used shapes, patterns and lines to create abstract effects. In particular there were films that sought to interpret music in abstract visual forms: *Pacific 231*, based on Honneger's music, Alexeieff's *Night on a Bare Mountain, Valse Mephistophilis* based on Liszt, and *Prelude in C Sharp Minor* based on Rachmaninov. These excited Dickinson to the extent that in 1936 he set up a project called *Facts and Fantasies*, with his own money, to finance the production of a programme of short films made by such figures as Len Lye, Basil Wright, Lotte Reiniger, and McKnight Kauffer. But the scheme collapsed during the 1937 film slump.

The most potent cinematic influence, however, on Dickinson was the French cinema of the 1930s. By the time he took over technical presentation at the Film Society, the great ages of Russian and German filmmaking were coming to an end, and during the 1930s the 'quality' films were largely French. The Russian cinema under Stalinism, the German under Nazism, and the Italian under Fascism were all being artistically stifled. But from France came the films of Carné, Feyder, Renoir, and Duvivier, all of which proved a revelation to Dickinson. When he began directing himself, he consciously adopted ideas and techniques from the French directors.

Dickinson, meeting Renoir in Berlin during these years, discussed with him his policy of shooting films in real buildings where he could and, where he could not, shooting window shots in real buildings so that real life could be seen going on behind the action of the film. This led directly to Dickinson in *Secret People* locating Serge Reggiani's lodgings in a building overlooking the main railway line into Paddington.

But Dickinson was particularly impressed by Marcel Carné, an admiration that had a direct effect on the form and style of his own films, as Barry Salt noted:

> In continental Europe long takes had often been used by film-makers right through the 'thirties, and this continued to be the case in the 'forties. As before these long takes were mostly done with fairly conventional staging of the action, and only a certain amount of camera movement. In England, on the other hand, where nearly all directors had used fast cutting through the thirties, the new American fashion for the long take had hardly any effect. Right at the end of the decade one or two directors such as David Lean briefly flirted with this approach, but after a couple of years they returned to their usual faster cutting. The only British director to pursue an interest in the long take right through the nineteen-forties was Thorold Dickinson, from *Gaslight* to *Secret People* (1950). In his particular case the original inspiration came from *Hôtel du Nord* (1938), and other Marcel Carné films, but though these films were highly regarded in England at the end of the 'thirties, there is no other sign of their influence on British cinema.[14]

Many of the people Dickinson was involved with in the Film Society, notably Sidney Cole and Ivor Montagu, also became involved in the running of the Association of Cinematograph Technicians (ACT), the cinema technicians' union. The ACT had been founded in spring 1933 by a group of technicians at the Gaumont British Studios, Shepherd's Bush, because of poor pay and long hours. It was initially not very successful, with an ineffectual general secretary (Captain Matthew Cope) and a small membership of about eighty. But when Dickinson joined, he and a small group of sympathetic activists galvanized it into action. They organized a vote of no confidence in Cope and his replacement by George Elvin, honorary secretary of the British Workers' Sports Association and son of the former Trade Union Council (TUC) President H. H. Elvin. George Elvin was to remain the union's secretary for forty years. He had been recommended to Dickinson by his younger brother Harold Elvin, working then in the Art Department at Ealing Studios and a prominent Film Society member, and Dickinson initially guaranteed half his salary after his appointment as general secretary.

It was Dickinson who suggested that the union should have a journal, and so *Ciné-Technician* was launched, with a cover designed by Joanna Dickinson, Thorold's wife. Dickinson was to contribute articles to it regularly over the years. In 1936 Dickinson became vice-president of the union, a position he held until 1953. As a result of these moves, the union's reputation and influence rose, and by 1936 its membership had risen to over 1,000.[15]

Dickinson was next instrumental in persuading Anthony Asquith to become president of the union in 1937 and to lead the union's campaign during the debates about the renewal of the film quota. Asquith was invaluable, as Dickinson later recalled:

> Not only was Anthony Asquith most energetic and resourceful, for he knew most of the ministers—or, if he didn't, they at any rate knew who he was; but his mother Margot, plunged into the fray too. She used to invite members of the government—Neville Chamberlain was Prime Minister at the time—to lunch in her house at 44 Bedford Square. The President of the Board of Trade was there and . . . oh! a lot of them at different times—and she had her son Anthony and George Elvin and me and some other members of A.C.T. there to meet the ministers and explain how the film crisis could be overcome. More than that, if the ministers weren't prepared to accept our arguments, she went for them, denounced them for not having the sense to see how important films were to the country, for they did not just entertain, they educated the public and showed the world what Britain was able to do. She was a stalwart fighter—a crusader in fact — and we owed a great deal to her.[16]

The ACT lobbied, petitioned, and pressured the Moyne Committee, which was reviewing the Cinematograph Films Act, and as a result managed to get safeguards for wages and working conditions written into the act, as well as a cost test, to eliminate quota quickies and restrictions on foreign technicians. So some success was achieved in the bid to revive the British film industry after the disastrous slump of 1936-37.

In 1937, Dickinson and Alan Lawson went as fraternal delegates from the ACT to attend the May Day celebrations in Russia. During their four-week stay, they visited studios, cinemas, the Film Training Institute as well as museums, the ballet, a tractor plant, and the Moscow Municipal Slaughterhouse. They interviewed Pudovkin and Dovzhenko. On their return, they wrote a detailed account of production, distribution, and exhibition of films in the U.S.S.R. for the *Ciné-Technician*.[17]

Dickinson's trade union activities raise the question of his political stance. A life-long Labour Party voter, a trade union activist, a maker of fund-raising films for the Republican cause in Spain, close associate of many avowedly left-wing figures, a stalwart of the Film Society with its left-wing flavour, friend of Communists such as Ivor Montagu and Sidney Cole, it would be very logical to assume that Dickinson was at the very least a Socialist. But he himself denied this. He was never active in party politics: 'I've never been a politician. I've never studied the techniques and practices of politics'. His decision to join the union and turn it into something more active and influential than it had been was more a product of personal experience than political dogma:

> After finishing *Java Head* and immediately being asked by Baker (the managing director of Ealing Studios) to get *Sing As We Go* ready for a trade show 42 days ahead, I worked on it, spending the final two weeks in the studio and never going out. I had my annual leave after that—two weeks paid holiday—and I was feeling so ill that I sent them a telegram saying 'I am staying away for an extra week' and when I got back, Baker said I could take the third week but they couldn't pay me for it. So they just cancelled my week's salary although they knew I had been working for 140 hours a week for two weeks and about 100 hours a week for several weeks before that. Something snapped and I went off and joined the Union.

Thereafter, Dickinson became strongly committed to improving conditions for his fellow technicians in the industry. His motive force, then, was hatred of injustice. This was one of the reasons that he undertook the trip to Spain to make a propaganda film on behalf of the Republicans. He characteristically chose to cover the Republican government's educational and cultural policies. He also wanted to do something to keep his filmmaking hand in. The visit to Russia in 1937 was prompted by his desire to study the film industry and filmmaking techniques of Russia rather than any interest in or sympathy with Communism.

Dickinson was first and foremost perhaps an intellectual. His bookshelves, with their complete runs of *Horizon* and *Penguin New Writing* and the novels of Graham Greene, Evelyn Waugh, Iris Murdoch, and Joyce Cary, proclaimed his adherence to a particular strand of English cultural life. He was a teacher and educationalist, seeking to import civilized and humane values and to raise the level of the public's appreciation of art, in particular cinematic art. He was, if anything, a middle-class liberal progressive, opposed to the extremism of right and left. When pressed, he grudgingly accepted Raymond Durgnat's description of him as a moralist. He admitted that his greatest political motive force had been the hatred of extremism, snobbism, and intolerance. It is this view that most forcibly explains his politics, his union activities, and the message of his films.

In assessing the influences on Dickinson, it is important not to forget his wife Joanna. Dickinson's cinematic testimony, *A Discovery of Cinema*, acknowledges his debt to her and she was also credited as cowriter and coeditor on his last feature film, *Hill 24 Doesn't Answer*. Her influence on and importance to him throughout his career was fundamental. An architect by training, she shared Dickinson's intellectual interests, his sense of humour, his forthrightness, and his hatred of snobbism and injustice. She was fiercely protective, some have suggested overly so, both of Dickinson and his career. They married in 1929 and remained life-long companions until her death in 1979. Throughout his life, she provided assistance and support to his work, contributing ideas, research, constructive criticism. She was also a perceptive critic in her own right, as her piece on Gracie Fields in *World Film News* testifies.[18]

Rather less of an influence than might have been supposed was the British documentary movement. Dickinson was always rather dismissive of the 'documentary boys':

> I am one of those who had documentary thrust upon them. I did not take it up by choice. In fact, when I first went into films in the pre-Grierson days of 1925 the word *documentary* was merely the lonely adjective of the noun *document*. In those days there were entertainment films, newsreels, cartoons, and interest pictures which were largely geographical. My first working contact with documentary was in the mid-thirties when I guided John Grierson to cut 25 minutes out of *BBC—the Voice of Britain* after his distributor had rejected it on the grounds that it was 'all knobs and washing'. Then I persuaded Associated Talking Pictures, for whom I was editing fiction films at Ealing Studios, to take over the distribution. I stayed with story films, except for ten weeks in republican Spain in 1938, until I went to work on five-minute propaganda films for the Ministry of Information and on training films for the War Office in 1941. . . . I went back to story films until a third war, the Arab-Israel conflict of 1948 triggered a film which blended fiction with fact, *Hill 24 Doesn't Answer* (1955). By this time my bent for fiction was broken and at the invitation of the United Nations Secretariat I took charge of their film production in 1956, convinced that Grierson's creative interpretation of reality was a bigger and more exciting challenge than the pursuit of pipe dreams.[19]

It is clear from this and comments he made in conversation that he was at best a reluctant documentarist until the United Nations beckoned, and his experience with them was to prove a further disillusioning experience.

It was the cinematic orthodoxy in intellectual circles in the 1930s and 1940s that since the coming of sound only two notable movements in cinema had occurred: the rise of British documentary in the wake of Grierson's *Drifters* and the 'sudden flowering of French cinema between 1935 and 1940 with the appearance of such films as *La Kermesse Heroique, Carnet de Bal, Hôtel du Nord* and *Quai des Brumes*'.[20] It is evident that Dickinson located himself firmly in the latter tradition and set out to make intelligent and dramatic stories in a visually elegant and eloquent fashion, which would raise both the intellectual and aesthetic level of the British cinema of his day.

NOTES

1. Thorold Dickinson, 'Working with Pearson', *The Silent Picture* 2 (Spring 1969), p. 6.
2. George Pearson, *Flashback* (London: George Allen and Unwin, 1957), p. 141.
3. According to Pearson, the film cost £9,000. His account of the filming of *The Little People* is in *Flashback*, pp. 140-43.
4. Dickinson, 'Working with Pearson', p. 6.
5. *Film Dope* 11 (January 1977), pp. 3-4.
6. Ibid., p. 4.
7. Sidney Cole, 'A Studio Passes', *Ciné-Technician* 4 (November-December, 1938), pp. 117-118.
8. Richard Norton (Lord Grantley), *Silver Spoon* (London: Hutchinson, 1954), pp. 163-164.
9. *Film Dope* 11, p. 5.
10. Author's interview with Sidney Cole, May 15, 1985.
11. On Phoenix Films, see Reginald Denham, *Stars in My Hair* (London: T. Werner Laurie, 1958), and Jeffrey Richards, 'Death at Broadcasting House', *Focus on Film* 26 (1977), pp. 46-47.
12. Author's interview with Sidney Cole.
13. On the Film Society, see Ivor Montagu, *The Youngest Son* (London: Lawrence and Wishart, 1970); Adrian Brunel, *Nice Work* (London: Faber Robertson, 1949), pp. 112-116; Caroline Moorehead, *Sidney Bernstein* (London: Jonathan Cape, 1984), pp. 21-29; *The Film Society Programmes 1926-39* (New York: Arno, 1972).
14. Barry Salt, *Film Style and Technology: History and Analysis* (London: Starword, 1983), pp. 292-293.
15. J. Neill-Brown, 'Pioneers', *Ciné-Technician* 4 (July-August 1938), pp. 48-49, and Rachael Low, *Film-making in 1930's Britain* (London: George Allen and Unwin, 1985), pp. 17-32.
16. R. J. Minney, *'Puffin' Asquith* (London: Leslie Frewin, 1973), pp. 90-91. On the battle for the quota, see Margaret Dickinson and Sarah Street, *Cinema and State: The Film Industry and the Government 1927-85* (London: BFI, 1984).
17. Thorold Dickinson and Alan Lawson, 'Film in the USSR—1937', *Ciné-Technician* 3 (August-September 1937) pp. 95-111.
18. Joanna MacFadyen, 'Gracie's Artistry Reflects the Psychology of the Masses', *World Film News* 1 (June 1936), p. 5.
19. *A.I.D. News* 3 (November 1972), p. 6.
20. Ernest Lindgren in BFI, *Film Appreciation and Visual Education* (London: BFI, 1944), p. 46.

THREE

First Features: *The High Command*, *Spanish ABC*, and *The Arsenal Stadium Mystery*

From his earliest days in the industry, Dickinson's desire had been to direct, and during the 1930s he took steps to break into that area of activity. He devised two story treatments and offered them to studios with the suggestion that he should direct them, but no one showed any interest. The first was a comedy thriller that he worked on with Peter Haddon, star of *The Silent Passenger*, which he had edited for Phoenix Films. The second was a drama, based on a newspaper item that he had read about the captain of a freighter who put two stowaways adrift in an open boat. The latter treatment, *You Can't Leave a Man to Die*, interested Dickinson sufficiently for him to revive it as a proposal in 1953. But there were still no takers.

His chance came, however, in 1936. Gordon Wellesley, script editor and scenario chief of Associated Talking Pictures (ATP), formed his own company, Fanfare, with the blessing of Basil Dean, who agreed to provide production facilities at Ealing. Wellesley obtained the screen rights of Lewis Robinson's novel *The General Goes Too Far* but ran into immediate trouble with the censors, to whom it was submitted with a view to screen adaptation. One proclaimed it

> a thoroughly objectionable story showing officers of the British army in a most offensive and objectionable light. Two are shown as murderers, and a third, Haverill, was certainly contemplating it. Morals are lax and the character of the Colonial Governor as a vindictive prosecutor of private spite is very objectionable. Another officer is shown as embezzling public money to support an expensive mistress. I strongly advise that the proposal to film this book be abandoned.[1]

Wellesley's wife, Katherine Strueby, was able to prepare an acceptable screenplay, however, that modified the objectionable elements sufficiently to ensure censorial approval. Wellesley offered the direction of *The General Goes Too Far*, as the film was known in production, to Dickinson. As he recalled in 1944:

> I always asked myself: when someone offers me my first job of direction with the subject already chosen, shall I gamble on being able to hide my ignorance of a possibly unfamiliar background or shall I turn the offer down? When the chance came, the background turned out to be West Africa. And the script was half-written. My heart sank. It was now or never. So I was canny. I influenced a number of exterior scenes into the script, persuaded the producers to pay for a modest location trip, learnt something of my background on the trip and gradually wormed a good deal of rewriting into the script as a result of our experiences. I know the results justified that research.[2]

When Dickinson proposed the location trip to Africa, ATP thought the idea ridiculous. But Wellesley backed the proposal, and eventually it was agreed that a small unit would go to West Africa to shoot some location footage, mainly long shots, using locally selected doubles, and all of it silent, so that sound equipment would be unnecessary. They would also study local colour, take research stills, and bring back props and costumes. The film was due on the floor at the start of November 1936, and a four-man unit left England at the end of August: Dickinson, the director; John Seago, the production manager; James E. Rogers, the location photographer; and Gordon Wellesley, the producer.

A two-week journey by ship from Liverpool took the unit to the Gold Coast (now Ghana), and then it was overland to Nigeria, a further two weeks spent on a 2,000-mile railway journey. The unit spent two weeks filming in Lagos and a further week inland in southern Nigeria. The plan was to complete a journey of some 11,000 miles in eight weeks, during which 16,000 feet of film was to be shot—enough for the location scenes of *The General Goes Too Far* and for a two-reel documentary short on Nigeria. There was obviously no point in wasting the trip to Nigeria.

The jobs to be done were divided up: the producer took the art direction and publicity stills and made contact with the civil and military authorities; the cameraman, who had worked in West Africa before and was familiar with tropical conditions, took charge of the camera equipment and film, the director shot the back projection plates, atmosphere shots, and long shots with locally selected doubles, and the production manager handled finance and commissariat. Working conditions were gruelling. All of the team suffered from fever at one time or another, and Wellesley went down with malaria. They would rise at 6:30 A.M., and work outdoors between then and 1:00 P.M., filming being resumed in the late afternoon. The middle of the day was impossible for shooting. The early onset of the rains kept them there a week longer than intended, and Dickinson finally flew back to London instead of sailing, as originally planned.

The Colonial Office had read and approved the script and generously made facilities available. The unit was allowed to film at Elmina and Christiansborg Castles, as well as around Lagos and up country at Kano. Dickinson was well pleased with the results: 'Our production was enriched by a number of invaluable shots and a great deal of authentic detail work in settings, story points, acting and general atmosphere, which we could never have injected into the film by merely having a gang of "experts" and working in their views second hand'.[3]

The 'local colour' footage was indeed to furnish two notable sequences. A tribal dancing sequence was integrated with studio footage to provide the background to a confrontation between the general and his blackmailer, and a montage sequence was created in which the faces of the principal characters were superimposed over scenes of activity in the colony to create a feeling of life in the fictional Port Mamba: General Sangye's face over scenes of drilling soldiers, Diana Cloam's over scenes of hospital visiting, Major Carson's over a polo game, trader Cloam's over scenes of a marketplace and shipping, and sergeant Crawford's, nose wrinkled disapprovingly, over the scenes of fruits and meats in the market. Although the naturalism of the location shooting does not meld wholly effectively with the more stylized, atmospheric lighting of the studio scenes, the location scenes do nevertheless add an authentic feel that enhances the mood of the film.

The bulk of the film was shot at Ealing, so Dickinson had no control of casting. Wellesley imported the British-born Hollywood star Lionel Atwill to play the general, to make the proposition attractive to the American market. He also signed James Mason on the recommendation of his friend, cinematographer James Wong Howe, who had been impressed by Mason's 'presence' during the filming of *Fire over England*. Dickinson found his cast charming to work with and recalled with particular pleasure the contributions and cooperation of the emigré continental actors Lucie Mannheim and Steven Geray.

The director did advise on cameraman. Dickinson had long admired the work of the Czech cinematographer Jan Stallich, particularly on *Ecstase*, which he had seen at the Film Society, and he engaged Stallich to shoot the interiors. After a week, however, Stallich wished to depart for another project and recommended his protegé Otto Heller to take over. Dickinson agreed; Heller worked with Stallich for a few days and then took over completely. The two were in such harmony that their lighting work dovetailed perfectly, and Dickinson developed a tremendous respect for Heller's work. He was very pleased with the finished film from the lighting point of view.

Naturally, Dickinson supervised the editing himself, but he invited his friend Sidney Cole to cut the film. Cole was excited and impressed by the film: 'It wasn't the ordinary sort of putting a few dialogue scenes together like I'd been accustomed to up to that time at British International where a lot of things were straightforward adaptations of stage plays. This was much more cinematic.' He remembered in particular the African dance sequence ('A lot of quite interesting rapid cutting') and the very visual opening in Ireland ('From Thorold, I learned the axiom I've always tried to convey— that film is a visual medium and therefore try and tell what is most important through visuals; the soundtrack is a decoration, an embellishment and goes into detail. But you should be able more or less to understand a picture by looking at the visuals'.).[4] The entire project was completed for a mere £30,000. But the title was changed to *The High Command* by Basil Dean.

The plot of the film is pure 'Sapper', resembling very strongly that host of short stories about 'The Breed', the behaviour of officers and gentlemen under stress in far-flung outposts of the Empire. It is a genre of stories that has its counterpart in thirties cinema in films such as *The Last Outpost* and *Another Dawn*. The film opens in Ireland in 1921 where Major John Sangye shoots in self-defence during an IRA ambush a fellow officer, Challoner, who has denounced Sangye as his wife's lover and the father of her child. Sangye passes off the officer's death as the work of the IRA. But another officer, Carson, has evidence of Sangye's guilt. The action moves on to 1937, and Sangye, now General Sir John Sangye V.C., is in command of British forces in a West African colony. Major Carson arrives in the colony, having travelled out from England with Diana, the wife of suspicious and narrow-minded trader Martin Cloam. Cloam hints at a relationship between Diana and Carson, but Diana is in fact in love with Carson's cousin, Major Jimmy Heverill. Carson courts Diana and tries to blackmail Sangye. Then Carson is found murdered, and Heverill, who is in debt and stands to inherit his money, is arrested and tried for the murder. But Diana reveals to the general that Heverill had spent the night with her and her husband had returned only at dawn. Sangye realizes that Cloam murdered Carson and has sought to frame Jimmy for the crime. However, the governor informs Sangye that the police have found the evidence of Sangye's complicity in the death of the officer in 1921 in Carson's belongings and that he is to be arrested. Sangye, wishing to spare his daughter the disgrace of the revelation and seeking also to secure justice for Heverill, tells Cloam that he knows who the murderer is and will denounce him tomorrow. That night Cloam comes to the general's quarters to plead for his life. But the general rejects his pleas and turns his back on Cloam, knowing that he is inviting death. Cloam shoots him and flees but is killed trying to escape. The governor destroys the evidence of Sangye's 1921 crime.

Taken straight, the story would be a typical 'Breed' melodrama. But it is not taken straight. It is quietly and subtly sent up, though not in such a way as to undermine the dramatic tension of the story and the climax. The decision to kid the Imperial archetypes and their behaviour was taken by Dickinson and Wellesley jointly. The abiding impression that Dickinson retained of colonial Nigeria was its snobbishness, clannishness, and elitism. He and the other members of his unit were in fact barred from the Lagos Club, because of the misbehaviour there of a previous film unit from a German company.

Dickinson was anxious to convey his disapproval of the colonial mentality that he had encountered and also to comment on the whole Imperial experience. But he did not do so at the expense of the traditional mystery and thriller ingredients of the conventional story that he had been handed. He did so by his lightness of touch and civilized amusement at the attitudes and mores of the expatriates and also in visual sequences that demonstrated the alienness of the English presence in Africa. The humour is clear early on in the film when Heverill greets Carson at the harbour with an airy 'I suppose you're all ready to share the white man's burden', and they exchange jokes about malaria.

General Sangye is played as tetchy, slightly deaf, and rather Blimpish and given a splendid throwaway exchange with the governor that irresistibly recalls Noël Coward's irreverent tribute to the *pukka sahib* tradition: 'I wonder what happened to him'.

> *Governor*: Whatever happened to old 'Stinker' Marchbanks of the Poona Horse?
> *Sangye*: He started a poultry farm in Surbiton. Calls it the 'Garden of Allah'.

The trial sequence is also done with a twinkle in the eye. The general's tetchy objection to the use of the term 'OK' by the prosecutor about what questions he will answer are actions in line with the Blimpish character already established. Then there is the 'surprise witness', Miss Tuff. Flown in specially from England, she is a diminutive, opinionated ladies' companion, with a large umbrella and an unmanageable solar topee, who resolutely refuses to give straight answers to the questions asked and is hopelessly prejudiced in favour of Heverill. She is an irresistibly funny comic creation, with an unanswerable exit line: 'Truth must out, even in a court of law'.

The darker side of colonial life is also highlighted, however. The hermetically sealed all-white community is unsparingly depicted as a handful of expatriates who all know each other and within whose ranks there is adultery, blackmail, and murder. The almost total absence of blacks emphasizes the enclosed nature of the world. When they do appear, they take the form of an ultraobsequious hotel owner in whose very servility there is an unmistakable hint of menace as he watches the comings and goings of the characters in the drama and revels in the knowledge of the secret meetings that he gathers from his position at the reception desk, and the terrified black servant Julius Caesar, bullied and hectored by the prosecutor into betraying his master.

There is also clear evidence of prejudice and snobbery in the attitude of the British to Cloam. Cloam is fussy, pompous, and self-important, but his attitude is partly a defence against the fact that he knows he is regarded as an outsider and an inferior. 'If your grand service friends want you', he tells Diana, 'they will have to put up with me'. His inferiority, partly based on his job (trader) and partly his foreignness (an implication of mixed blood), is brought home in another of Dickinson's almost throwaway touches: the military band at the British Club playing 'Little Brown Jug' derisively as Cloam's car arrives and, as he stares angrily out of the window, resuming their previous tune.

One of the best and most evocative scenes in the film suggests the fragility and vulnerability of this enclosed colonial world. It is a scene, too, that vindicates the West African trip undertaken by Dickinson, for it was his experience of a *hamatan* (the evening windstorm of Nigeria) that led him to incorporate it into the film. The scene is the British club, where the whites gather over their whiskies and sodas. The governor arrives, and as he enters the club, the band strikes up the national anthem. Everyone stands to attention. Suddenly the evening wind gets up, howling through the club, blowing the curtains forth in billows, shattering a window and setting the lights over the billiard table swaying dangerously. A servant moves forward to close the windows while the anthem is playing, but the general signals him to stay still. The fundamental incongruity of the British presence in Africa is encapsulated in those images of the officers at attention, the national anthem playing, and the wind howling through the club, precursor of the wind of change that is ultimately to sweep the British and their Imperial mission away. When the music is over, the servants bustle to close the windows and clear up the mess and life goes on. Graham Greene commented admiringly of this scene, 'British West Africa comes alive as it never did in Mr. Korda's lavish and unimaginative *Sanders of the River*'.[5]

It would be overstating the case to argue a programmatic denunciation of Imperialism in this film. But Dickinson's trip to Africa had inspired him with a love of the continent, a sympathy for African aspirations, and a dislike of racialism and expatriate snobbery. His interest in the Empire was to find fuller expression in the later and more profound *Men of Two Worlds*.

But just as the film testifies to an early interest in contemporary world problems, it also supports an *auteurist* interpretation of Dickinson's work. For it is his first exploration of the 'secret people' theme, the recurrent concern with exploring the tension created by the existence of an inner person concealed beneath the outer surface. The very title *The High Command* has a double-edged implication. The high command is, in the military sense, the general and the officer caste and, in a moral sense, the biblical commandment 'Thou shalt not kill'. Similarly, it is not just that the characters involved have secrets (Sangye and Cloam are killers, Carson is a blackmailer, Diana has a lover, Heverill's mess funds are deficient) but also that an inner person is revealed when the circumstances demand it. Diana is prepared to sacrifice her reputation by testifying that Heverill was with her on the night of the murder. Sangye is prepared to sacrifice his life to preserve his daughter from the scandal that will accompany the revelation of his murderous deed years before. Cloam is willing to sacrifice his career (significantly, we see him looking through press cuttings about his career before he sets off to murder the general) to get rid of his wife's admirers and the man who has deduced his guilt. Each of these three characters faces a moment of truth, and the secret person is revealed—the destructive force within Cloam, the self-sacrificing force within Diana and Sangye,—pointing up the essentially Manichaean worldview that underlies so much of Dickinson's work: the positive interaction of the powers of good and evil.

The High Command is a straightforward linear narrative within the traditional mystery story framework—the establishment of characters, milieux and clues and the final elucidation of the mystery. The pace of the film is careful and measured, which is perfect for the first three-quarters of the film, but it slows down at the end. Here the script calls for lengthy exposition scenes when the audience's requirement is really for the speedy winding up of the plot and the punishment of the murderer.

On the whole, however, Dickinson tells his story economically, avoiding camera trickery but using camera movement as the grammar of the narrative. In the first half of the film, there are only three close-ups: one in which Carson recognizes the bullet from Challoner's body and the consequences that flow from it; a second, a conventional romantic close-up of Diana reclining, establishing her as the centre of amatory interest; and a third in which Diana recognizes her lover Heverill as she disembarks from the ship. The close-up is being used sparingly as a point of emphasis. In the second half of the film, there are close-ups of Sangye and Julius Caesar giving important testimony at the trial. But the most important use of the close-up is the intercutting of close-ups of Sangye and Diana in the key scene in which she gives Heverill an alibi and he deduces Cloam's guilt. In story terms, the significance of the scene is that it is the one in which the 'secret people' within Diana and Sangye are released. In cinematic terms, it marks a dramatic departure from the method of shooting conversations that Dickinson has employed throughout the film—the medium two-shot with both speakers on camera, the dialogue scene being used essentially to convey important information. In the Sangye-Diana scene, it is being used to do more than that. It represents the moment of truth.

There is a similarly grammatical use of the rapid dolly-in. This is the method traditionally used to indicate the realization of something. The camera dollies in to Carson's face when he realizes that Sangye has killed Challoner, into Cloam's face when he realizes that Sangye knows he killed Carson, and into Sangye's face when he realizes that the authorities know about his involvement in Challoner's death. It is used dramatically in reverse for the farewell scene of Belinda and Sangye. On the foggy quayside of the fort, the general sends his daughter off for the evening. She is saying good-bye and expecting to see him in the morning, he is saying good-bye knowing that he is to die that night. The farewell is done in close-up, as befits the emotional intensity of the scene, and then as the general stands and waves good-bye, the camera adopting the point of view of the departing boat pulls away from the quay, emphasizing both the separation and the general's loneliness.

So the camera angle and the camera movement punctuate and emphasize the narrative. Cutting, on the other hand, controls the pace.

The opening sequence is masterly in this regard. 'Ireland—1921', says the title. The camera pans slowly across the bleak moorland to a sign reading 'Curfew'. The sign is splattered with mud, and a group of hostile locals turn out of a pub to pelt a passing army car with tomatoes as the camera pans up a sign saying 'Up the rebels'. Thus, in no more than a dozen shots, the time, place, and ambience are established. The IRA ambush is also effectively done, recalling the menace and mystery that John Ford evoked in his besieged oasis in *The Lost Patrol*. The ambush is staged in the fog, the rebels are never seen, just the flashes of their gunfire in the gloom, and then they disperse at the sight of the approaching headlights of the relief column.

Equally effective is the scene when a jungle picnic at which many of the internal tensions in the white community have become apparent is interrupted by the sound of African drums. Like the *hamatan*, it is another unwelcome intrusion of Africa into their world. There is a sudden and dramatic succession of staccato close-ups of the whites as they listen, more close-ups in a few seconds than in the previous three-quarters of an hour. Both these sudden changes of pace and style have the effect of jolting the audience upright in their seats. Then in a succession of highly atmospheric shots, mostly location work, drums beat, fires flare, the natives ride their horses through a forest of eerily spiky trees, and then they dance as the whites look on.

Apart from cutting for pace, there is cutting into montage, and several sequences indicate the influence of Eisensteinian juxtaposition. This is most noticeable in a little vignette in which Jimmy Heverill and Diana Cloam watch a bushbaby in a tree as it is struck by a waiting snake and killed and Diana falls weeping into Heverill's arms. Jimmy and Diana are the innocent bushbabies and the lurking snake is Cloam, already seen gliding through the bushes watching them. Later at the tribal dance, dramatic and vivid shots of drums and fire are intercut with high key shots of Carson's bid to blackmail Sangye. The passion and suppressed violence of the verbal encounter are thus counterpointed by the primal imagery of drum and flame.

The critical reaction to *The High Command* was generally rather lukewarm, but several discerning critics heralded the debut of an important new director. Graham Greene wrote in *Night and Day* (July 1937):

> It isn't so often that the English cinema throws up a new director of promise and when a new face does appear among the old gang, it is often greeted with rotten vegetables. That the critic of so distinguished a paper as *The Sunday Times* should dismiss Mr. Thorold Dickinson's *The High Command* in two glib sentences is rather shock-

ing. 'As for *The High Command*, this is a picture made by Fanfare, a new British film company. Its avoidance of reality and its slowness make it a first-class soporific in this sultry weather.' No one will deny that *The High Command* is full of faults. The story is wildly improbable. . . . [T]he first half suffers from a slow, jerky and obscure script. Then the sets sometimes reveal too obviously the strict economy with which the film was made. . . . The devil's advocate indeed has plenty to play with in this picture, but a film critic should be capable of distinguishing from the faults due to a poor story, an uncertain script and mere poverty, the very high promise of the direction.[6]

He went on to describe the 'the beautifully cut documentary scenes' of West Africa and the handling of some of the big scenes, which he said had 'a touch of lyrical imagination which one seeks in vain in most English films'.

Basil Wright in the *Spectator* echoed Greene: 'It is difficult to understand why this slow and overcomplicated plot should have been selected for the first production of a new company and a new and very promising director'. He praised the cast, the 'atmosphere of heat and humidity well established' and 'the well shot and authentic scenes of landscape and native life'.[7]

Jympson Harman in the *Evening News* proclaimed the film:

> an excellent murder drama built on unusual lines. . . . The film is well acted. . . . The direction of Thorold Dickinson is good in a straightforward and dramatic way, but it is a trifle too slow. . . . *The High Command* stands out miles ahead of the average independent British production.[8]

The High Command had in fact demonstrated Dickinson's distinctive characteristics: his intelligent concern with contemporary issues, his deep sense of humour, his fascination with 'secret people', and, as a filmmaker, his command of narrative, strong feel for pace and atmosphere, and visual sense. But there was no more work to follow *The High Command*. He prepared a screenplay with Peggy Thompson from Lady Eleanor Smith's novel *Ballerina*, an indication of his continuing fascination with the love of music. But the British film industry was in crisis. There had been a major financial collapse, and the industry was waiting to see on what terms the quota would be renewed. Eighty percent of the workers in the film industry were unemployed, and Dickinson devoted his energies to promoting ACT policy on the Cinematograph Films Bill. *Ballerina* was never filmed in Britain. But, in 1941, Gregory Ratoff directed a version of it in Hollywood called *The Men in Her Life* from a different screenplay. It starred Loretta Young and Conrad Veidt.

In January 1938, Ivor Montagu, Dickinson's old Film Society associate, asked Dickinson to join a unit he was taking to Spain to make three documentary films for showing to public and private meetings to raise funds for the Spanish Republican cause. Montagu's Progressive Film Institute had raised £3,000 to cover the cost of the trip. Dickinson agreed to go for two reasons:

> The negative reason was that there was a slump in film production in Britain while we all waited for the passing of the second Film Quota Act, now a year late. The positive reason was more serious. By international law the elected government of a nation has the right to buy from abroad weapons with which to defend itself and this right was denied to the Spanish Republic by the non-intervention agreement signed by France and Britain in 1936. This attempt to persuade the socialist and fascist powers to withold their support of the Government and the rebels soon proved abortive and revealed in Britain a strong bias of support for the fascists, particularly among capitalists and the wealthy by birth. In the field of cinema, only one newsreel, Paramount News, ever showed an item from the Republican side. The other four competed for items from rebel territory. Newspapers were equally biassed.[9]

This very precisely articulated view distances Dickinson somewhat from those who were totally committed ideologically to the Republican cause. For Dickinson's view is not Socialist or Communist but Liberal. He hated the injustice of the international reaction and the unfair nature of the reporting. He was opposed to Fascism but not in favour of Communism.

A unit of seven was formed, many of them Film Society stalwarts. Montagu was producer, Dickinson and Sidney Cole directors, Philip Leacock and Ray Pitt cutters and assistants, Arthur Graham and Alan Lawson cameramen. They travelled by train through France to Perpignan and then proceeded by car to Barcelona, arriving there on January 14, 1938. They divided into two units, one headed by Cole, which was based principally in Madrid and one headed by Dickinson, which was based principally in Barcelona. Montagu acted as coordinator and administrator. Dickinson recalled the conditions they discovered there:

> Wherever we moved in Spain, the hotels were comfortable when their windows were unbroken, but the hunger was intense. This was not so bad when we were busy working, but on the many occasions when we were waiting for assignments to be laid on or for people to come and brief us or guide us to locations, hunger consciously nagged us. Breakfast was usually four Barcelona nuts, the size of hazel nuts, and a cup of milkless 'coffee' made from ground acorns. Lunch was a bowl of hot water flavoured with shreds of vegetable and stewed squid. . . . There might be some flakes of tough meat in consommé and an occasional bread roll for dinner. Only the food parcels brought from our families by Montagu on his journeys to and fro kept us in reasonable trim. In the 10 weeks which we spent there, the sustaining element was the courage and the intelligence of the Spanish people.[10]

The subject of Dickinson's film *Spanish ABC* was to be the educational and cultural policies of the Republic, subjects close to his heart.

> Soldiers and civilians were now receiving 10 pesetas a day in place of the average of two and a half pesetas they had been paid in peace time. They were also receiving adult education to reduce the prevailing national illiteracy. Public libraries and theatrical performances were growing in size, numbers and quality in spite of the shortage of manpower, and a determined though none too successful effort was being made to substitute national for neighbourhood interest, to unify Catalan, Basque and other regional interests into a national devotion.[11]

There was no scenario. The film was put together using information and statistics gathered locally. Dickinson and his unit visited schools, factories, and mines in and around Madrid and Barcelona, and they even visited front-line trenches. 'We found literacy classes of Republican soldiers off duty within a few hundred yards of the front line'.

Dickinson and his unit had been filming near Madrid when they learned that Franco had launched his spring offensive against the northern coast of Valencia. Afraid of being cut off, they hastily collected their developed negative and positive rushes and raced back to Barcelona by car to complete the filming. March in Barcelona was a time of heavy bombing and high casualties. But the Republicans attempted to carry on life as normal. Dickinson and Arthur Graham found time to attend a performance of *Samson and Delilah* at the Barcelona Opera House. There were two air raids during the performance. But the audience sat through them, talking and listening to the orchestra who played the Catalan National Anthem until the bombing was over. Dickinson got back to his hotel at 3 A.M.

But Dickinson had another, more chilling experience:

> One day, an official drove Arthur Graham and myself out to a large windowless building to see whether we could film its interior. The only light came through its entrance door, inside which there was a lobby with large doors beyond. The official pushed them open and we entered to a strange smell. Arthur said he would need a generator as our eyes began to adjust to the gloom. Wherever we looked, there were deep shelves stretching away into the dark. Piled thick on all the shelves up to the roof lay, painfully twisted and with their heads towards us, hundreds of human corpses stiffened in terror. My body must have gone on functioning but not my mind. The next thing I remembered was sitting in a dark, candle-lit café in front of a glass of sticky Spanish vermouth with my friends around me. That was four hours later.[12]

The need for the films was now imperative, so filming was completed and they duly returned to London. Dickinson and Cole cut the two films, and although they shared the credits on both, *Spanish ABC* was largely Dickinson's work and *Behind Spanish Lines* largely Cole's. Dickinson denied that the films were documentaries, preferring to call them 'reportage': 'These were not documentary films but news reports; any eloquence depended on the immediacy of the images captured on the spur of the moment, snapshots in every sense of the word.' They were put to immediate use in fund raising and were shown at the Albert Hall and also at the Film Society.[13]

Behind Spanish Lines was a general propaganda piece depicting day-to-day life going on as normally as possible in Republican Spain, despite constant bombing raids, in which German and Italian involvement was stressed. The film emphasized the legitimacy, democracy, plurality, and humanity of Republican Spain, including scenes of the government functioning, freedom of the press being maintained, humane prison and progressive hospital systems being instituted, a workers' cooperative running a mine, and the people enthusiastically volunteering to defend their state against Fascism.

Spanish ABC, on the other hand, concentrated specifically on the work of the Ministry of Public Instruction. It was a forceful, well-argued, and succinct manifesto on behalf of a society and a programme that were clearly close to Dickinson's heart. It demonstrated his ability to organize material, deploy statistics, and choose the apposite image. Particularly telling was his use of shots of a bombed children's home, with the camera picking up all that remained of its occupants' possessions: a sandal, a toy, a torn book, and his demonstration of letters from newly literate soldiers.

'Although Spain is at war, Spain is building', says the narrator, and we see a school-building programme in operation and the implementation of modern teaching methods. Institutes are set up to raise the low educational standards of the workers, and classes are set up in factories and mines, and even at the front, where 75,000 soldiers have been taught to read and write. Monthly reproductions of famous paintings teach art appreciation, and the soldiers own and run their own newspaper and are encouraged to write and draw. This is all in pointed contrast to the Fascists, who are seen closing schools. The commitment to Spain's cultural heritage is stressed in the removal of paintings from the Prado Museum to places of safety and the enclosing of public statues in brick casings. Schools are even set up in the mountains to educate refugee children. 'All Spain goes to school', concludes the narrator, who quotes a Fascist newspaper: 'All the misfortunes of Spain come from the folly of teaching men to read'. The narrator counters with the Republican belief that knowledge is the strength of Spain, and the invader can never take this away. The last image is of a small boy writing.

Back in England, Dickinson got work as second unit director on Victor Schertzinger's production of *The Mikado*. It was well paid, he recalled, but he did comparatively little on it. He shot Koko's song 'They Never Will Be Missed' and to illustrate it shot a caricature with Chamberlain, Stalin, and Hitler in Japanese dress. It was omitted from the release print of the film. Dickinson described this as 'the only real satire I've ever done'.

But he got his second chance to direct a feature with *The Arsenal Stadium Mystery* in 1939. This was one of three dramas produced at Denham Studios by G. and S., a company set up by Captain Hon. Richard Norton and Josef Somlo to produce quality quota films with distinctive British settings. The other two were *A Window in London*, with a background of the building of Waterloo bridge, and *On the Night of the Fire*, set in Newcastle.

It was Dickinson's idea to do a popular thriller based on actuality, and he took 'an appalling *Daily Express* serial' by Leonard Gribble and did a screen treatment with Alan Hayman. He showed it to Somlo, who liked it and arranged to add it to the schedule of G. and S. On this film, Dickinson had far more creative control than on *The High*

Command in that he prepared the original treatment and then worked on the script, he controlled the casting (introducing his old friend Leslie Banks), and, as usual, he supervised the editing. The result was to be a completely assured and accomplished work, lacking the flaws of the previous film and indicating that Dickinson had mastered the mystery thriller genre completely.

The screenplay was actually written by Donald Bull and Patrick Kirwan, Bull blocking out and doing the basic work of organization and Kirwan supplying much of the humour. Dickinson got on well with Kirwan ('a very amusing man with a strong, impudent wit'), and they batted ideas to and fro between them, sparking each other off in a truly creative relationship.

The story begins on the day of the charity soccer match between Arsenal and the Trojans, a leading amateur side. Trojan star Jack Doyce drives to Highbury with Gwen Lee, with whom he is having an affair, even though she is the fiancée of another player, Phil Morring. In the car, Gwen breaks off the relationship to the astonishment of Jack. At half-time Jack receives a parcel containing a ring. It scratches him, but he goes out for the second half, takes a penalty, and drops dead. Inspector Slade, who is in the middle of producing the police revue, is called in, examines the body, notices the scratch, and deduces poison, a conclusion subsequently confirmed by the police pathologist. He questions the players on both sides and then goes to Doyce's flat, where he learns that a mystery girl had spent the night. A mystery girl also asked Arsenal manager George Allison about Doyce's condition, and he accidentally discovers from an advertisement that she is photographic model Gwen Lee, Morring's fiancée.

From his enquiries, Slade establishes several suspects. Gwen, with whom Doyce had been having an affair; her cousin Inga, secretly in love with Phil; Phil Morring, who had found out about the affair; Dick Setchley, to whom Doyce lent money to develop a new drug— the drug that killed him; and George Raille, who was known to dislike Doyce.

Gwen is found dead, killed by the new drug. Slade now discovers that Doyce, Morring, Setchley, Raille, and manager Frank Kindilett were all once part of the Saxon Rovers team at Wynchester. A search of the newspaper files reveals that Kindilett's daughter had committed suicide after being rejected by an unnamed man. The supposition is that it was Doyce, and Kindilett is therefore suspect.

Slade discovers the poisoned ring, hidden in a liniment bottle, and seals the treatment room on the day of the replay. He covers the ring with marking ink and returns to Scotland Yard, ordering Sergeant

Clinton to arrest whoever gets a black mark on his hand. The culprit turns out to be Raille, who had been in love with Mary Kindilett and killed Doyce for betraying her and then Gwen Lee when she found out. Spotting the waiting policemen, Raille scratches himself with the ring, scores a goal, and is arrested knowing he will die. Inga and Phil are united, and Slade gets on with his show.

Dickinson took a straightforward mystery thriller but lifted it onto an entirely different plane by the application of a quirky, inventive sense of humour and a love of location shooting and realism. Much of the comedy in the film was scripted but Dickinson allowed himself room for the improvisation that he believed brought the breath of real life into a film and freed the director from the shackles of the accountants and administrators, improvisation but within a preplanned framework. For instance, the sort of improvisation he envisaged is the exchange between the referee and a spectator in the crowd ('I've had me eye on you throughout the whole game'). This was suggested by the actual referee, was based on something that had really happened, and was delightedly incorporated by Dickinson. The continuing comic business in which Inspector Slade (Leslie Banks) changes his hat to suit each mood was devised by Dickinson and based on a habit of the old Universal serial director Henry Macrae with whom Dickinson had worked on *Lloyd of the C.I.D.* The delirious upside-down shot of Eddie Hapgood's view of the dressing room was devised by Dickinson to distract the audience's attention from the fact that the Arsenal trainer was so nervous that he could hardly get through the line he was supposed to deliver at that point as he entered the dressing room. There were two other notable pieces of improvisation. Banks's habit of answering the phone by saying hello before he picked up the receiver Dickinson based on a trait of his own. The scenes of the players practising heading balls was added to the film when Dickinson saw Arsenal players doing it and thought it would add some authentic colour.

To ensure realism, Dickinson shot the exteriors at the Highbury stadium, establishing shots of the ground and the games themselves. The plot called for two games between Arsenal and an amateur team, the Trojans. These were done in two parts. An actual match was filmed at Highbury between Arsenal and Brentford, the latter agreeing to forego their usual red and white stripes and wear the white shirts and black shorts of the Trojans. Fourteen cameras were used to get long shots of match action and the crowds. Then close shots were filmed, with the cameras pointing down at the pitch to disguise the absence of the crowd, and in these scenes the Trojans team was played by Oxford and Cambridge blues. This latter part of the shooting involved Dickinson in one major problem. When the shooting was halted by bad weather and he took the unit back to Denham, Dickinson returned to find that the grass of the pitch had been mowed in an angular pattern and now looked completely different than it had in the earlier shots, and so it had to be treated to make the grass uniform in the game sequence.

To ensure further realism, Dickinson had the entire Arsenal team play themselves, as well as the famous Arsenal manager George Allison and the commentator E. V. H. Emmett. The interiors of the Highbury stadium, the dressing rooms, treatment room, and so forth, were re-created at Denham, and the Arsenal staff came out to film. The players enjoyed themselves enormously, playing practical jokes and making so much noise that Somlo, in the only *contretemps* Dickinson had with him, reproved him for lack of discipline on the set and took him over to the neighbouring sound stage when Brian Desmond Hurst was shooting *On the Night of the Fire* to show him how a well-disciplined set should be run. Dickinson simply suggested that Somlo should come down and try to keep order himself, and Somlo retreated to his office.

A major problem to solve was how to introduce the audience to twenty-two characters at once. Dickinson got around this brilliantly by shooting an imitation Gaumont British newsreel that begins straight, setting the background to the Arsenal-Trojans match and introducing the players individually. Then it is suddenly interrupted by a head in front of the screen, and the camera pulls back to reveal the two teams watching the newsreel, cracking jokes and laughing. The life and atmosphere of a great soccer club is depicted with a sharp eye for detail and humour. For instance, the social milieux of the two sides in the charity match is tellingly established in a vignette outside the ground. A gentleman in a pinstripe suit and monocle, who supports the Trojans, engages in an argument about the respective merits of their teams with an Arsenal supporter, depicted as a roughly dressed young ragamuffin, bedecked with scarf and rosettes. But on the whole Dickinson is not much interested in exploring the social implications of a meeting between a team of professionals and a team of gentleman amateurs, clearly modelled on the Corinthians.

Every facet of the prematch build-up and the match itself is observed. There is the team talk from the manager, using a scale model of the pitch. There is the dressing room, with its bustle and comic byplay, one player, for instance, putting on all the shirts. There is the treatment room and the bath, where one of the players, Leslie Jones, is in fact interviewed by the inspector. There are scenes of training and of the half-time pep talk delivered as cups of tea are served to the tired players. On top of all this there are two games, excitingly put together, to capture all the passion and tension of the sport.

In unfolding the process of detection and deduction, Dickinson puts his humour and inventiveness to invaluable use. He never allows the audience to get bored with the constant exposition and explanatory dialogue by the expedient of covering all the dialogue scenes with comic business and comic minor characters.

Detective Inspector Anthony Slade is a delightfully whimsical creation, introduced by one of Dickinson's characteristically witty bridges. After Doyce's death, Arsenal manager Allison picks up the telephone and asks for 'Whitehall one-two', and Dickinson dissolves to a line of policemen in ballet skirts dancing onto a stage and a voice saying 'One-two-one-two'. Inspector Slade is busy producing the annual policemen's concert and remains preoccupied with that task throughout the case. Dickinson gives him a slow-witted sergeant to whom he can explain everything while making gentle fun of him.

Once Slade begins his investigations, putting on a different hat for each occasion, Dickinson sets to work to vary the manner and setting for each episode of questioning and deduction. In establishing the movements of the murdered Doyce, Slade questions Leslie Jones in the bath, is harassed by a garrulous Irish porter at the block of flats who will not come to the point and encounters a huge fat man, Doyce's neighbour, who is playing awful, tuneless music on his piano and whose attention Slade attracts by the device of banging on the wall.

At the golf club, the important facts emerge while the rain-bound soccer players are debagging one of their number, Dick Setchley, and Slade himself is apparently absent-mindedly questioning Morring while practising putting and breaking a vase in the process. Later, when he has to question Gwen and Inga, Slade arrives at their flat with Sergeant Clinton and breezes in, demanding coffee and cake. Inga responds by putting epsom salts in the coffee. Again, at Setchley's laboratory while Slade, who has broken in, is searching for evidence, he makes deductions while chasing a frog that escapes and tinkering with various scientific gadgets. All these different scenes convey information, but in every one of them Dickinson also engages the audience's amused attention in the inspector's unconventional antics.

Dickinson employs the same visual style in *The Arsenal Stadium Mystery* as in *The High Command*. In the first half of the film the only close-ups are of the ball at the kick-off and of the fatal ring that will poison Doyce, though there are medium-close reaction shots of the key characters during the match. All the conversations in the early part of the film are in medium two-shot with no intercutting. This convention is first broken with when Inga and Gwen discuss Doyce's death. Dickinson intercuts between them, establishing their rivalry and hostility. Similarly, when Slade and Clinton visit the flat, Dickinson intercuts between them and Inga and Gwen, establishing their roles as questioners and questioned. The first big close-up of an actor comes when Gwen tells Phil that she can ruin him because of information that she possesses about him. The audience is thus made aware of the importance of this information and points to her subsequent murder. Dickinson's method then is clearly to use the close-up sparingly, to shoot dialogue scenes in medium two-shot, and to use 'business' to cover the transmission of information. In this way he is able to engage the audience gradually in the story, increasing close-ups as he goes along and distracting them with comedy.

Like its predecessor, *The Arsenal Stadium Mystery* earned the admiration of Graham Greene:

> Mr. Thorold Dickinson who will be remembered for his promising first film *The High Command* has admirably succeeded in keeping his detection alive as well as obscure—this picture is as good to watch as either of *The Thin Man* films, and he gives us wit instead of facetiousness—wit of cutting and wit of angle.[14]

This time, however, a Dickinson film was uniformly liked by the critics, who praised Leslie Banks, the realism, the comedy, and the construction and pacing of the story.

In retrospect, Dickinson described his first two features as 'second raters'. Admittedly, they were familiar enough subjects in thirties cinema—murder mysteries—but he brought to them a freshness and imagination that transcended their limited budgets and B picture circumstances. He was now ready to move on to something more demanding.

Before that, however, there was almost a third thriller. Captain Hon. Richard Norton was put in charge of Alexander Korda's London Films when Korda departed for Hollywood to complete the production of *The Thief of Bagdad*. Anxious to utilize some of the footage of Korda's various uncompleted projects, he asked Dickinson if anything could be done with the *I Claudius* material shot by Josef von Sternberg. Five reels of this ambitious Roman epic had been shot in 1937 before the project was abandoned following a car accident involving Merle Oberon, who was playing the Empress Messalina.[15] Dickinson came up with the idea for a sequel to *The Arsenal Stadium Mystery* to be called *The Denham Studio Mystery*. The basic idea was for a murder to be committed during the shooting of an epic film and for Leslie Banks to be called in to solve it, re-creating his role from *The Arsenal Stadium Mystery*. It would have been extremely economical, for the film in progress would have been *I Claudius* and the settings for the film would have been provided by Denham Studios itself. Dickinson contacted Leslie Banks, who was enthusiastic, and Patrick Kirwan, who agreed to write the script with him. Dickinson had even worked out the idea for a marvellous gag opening:

> A night shot of Parliament Square with the camera roving over it and coming into the courtyard of the Commons and in the middle of the courtyard, an enormous foot. The camera pulls back to show Leslie Banks sitting astride the Houses of Parliament moving the hands of Big Ben.

This would have thus mocked both Korda's trademark and the studio's recurrent use of models. But just as preliminary discussions were underway, Dickinson was offered the chance to direct *Gaslight*. *The Denham Studio Mystery* was shelved permanently.

NOTES

1. *BBFC Scenario Reports 1936*, no. 69.
2. BFI, *Film Appreciation and Visual Education* (London: BFI, 1944), p. 5.
3. Dickinson's account is in his article, 'Mad Dogs and Location Units', *Ciné-Technician* 3 (June-July 1937), pp. 56-57. I have been unable to uncover any evidence that the documentary was actually filmed.
4. Author's interview with Sidney Cole, May 15, 1985.
5. Graham Greene, *The Pleasure Dome* (London: Secker and Warburg, 1972) p. 157.
6. Ibid.
7. *Spectator*, July 30, 1937.
8. *Evening News*, July 23, 1937.
9. Thorold Dickinson, 'Experiences in the Spanish Civil War', *Historical Journal of Film, Radio and Television* 4 (1984), p. 189. Sidney Cole's account, 'Shooting in Spain', *Ciné-Technician* 4 (May-June 1938), pp. 1-2.
10. Dickinson, 'Experiences in the Spanish Civil War', p. 190.
11. Ibid., p. 191.
12. Ibid., pp. 191-192.
13. A third film, shot later by Alan Lawson, for PFI was *Britain Expects* about the British blockade runner, Captain 'Potato' Jones. Dickinson's *Spanish ABC* was the only one of the PFI films to be registered for the quota, and it received a 'U' certificate from the censors. See Rachael Low, *Films of Comment and Persuasion of the 1930's* (London: George Allen and Unwin, 1979), pp. 185-190.
14. Graham Greene, *The Pleasure Dome*, pp. 266-268.
15. On Sternberg's *I Claudius*, see John Baxter, *The Cinema of Josef von Sternberg* (London: Zwemmer, 1971), pp. 136-149.

FOUR

Victorian Values: *Gaslight*

Dickinson was asked only three weeks before shooting began to take on the film version of Patrick Hamilton's play *Gaslight* with Anton Walbrook and Diana Wynyard. A director had been provisionally engaged, but the stars had vetoed him. Dickinson's agent, who was also their agent, suggested his name and had *The High Command* run for them. Walbrook and Wynyard were so impressed by the sequence of Diana Cloam's return home, handled without dialogue and played simply by glance and gesture, that they agreed at once to Dickinson being hired.

The film was being produced by British National, a company headed by the millionairess Lady Yule that mainly turned out inexpensive programmers. This too was planned as a cheap production. But Dickinson leaped at the idea of doing it. 'I'd seen the play and been shaken by it and jumped at the chance to expose the worst side of the Victorian male's attitude to women'.

The play had opened in 1938 in Richmond with Gwen Frangcon-Davies and Dennis Arundell as Jack and Bella Manningham. The plot was straightforward. The husband has murdered his aunt for her jewels but cannot find them and searches the house at night. He is also seeking to drive his wife insane because she has innocently come across information that points to him as the murderer. He is eventually exposed by a retired detective who has been studying the unsolved murder of the aunt. The play was hailed as a powerful psychological study in sadistic torment. In the United States, under the title *Angel Street*, the play ran for three years on Broadway with Judith Evelyn and Vincent Price in the leading roles. The stars of the film version were already cast, but Dickinson was able to cast the supporting roles, notable Frank Pettingell and Robert Newton.

But Dickinson was extremely unhappy with the A. R. Rawlinson script. He found it heavy-handed, unsubtle, and overobvious ('a real blood and thunder B feature job, giving the whole show away from the start'). As Dickinson told it, he together with Bridget Boland reworked the script to make it less obvious and enhance the atmosphere and tension. He introduced a new opening and invented a new character (the cousin Vincent Ullswater). It was also Dickinson's idea to follow the roll-up titles at the start with an embroidered sampler giving the name of the victim and the date (Alice Barlow—1865). Dickinson recalled that he had Miss Boland telescope the last two acts of the play to make it more dramatically effective. They added the details of family life above and below stairs, the morning prayers sequence being based on Dickinson's memories of his own childhood in Bristol.

However, when Dickinson outlined his account of the script revisions in a letter to *Radio Times* on the occasion of the first television showing of *Gaslight* on BBC I in 1978, Bridget Boland wrote to him (August 17, 1978), rejecting his version entirely. 'The script was already finished when you arrived on the scene and was never altered in any way', she wrote. ('Nonsense' was Dickinson's scribbled marginal comment.) She suggested that he did not and could not have altered plot and dialogue in the time available. On the face of it, the two versions of events are irreconcilable. But the most likely explanation is that in preparing his shooting script, Dickinson reconstructed the script somewhat, tightening, cutting, rearranging, and conveying information by visual means rather than dialogue, much as he did in the case of the later *Queen of Spades*.[1]

Unusual for that time, the film was shot in continuity and a rough cut was made as shooting proceeded. Dickinson decided to eschew the freedom to improvise that he had allowed himself in previous films. Instead, he worked out an absolutely precise shooting plan in advance, from which he permitted no deviation, thus allowing the built-in nervosity of the subject and the tension of the actors to play off against the perfectly regulated shooting. 'I wanted a precise film not merely in composition of shots but in continuity of shots. The whole thing was precisely set before we started.'

To this end, Dickinson and Sidney Cole, whom he brought in as editor, prepared an enormously complex chart preplanning every shot. The finished film contained only two extra shots not in the plan, and the only improvised sequence was the one in the music hall, for which he obtained the services of a Hungarian dance troupe, the Darmora Ballet, stranded in London. The can-can sequence was shot in a single day. The dancers were rehearsed from 10 A.M. until lunch, and then between 2 P.M. and 4 P.M. four complete performances were shot with six cameras, resulting in an hour of film, taken from many different angles. Cole studied and edited it down to ten minutes. Then, with Dickinson supervising, Cole selected the high points from each shot and assembled a minute and a half, for which the music was rerecorded and added on, to create what Cole calls 'the fastest can-can that has ever been danced'.

The film was able to be shot in sequence because art director Duncan Sutherland constructed the entire house, where much of the action takes place, with four removable walls, allowing for dramatic changes of camera angle and reverse shooting. Dickinson's method of work initially caused problems with Walbrook. He felt that he was not getting enough direction and that the production was too restrained and unemphatic. But Dickinson was able to show him the rough cut as it was being assembled, which converted him immediately. Thereafter, he was extremely cooperative. Dickinson recalled:

> We got on extremely well once he got his faith restored after the first fortnight. He'd never steal a picture from anybody. He had this extraordinarily mobile face and in both the films we made there are close-ups that you wouldn't dare try to get from the ordinary actor.

The production overran somewhat because the leading actors succumbed to influenza. But it was nevertheless completed in nine weeks and at a record-low cost (£39,000). A week later it was edited, and six weeks after that it was ready to be shown at the Leicester Square Odeon. Its rapid processing was due in part to the fact that Denham Studios currently had no other film in production. But it was also due to the economical preplanned method of shooting. Sidney Cole recalled in 1944 that the editing of *Gaslight* was

> among the best I have done. Yet it presented not a tenth of the difficulties I've had with many a worse picture. . . . The . . . material was a delight to work with, being susceptible of the utmost subtlety in cutting. This was only because the film had been made with the requisite consideration of the demands of editing, and because the director had conceived broadly in his mind the final shape of the picture, and had allowed himself the necessary margin of material to achieve the planned result.[2]

In 1985, Cole recalled not only Dickinson's great professionalism but also his great kindness.

I hadn't cut a film apart from the Spanish republican thing for quite a while. The first sequence I cut was the sequence at the beginning of *Gaslight*. . . . with Walbrook dashing around killing the old woman, and dashing around the house madly and Thorold shot all these shots, which are very impressionistic shots. I looked at them and decided on an order which I thought would be best, which was a mounting sort of accelerating rhythm, and with great trepidation took it into the theatre to show Thorold, and Thorold said when the lights went up, 'Oh, that wasn't really what I meant at all', and I said, 'I'm very sorry', and he said, 'No, no, let's see it again', and he ran it again and he said, 'Ah, yes, I see, I see, I think it works,' and we ran it a third time and he made one or two suggestions, and now it is in. The film is basically the way I cut it with one or two touches from Thorold, and that absolutely restored my confidence in my ability to edit, which had been a bit sapped by eighteen months of not actually doing it. But that's a very typical story to me of Thorold as a person of understanding and also in purely professional terms, a willingness to accept something from other people. He was very like that.[3]

Gaslight is Dickinson's first mature masterpiece. It reveals the extent of the Film Society's influence on him, and it was itself to influence a whole genre of British films of the forties, set in upper-middle-class Victorian households and dramatizing the myth of Victorian 'hypocrisy', by contrasting the surface appearance of regularity, order, and social hierarchy with the concealed reality of tyranny, intolerance, and familial strain. *Pink String and Sealing Wax*, *Hatter's Castle*, *So Evil My Love*, and *Madeleine* all follow in the footsteps of *Gaslight* and represent a critique of nineteenth-century family structure and middle-class mores, which came to the fore in particular during World War II.

For Dickinson, there was the continuing interest in 'secret people', here capable of much deeper and fuller expression than in *The High Command* or *The Arsenal Stadium Mystery*. For the removal of the whodunnit aspect changed the emphasis of the plot. The film opens with the murder of old Alice Barlow and the ransacking of her house. Thereafter, in almost the first dialogue of the film, Rough, the retired detective, remarks to his assistant on how much Paul Mallen resembles Louis Bauer, the nephew of the murdered Alice Barlow. The audience will rapidly deduce that Mallen is the murderer and is deliberately seeking to drive his wife mad. The tension of the story then shifts from whether he is seeking to drive her mad or even why (because she found a letter addressed to Louis Bauer) to whether he will succeed. It becomes a battle of wills, a psychological drama rather than a mystery thriller. It is clear that this aspect is what fascinated Dickinson most. For in Mallen there is a set of contrasts and concealments: the loving husband versus the ruthless tormenter, the monogamous bourgeois versus the philandering gentleman, the pious *pater familias* versus the thief and murderer. He is a classic 'secret person'.

But the recurrence of religious motifs in *Gaslight* in conjunction with some act of devilry by Paul Mallen indicates that the exposure of 'hypocrisy' is also one of the film's preoccupations. For instance, Rough's first expression of suspicion about Mallen is made as the Mallens leave a Sunday morning church service, and following their return home from church we get the first big scene of Mallen tormenting Bella. Later, he deliberately conceals a letter from her, denying its existence, and calmly goes on from that to preside over morning prayers with the servants kneeling and Mallen himself sanctimoniously reading from the psalm. Later still Mallen compels the servants to kiss the Bible in token of their innocence of stealing Bella's brooch, which he himself removed. Bella insists on doing so too, provoking a denunciatory outburst from Mallen, who accuses her of being insane and drives her from the room.

Together with the religious hypocrisy there is also an oblique sexual motif. The generalized repression of *Gaslight* was to become in later films more specifically sexual repression and the contrast between surface respectability and inner drives and tensions to become split personality in such flamboyant Gainsborough melodramas as *Madonna of the Seven Moons*, *Caravan*, and *The Wicked Lady*. The refinement of cruelty with which Mallen tortures Bella psychologically is sadistic. While pretending concern for Bella's sanity, he also inaugurates a clandestine affair with the maid Nancy. He propositions the willing Nancy while he is lying on a chaise longue and she removes his boots. He chews on the end of the overhanging aspidistra leaf, a situation that seems absurd when written down but works on film as an expression of a languid and insidious sensuality. The more overtly passionate aspect of their relationship is visually expressed when they visit a music hall and watch a display of can-can dancing. The camera tracks past the kicking legs and frilly underwear, cutting to Mallen and Nancy in the box, establishing the link between the uninhibited sexuality of the dance and the nature of their liaison.

Gaslight works as a film because all the elements dovetail together to create tension and suspense. In particular, the camerawork, the acting, and the construction of the scenes combine to this effect. When Patrick Hamilton saw the film, he described it as 'a French film in English', something that delighted Dickinson since his style was deliberately modelled on that of Carné. The average shot length of *Gaslight* is ten seconds, approaching the average shot length of Carné's *Hôtel du Nord* at fourteen seconds, the culmination of Carné's steadily increasing shot length, and contrasting with the average shot length of the typical British film of the period, including Dickinson's previous two films, at seven seconds. It also opens with a long crane shot from the name of the square and a flickering gas lamp across Pimlico Square to number 12 and then up to the first floor, the scene of the murder, an introduction also reminiscent of *Hôtel du Nord*.

Throughout *Gaslight*, Dickinson employs longer takes, fewer close-ups, and a more mobile camera than was usual in the contemporary British cinema. The constant camera movement and abrupt changes of angle convey the nervous tension of the conflict, contrasting with Anton Walbrook's icy control as Mallen and also playing off the measured build-up that is implicit in the longer average shot length. The very sparing use of close-ups similarly enables a build-up of tension until the final long and full close-ups of Mallen as his mind snaps.

Dickinson's philosophy of 'getting the aircraft airborne' as soon as possible and conveying to the audience essential 'matter' as economically as possible is magnificently resolved in the opening sequence, in which he conveys virtually without dialogue all the essential background information for the audience's appreciation of the main story. The murder of Mrs. Barlow, strangled by the hands of an unseen murderer, and the subsequent frantic search of her house for something, are done in a series of diagonal wipes and dissolves, with the music underlining the frantic urgency of the search. This montage culminates in a slow tracking shot across the disordered room to the body. Then there is a whip pan from the concerned group surrounding the distressed maid on the front steps of the house to the search of the interior by the police, a visual device that eliminates the need for exposition. Finally, there is a rapid dolly shot in to the headline of a newspaper proclaiming the murder. A 'For Sale' sign goes up outside the house, and two men plant a tree in the park opposite. The scene dissolves to the tree fully grown and beyond it the 'For Sale' sign weathered and dirty. The sign is taken down, repairs are executed to the house, a carriage arrives, and the Mallens move in.

Although the narrative of the film intertwines two main plot themes, Mallen's gradually escalating plot to drive Bella insane and Rough's patient and persistent sleuthing to unmask Mallen, the film's 'big' scenes are the ones involving the tormenting of Bella, and here the blending of the main elements of the film is vital.

Anton Walbrook's Paul Mallen is an unforgettable portrait of cruelty, his engaging charm and continental suavity giving way with terrifying suddenness to a freezing, sadistic contempt, his complete authority over Bella so well established that in an electrifying scene where he finds her in a candy shop buying sweets for street urchins, he has only to utter the word 'Bella' in a baleful tone for her to wilt visibly and come to heel. Diana Wynyard is equally good as Bella, desperately trying to please her husband but increasingly driven by his calculated violent changes of mood and continual public humiliations of her to doubt her sanity and finally pushed to the verge of a breaking point. Both performers begin by establishing a stereotype, the coldly authoritative husband and the meek, submissive wife, and then build on this and round it out by varying mood, response, and reaction, so that they eventually create much more complex and feeling studies. Dickinson's camera never fails to capture all the nuances and subtle changes of expression, charting what is essentially a battle of wills between the two leading characters.

The construction of the big scenes is also well done, so written as to lull the audience into a false sense of security and then to snap them out of it as Mallen tries another of his ploys against Bella. The acting and the construction then meld with the camera work, as the first scene between Mallen and Bella demonstrates. Mallen, back to camera, hands clasped together, talks in cold, mocking tones about her desire for muffins for tea when the muffin man has already gone and then further upsets her by openly flirting with the maid Nancy when she brings the tea. Bella tells him that she feels humiliated. But he talks of her eccentricities, her stealing of things from the house and hiding them, and he warns her of incipient madness. She denies the accusations and says that she has been much better of late because he has been kind to her. At this stage, Dickinson intercuts medium close shots of the two, but he brings them together in the same shot as she insists that she is getting better, he relaxes, kisses her, unbends, and plays the piano as she dances happily round the room, followed by the camera. Cut to Mallen, who rises and advances smiling and humming towards Bella. Suddenly he stops and his face freezes as he points to a spot on the wall where a picture is missing. Dickinson resumes the intercutting as Mallen orders her to return it; she denies taking it and retreats up the stairs, followed by Mallen. The picture is discovered behind a statue. Bella denies putting it there and flees to her room, pursued by Mallen ('I don't know how much longer I can keep my patience'). He covers his face with his hands. There is a rapid pan from her, crumpled and crestfallen, to a medium shot of him, hands over face. Suddenly the fingers part, his eyes flicker downwards, and he slips a cameo brooch from her dressing table into his pocket and leaves, seen retreating in the mirror. The stage is thus set for the next humiliation. Thus, the construction of the sequence—accusation, mollification, fresh accusation, collapse of Bella—maintains audience involvement and tension. The tracking and dollying of the camera, changes of angle in the baiting sequences, the intercutting between the two give visual expression to this tension, while it is reinforced by the acting, in Walbrook's icy savagery and Wynyard's timorous desperation.

The second episode of torment occurs when Mallen agrees to take Bella to a charity concert at Winterbourne House if she will wear her cameo brooch, which we know Mallen himself to have abstracted. She cannot find it and pretends that it does not go with the dress. When Mallen accepts this explanation, the audience relaxes. The Mallens go to the concert, but there he slips his watch off its chain and into her handbag. During the concert, he starts whispering to her, insisting that she has taken the watch; she denies it, he takes her bag, searches it, and finds it; she breaks down and he escorts her sobbing from the hall. This interchange between them is done entirely in medium two-shot, the tension between the characters now enough to sustain the interest. It is varied only by reaction shots of the pianist annoyed at the interruption and the audience angry at being disturbed. On the way home, they sit in the cab, again facing the camera in medium two-shot. She begs him to speak to her, but he stares coldly ahead. The coldness is more effective than rage, and once again the tension between the characters makes intercutting unnecessary.

The first use of full close-up occurs in the next big confrontation. After her cousin Vincent Ullswater has been sent away by Mallen without seeing Bella, she rushes down from her room to confront her husband. She says that he turned against her after the discovery of a letter addressed to Louis Bauer and asks who Louis Bauer is. In intercut close-ups and medium two-shots, he denounces and rejects her and says he will have her certified and committed in the morning. She collapses on the ground. The sequence ends with a huge close-up of Paul mouthing the name 'Louis Bauer'.

The biggest and longest close-up is literally the climactic moment of the film. After Rough has exposed Mallen's plot and overpowered him, he is left alone with Bella. Although tied up, he attempts once more to exert his will, ordering her to free him. This is done with intercutting, including enormous close-ups. She advances with knife in hand, saying that he has tried to drive her mad and if she is mad, no one would blame her for killing him. ('What *knife*? Are you suggesting this is a *knife* I have in my hand? There was a *knife* but I lost it'). This episode is consciously modelled on the celebrated sequence in Hitchcock's *Blackmail* in which a distracted Anny Ondra, having committed murder, has to listen to a neighbour talking constantly of a knife. At this point, Dickinson makes his most obvious use of point-of-view shots, tilted shots of Bella advancing on Mallen, their imbalance reflecting his incipient madness. Finally, in a seventeen-second close-up, Mallen's mind snaps; he tears himself free and grabs at the rubies before being seized and led away. Walbrook's sudden lapse into insanity was assisted by cameraman Bernard Knowles putting a filter over the camera at the crucial moment, so that the manic gleam in his eyes suddenly and dramatically dulls. Bella, freed from his spell, goes out onto the balcony. The camera reverses the opening crane shot, cranes back across the square, and comes to rest again on the flickering gaslight. This reverse of the opening provides a symmetry to the story, just as the shooting entirely in the studio provides the necessary claustrophobia.

Stylistically and thematically, *Gaslight* was an important step forward in Dickinson's career. He was able for the first time to explore the concept of 'secret people' in depth. He was also able to apply the techniques and approach to filming he had learned from his years with the Film Society. The French influence was paramount. But the film also shows that he had absorbed the Russian theories of montage. Particularly noticeable under this heading are the intercutting between a Punch and Judy show in the street in which Punch is battering Judy and the second baiting session inside the house as Mallen torments Bella after bringing her back from the candy shop, and the music hall sequence, in which Dickinson intercuts between the dancers and the lovers in their box, and also between the dancers and Rough trying to convince Bella of her husband's guilt. The first set of intercutting establishes the sexual nature of the Mallen-Nancy relationship; the second lends what is on paper a mere discussion the full crashing weight of a climacteric. Above all, the construction of the film and the carefully plotted camerawork demonstrate Dickinson's supreme quality as a storyteller and his constant awareness of the audience, whom he plays on with consummate skill.

The story is given a wider social relevance by the personalization of the contrast between the respectable ordered surface of Victorian middle-class life and the inner tensions and frustrations that it concealed. The precise detail of this surface life is impeccably evoked with the help of Duncan Sutherland's atmospheric period sets, and the Victorian era is brought to life in both its rituals (morning prayers, the walk in the park, Sunday church services) and its safe, comfortable externals (the muffin men, the flaring gaslight, the horse-drawn omnibuses, the pennyfarthing bicycles, the road sweepers). Mirrors are very important both historically and symbolically, but they kept reflecting the camera movement. A researcher discovered that the Victorians regularly used transfers to decorate their mirrors, and this resolved the problem. The very normality of the surroundings contrasts pointedly with the growing torture and insanity in the Mallen household.

Sidney Cole thought *Gaslight* 'one of those films in which everybody without exception was at the top of their form', and critically the film was very well received. The *Daily Mail* called it 'a thriller that will make you forget everything else while you are watching it. Atmosphere has been splendidly created and suspense admirably maintained'.[4] It praised also 'the clever scenario writing, brilliant direction and superb acting'. The *Evening Standard* thought it 'a fascinating period piece and the best home-made film we have seen for some time'.[5] The *Observer* proclaimed it 'the best English film drama of the year— an exquisite Victorian horror arrestingly handled by Thorold Dickinson and just right for the fine-drawn playing of Diana Wynyard and Anton Walbrook'.[6] The *Sunday Pictorial* declared it 'one of the best and creepiest psychological thrillers that the screen has seen'.[7] The *Daily Worker* thought it 'perfect'.[8] The *Daily Sketch* called it 'an outstanding film— not only an outstanding British film. . . . [T]he atmosphere of suspense is brilliantly sustained, thanks to the direction of Thorold Dickinson and the grand acting of the principals'.[9] Quite apart from the published tributes, Dickinson received many private letters of congratulation on his achievement, including ones from Paul Rotha, Ralph Bond, and Margot Asquith.[10]

Patrick Hamilton had intensely disapproved of the casting of Anton Walbrook in a part originally written for an Englishman, but when he saw the finished film, he too loved it. Another admirer of the film was David O. Selznick, who sent Dickinson one of his celebrated 2,500-word cables inviting him to Hollywood to remake it. Dickinson refused to leave Britain while the war was on and thus sacrificed a possible Hollywood career; how he would have taken to the Hollywood system remains an open question.

Although *Gaslight* was not about the war, it did have overseas propaganda value, as did all well-made British films even if not about the war. Dickinson recalled that the Ministry of Information

> believed quite rightly that the British propaganda people in neutral countries could introduce the idea to them—'We've got another British film to show you' and having drinks with the press afterwards, they'd say 'Well, you saw that thing in *Das Reich* last week about the state of conditions in Britain. Do you think they could make a film like that if the conditions were as stated in the German press?' Whether the film itself had anything to do with the war or not, people in South America and South Africa and so on would say, 'For Christ's sake, they're making films just as they did before the war or better.' So anything that clicked that came out of Britain was excellent as war propaganda. [Sidney] Bernstein told me that *Gaslight* was so unexpected to come out of a nation in wartime that it was much more valuable to them than many a patriotic endeavour full of troops and flags. Incidentally, it brought in foreign currency as well, which was very valuable.

But the film had a less happy aftermath too. M-G-M bought the rights of the film with the intention of remaking it in Hollywood. Part of the agreement was that all the existing prints of the British version be destroyed. This created a furor in Britain. Sidney Cole wrote an open letter to Lady Yule, which was printed in the *Ciné-Technician* in 1944. It was reprinted by C. A. Lejeune in the *Observer*. Headed 'Murder by Gaslight', it denounced the suppression clause in the M-G-M contract.

> We know that if we make bad pictures in this country the Americans don't want them—even our own countrymen are not very keen on bad English pictures. Perhaps even less do the Americans want *good* British pictures. Since when has a powerful industry encouraged foreign competition?[11]

Taking a lead from Ellen Wilkinson's book on Jarrow, *The Town That Was Murdered*, Cole dubbed *Gaslight* 'The film that was murdered'. But determined to prevent its destruction, Dickinson and Cole secretly had a print struck from the negative before it was removed and eventually deposited the print with the British Film Institute. Eventually prints of the British version began to circulate in the United States in art house cinemas under the title *Angel Street* during the 1950s and it was subsequently shown on American television. But it remained unseen in Britain for many years, and there is no doubt that its suppression throughout the period of Dickinson's active directorial career led to the belief that it was a lost film. When it was subsequently resurrected and hailed as a lost masterwork, there were inevitable claims that George Cukor's 1944 Hollywood remake had been a vulgar travesty. But this charge is unfair, and it is instructive to compare the two films.

Cukor's *Gaslight* is very different from Dickinson's. It retains the plot line and the key scenes of the original but is completely reworked as a full-blown Hollywood melodrama, nearly two hours long, lavishly designed, sumptuously photographed, richly scored, and full of close-ups geared to the presence of star performers in the leading roles. There are also several significant changes. Rough, the retired old detective who finally unmasks the murderer, becomes Brian Cameron (Joseph Cotten), handsome young assistant to the commissioner of police, providing a promise of future romance for the tormented heroine Paula (Ingrid Bergman). The film adds a visit to the Tower of London and a delightfully nosey neighbour but eliminates much of the detailed routine of bourgeois life. The affair with Nancy the maid is eliminated, and the central relationship between husband and wife takes on an infinitely more sexual dimension than in Dickinson's film. Sex never loomed large in Dickinson's oeuvre or in British cinema in general, for that matter. It is not part of the Mallens' relationship and is sidelined into Mallen's liaison with the maid, which is seen to be illicit.

But sex is central to Cukor's film and emphasized in the long introductory sequence of romance and marriage. Although she is in Italy studying singing, Paula Alquist's heart is not in it, and her teacher recognizes that she is in love. Paula admits it and is soon in the arms of her accompanist Gregory Anton (Charles Boyer). The radiance of a young woman in love with one of the screen's great Latin lovers is well established both in Bergman's luminous playing and Cukor's caressing close-ups. Italy, an ornate balcony and elegantly designed stone staircase, trailing vines, lapping water, and a gondolier singing in the distance provide the perfect Hollywood-Romantic setting for a honeymoon, and the loving relationship of the couple is cemented. All this makes Gregory's withdrawal of love all the more hurtful and destructive of Paula. Her off-screen cry 'Please, please, take me in your arms' when he has escorted her to her room after yet another session of accusation and humiliation, only to be met by the cold response 'I hope to find you better in the morning', goes to the heart of it.

The final confrontation is softened by Cukor, though. Paula pretends to be mad when Gregory asks her to help him escape and then defiantly denounces him and orders his removal in a glorious final release, far more full-throated than Dickinson's. Gregory does not go mad but departs with a regretful smile and impassive dignity. The film is superbly acted by Bergman and Boyer, who are more sensual than Wynyard and Walbrook, and Cukor's policy of relying far more on close-ups than Dickinson dwells more on her suffering.

Andrew Sarris has made a comparison of the two versions and declared his preference for the Cukor version, insisting that it is both better acted and better directed:

> On the whole Thorold Dickinson keeps his distance from the characters so as to focus on the period decor. He thinks nothing of interrupting his film to present his affectionate portrait of a Victorian music-hall performance to which the husband has taken the saucy parlour maid. There are also little vignettes with lower class touches in the vicinity of what started out on stage as unfashionable Angel Street, and became progressively more elegant in its two screen adaptations.

He accuses Dickinson of deliberate aestheticism in which

> he time and again deserts the characters and the narrative for a studied pose or an essay in the decor. By contrast Cukor abandons his backgrounds as often in order to contemplate the intense expressions of his players. It is a subtle, almost imperceptible process of displacement, in both instances, but it provides nevertheless an invaluable comparison of two divergent directional styles from two different countries in almost the same era.[12]

The disparagement of Dickinson is unfair, almost wilfully misunderstanding the function of the music hall sequence and the period detail, which are not redundant but intrinsic to Dickinson's interpretation. But Sarris's response was prefigured by the *New York Times* review of *Angel Street* in 1952.

> A studied, mannered, decorous piece of period cat and mouse play for those who have never seen it acted. Others though will probably find that it brings no fresh interest to its oft-told story. This *Angel Street* invites comparison with the other versions and loses by it. . . . Except for its production trappings, the British *Angel Street* is an ordinary piece of movie work and certainly in no condition to cope with the handicap of familiarity.[13]

This review suggests that responses to the two *Gaslight*s essentially reflect differences in national character and outlook rather than pure aesthetic judgement. The British cinema has traditionally been more puritanical and more restrained than the American, overt American emotionalism sometimes causing British viewers and critics embarrassment and discomfort. The American version of *Gaslight* is different from but not thereby necessarily superior to the British. For this is not a matter for value judgements. Both films are superb representations of the style and essence of their own countries and their national film industries.

NOTES

1. Letter from Bridget Boland to Thorold Dickinson, August 17, 1978, Dickinson papers.
2. BFI, *Film Appreciation and Visual Education* (London: BFI, 1944), p. 18.
3. Author's interview with Sidney Cole, May 15, 1985.
4. *Daily Mail*, June 14, 1940.
5. *Evening Standard*, June 15, 1940.
6. *Observer*, December 29, 1940.
7. *Sunday Pictorial*, June 16, 1940.
8. *Daily Worker*, June 24, 1940.
9. *Daily Sketch*, June 14, 1940.
10. These letters are in the Dickinson Papers.
11. *Ciné-Technician* 10 (January-April 1940), p. 1.
12. Andrew Sarris, 'Two or Three Things I Know about *Gaslight*', *Film Comment* 12 (May-June 1976), pp. 23-25.
13. *New York Times*, November 11, 1952.

FIVE

Tracts for the Times: *The Prime Minister* and *The Next of Kin*

For much of the war, Dickinson's filmmaking activities were part of the propaganda offensive, and he worked closely with the Ministry of Information. He was later to praise the effect the Ministry had on British film production:

> The internationals sought work in the U.S.A. along with a few British individualists, leaving the field open for a new generation of filmmakers who were to receive generous guidance from the reconstituted films division at the Ministry. The argument there was, that while the propaganda film is invaluable, the skilful film of entertainment has the double advantage of diverting the native and impressing the foreigner as evidence of British morale. The films division was given control of all negative film which was made available to producers only after approval of each script. This veto, intelligently applied, raised the quality of the British product without removing the element of competition from the lack of which a nationalized output is liable to suffer.[1]

Dickinson and other filmmakers had offered their services to the Ministry of Information at the very outset of the war. But Sir Joseph Ball, the head of the Films Division, told them that all the cinemas and theatres were going to be closed down as air raid hazards, so their services would not be required. As Dickinson later recalled:

> I was horrified. 'No cinemas! No theatres!' I exclaimed. 'Theatres' he replied, 'will be open only in the middle of the day—not after dark. Cinemas will not be open at all'. Nothing more inconceivable or in-

deed nonsensical could have been given out as official policy. I said: 'But you will need cinemas. They are vitally important for purposes of propaganda—to keep the public fully informed of what is happening—for raising morale. There are all sorts of things that the public will have to be told—about rationing, fire-fighting, coal-supplies, conserving one's water supply, and so on. And then there is the very important need to show short documentary films about recruiting for the services and for the coal-mines and for training those who volunteer to help—men as well as women. . . .' He interrupted. 'It's a Cabinet decision' he said. I went at once to see Anthony Asquith, and his mother lost no time in inviting a number of Cabinet Ministers and Members of Parliament as well as myself, George Elvin and other A.C.T. members to 44 Bedford Square. She denounced the Government. Films were vitally important not only for the people in Britain, but for keeping foreign countries, especially neutral countries, informed about what we were doing. Her attack was devastating; it galvanized the Government into action. Sir Joseph Ball was replaced by Sir Kenneth Clark, who was Director of the National Gallery and Surveyor of the King's Pictures. . . . He reversed the earlier decision and we were able to continue to make films and show them in cinemas all over the country.[2]

This account runs together two separate developments. The cinemas were closed down on September 3, 1939, but this ban was lifted for cinemas outside urban districts on September 11 and for cinemas in city areas from September 15. No doubt the agitation organized by Margot Asquith played its part in this. Ball continued in office until the end of 1939, when he was replaced by Clark, but Ball was under mounting attack for his failure to provide a comprehensive policy of cinematic propaganda and his inclination to rely merely on the newsreels. Clark was to produce a much more thorough plan for use of feature films, documentaries, and newsreels as part of a concerted effort to put across 'the principles underlying British wartime propaganda'. This was clearly much more to the taste of Dickinson, Asquith, and the other activists of the film industry. Clark himself did not stay long in the post of director of the Films Division, being promoted in April 1940 to controller of Home Publicity. His successor at the Films Division was Jack Beddington, who had been head of publicity at Shell and whom Dickinson thought 'brilliant, absolutely right'.

Dickinson became involved in directing *Gaslight*, but as this film was going through the labs, he was contacted by Dallas Bower, an old friend who had been a sound engineer at Stoll Studios, for Cricklewood, when Dickinson worked there and was now with the Ministry of Information (MoI). He had been put in charge of the project to make five-minute MoI instructional films, to be shown in all cinemas as part of the regular programme. The MoI wanted a pilot film, and the plan was to strike a thousand prints and get them into 4,000 cinemas within a month. The MoI had no idea about a subject and asked Dickinson to come up with one. He found a letter in the *News Chronicle* from a mother complaining about the evacuation of children, contacted her to discuss her criticisms, and proposed a film justifying the evacuation policy. He gathered together a production team, including his old Stoll colleagues, cinematographer Desmond Dickinson, editor Sidney Cole, and the writer Donald Bull, all of whom had worked on his recent feature films. The day after *Gaslight* opened, they were at Paddington Station filming the evacuation of children. They travelled to Torquay to film the arrival and then back to Denham Studios to put the film together. It was finished at a cost of £450 and previewed at the Dominion Cinema, Tottenham Court Road, exactly two weeks after shooting began. It successfully launched the five-minute programme.

The film *Westward Ho!—1940* is a taut, pacy little film, with its message spelled out at the beginning and the end: 'Controlled Evacuation, planned and executed in good time, is right'. It utilizes Bliss's minatory *Things to Come* music as a score, and in tracing the evacuation of children from Woolwich via Paddington to Cornwall, it employs some effective point-of-view sequences, from the local train passing through successive stations and collecting children en route, with parents lining the railway bridges to see them off; from the Devon-bound train, the children's view of the passing green fields. On arrival in Torquay, the children are bussed to local schools for meals, dispersed to local families and finally seen playing happily on the beach. Voice-overs by the children themselves cheerfully describe their experiences.

The film ends with the importance of evacuation attested by refugee women from Norway, Holland, Belgium, and France, superimposed on the map of Europe and warning that their countries were overrun before they could evacuate the children and urging Britain not to make the same mistake. Dickinson recalled that there was concern that this passage might do more harm than good to morale, and so they had to soften it. But the print as it stands contains the sequence and ends with a Scottish soldier declaring that he has evacuated his children and urging the audience to do the same. So either it was decided not to alter it or a similar but even more powerful sequence was replaced by the present one. It was, however, pronounced a success and Dickinson embarked on more.

With Donald Bull Dickinson scripted *Miss Grant Goes to the Door*, to illustrate the need for constant vigilance. It told the story of two spinsters unmasking a German parachutist and successfully handing him over to the authorities. But this was given to Brian Desmond Hurst to direct, because the Ministry of Labour wanted Dickinson to work on a film to encourage white-collar workers to retrain as engineers for the war effort. Working again with Desmond Dickinson, Cole, and Bull, Thorold directed and produced the five-minute *Yesterday Is over Your Shoulder*. This charming, crisp little film featured Robertson Hare, who also wrote and sang the jaunty title song. The commentary was spoken by Herbert Hodge, London taxi driver turned writer and radio personality, to give the film a wide demotic appeal.

Opening on the familiar bald pate of Robertson Hare, it established him in a few deft strokes as a clerk in a safe, steady job but anxious to contribute to the war effort. In a crowded commuter train, he sees an advertizement for 'untrained men to help their country'. He retrains in a factory as an engineer and earns a pat on the back from Minister of Labour Ernest Bevin, who is inspecting the factory. Having made the grade, he marches home in his overalls, to be received by his horrified wife (Joyce Barbour) with 'What will the neighbours say?'. 'Bugger the neighbours. I'm a British worker now', he replies. Although the 'bugger' is muffled by the slam of the garden gate, it is unmistakable and signals that loosening of censorship in the matter of language that the war was to usher in and shows Dickinson taking a characteristic swipe at one of his pet hates, class snobbery.

Dickinson's next five-minute film was to be *The Horse-shoe Nail*, from an idea by the playwright Clemence Dane, a story about the danger of careless workers putting an inadequately heated rivet into an airplane body. It was to climax in the plane crashing because of the defective rivet. But Lord Beaverbrook, the Minister of Aircraft Production, whose cooperation was needed, vetoed the film as an insult to aircraft workers. When Ernest Bevin, whose help Dickinson had enlisted, told him that it was based on an actual incident, Beaverbrook said that this was all the more reason to keep it quiet and the film was abandoned.

The MoI was at this time also anxious to make full-length feature films, and Dickinson was asked in the summer of 1940 to prepare a film version of an anti-Nazi play by Vicki Baum. But this was cancelled on orders from Churchill, who said that Britain was no longer fighting the Nazis but the Germans and so the main thrust of the film would have been wrong.

Dickinson had received several Hollywood offers following the success of *Gaslight*, including one from David O. Selznick, but he refused to leave Britain while the war was on. Instead, he accepted an offer from Warner Bros. to direct in Britain a biographical film about Disraeli, *The Prime Minister*. It was a presold package: an unproduced script sent over from Hollywood and two stars already cast, and Dickinson had very little say in either writing or casting. He was subsequently to dismiss the film as a piece of hackwork ('The less said about *The Prime Minister* the better'), and he refused to allow the National Film Theatre (NFT) to include the film in his eightieth birthday retrospective. When pressed, he would complain about the miscasting of Gielgud and Wynyard; the humdrum lighting and art direction and cramped conditions at Warner Bros.'; and ill-equipped and badly soundproofed Teddington Studios, where shooting, which lasted from September to December 1940, was constantly interrupted by air raids.

Sir John Gielgud has similar unhappy memories of the film. He recalled that it had been turned down by several stars before he was cast and

> was now to be made on a very small budget . . . with a couple of pillars and an arch that were moved around for exteriors, and grass matting for a stagey-looking garden. 'When in doubt', Thorold Dickinson said, 'We make it a night scene'. . . . The art director was cramped for space and the research had been skimped.[3]

These circumstances undoubtedly explain in part why the film emerged as a staid, cramped, and talky production, wholly lacking the dynamism of Warner Bros.' celebrated Hollywood biopics. But the script (by Michael Hogan and Brock Williams) was also part of the problem. For, in effect, it was two films crammed uneasily into one: the first half, set in the 1830s, detailing the courtship and marriage of the young Disraeli and showing his transformation from dandy novelist to respected statesman, and the second half, set in the 1870s, dramatizing his premiership and in particular his conduct of foreign affairs. This necessitates endless montages of newspaper headlines and lengthy intertitles to explain complex events and to bridge the passing of time, further slowing down the narrative flow. Under the circumstances, Dickinson handles it quite conventionally, contenting himself with realizing the script as efficiently and unobtrusively as possible, filming parliamentary debates in tableau long shot and conversations in standard two-shots, tracking on movement, and so forth.

Curiously enough, however, the film does fit one of Dickinson's continuing preoccupations— 'secret people'. Disraeli, the flashy, witty, conceited, dandy novelist, does contain a secret inner person—a deeply serious, patriotic statesman, anxious to serve his country. This is discovered both by the young widow Mary Anne Wyndham-Lewis and the Liberal Prime Minister, Lord Melbourne ('I think you can do great things for England'), who both encourage him to enter politics and support him at his lowest ebbs. This aspect may have attracted Dickinson. But the conventions of the historical biopic leave little room for the psychological exploration of this tension.

The lifelong romance of Disraeli and his wife Mary Anne, seen as entranced young lovers in the first half and Darby and Joan in the second half, is charmingly played by Gielgud and Wynyard. The film also explores Disraeli's special relationship with a supportive and sympathetic Queen Victoria, played by a badly miscast Fay Compton with too obviously padded cheeks. Gielgud, in a part that is a gift to an actor, enjoys himself hugely both as the flashy dandy and the canny elder statesman.

But the principal interest of the film lies in its propaganda content, which may well have been another of the film's attractions for Dickinson. The MoI had developed an attitude to the past that its officials were encouraged to disseminate. It centred on

> Britain's past record in achieving social justice while at the same time preserving the rights of man. The conjunction of the ideas of Britain as a pioneer of freedom and justice, against both domestic and foreign tyrants, and of balanced gradual social improvement.[4]

Disraeli in the context of 1940 clearly stands for Churchill. Patriot and imperialist, mistrusted as an outsider by the establishment, he comes to stand above party as a symbol of the nation. But, also in line with the MoI's directives on history, he shows concern for social reform, passing a series of acts (Public Health, Education and Factory Acts) designed to improve the lot of the poor. This programme for reform is significantly achieved by parliamentary methods and not by the revolutionary violence of the Chartists, seen earlier in the film. Disraeli thus stands for 'one nation' Toryism and is seen to have the love and backing of the people.

His great opponent Gladstone, on the other hand, is clearly Chamberlain. He preaches the policies of the now discredited National Government of the 1930s: peace, retrenchment, reform. But he is in the pocket of the industrialists and the party establishment ('The Old

Gang'), and his policies are denounced by Disraeli ('Peace at the cost of honour, reform at the cost of the constitution, retrenchment at the cost of national security').

When Disraeli becomes prime minister, he is handicapped, as Churchill was, by having a cabinet full of Old Gang stalwarts. A great continental alliance of Germany, Austria, and Russia threatens to dominate Europe in the 1870s just as in 1939 the Russo-German treaty gave both Hitler and Stalin the chance to further their territorial ambitions. When in 1878 Russia threatens Turkey, the cabinet refuses to honour its pledge of support and seeks to appease Germany and Russia. But Disraeli insists on mobilizing in support of Turkey ('Peace can be purchased at too great a price'). In 1939, Britain and Turkey had a similar mutual assistance pact. But Turkey can also be seen in the nineteenth-century context to stand for all those countries lost to Germany by appeasement.

Although Gladstone denounces Disraeli as a warmonger, the mobilization halts the Russian advance on Constantinople. As Nigel Mace has pointed out, the whole film is designed to exorcise the ghost of the Munich agreement by visually imitating the newsreels of Chamberlain's flight to and return from Munich in the guise of Disraeli's progress of 1875.[5] Like Chamberlain, Disraeli travels to Germany to confront the German chancellor. At one point, he even waves a piece of paper above his head in the familiar Chamberlain gesture. But unlike Chamberlain, he stands up to the dictators and by showing a willingness to fight forces Bismarck to back down so that he brings back a real 'peace with honour' and, unlike Chamberlain, deserves the plaudits of the grateful populace as he stands on the balcony of Buckingham Palace with his sovereign.

Interestingly, no mention whatever is made of the fact that Disraeli was a Jew. Film companies, both British and American, although often run by Jews, were notoriously diffident in the 1930s about tackling Jewish subjects and in particular tackling anti-Semitism. There were a few notable 1930s examples of such films—*Jew Süss* in Britain and *The House of Rothschild* in Hollywood—but in the main the cinema skirted the issue. Lester Friedman has suggested that this was in part because studio bosses wanted to be integrated into non-Jewish society and were reluctant to draw attention to the 'otherness' of Jewry.[6] Despite the war, little was made of the plight of the Jews in British wartime films, and anti-Semitism remained a feature of British life.

Despite Dickinson's apparent discontent with his script and cast, he signed a contract with Warner Bros. on completion of the film. It was released in March 1941, and the critics almost unanimously pronounced it worthy but dull and a disappointment coming from Dickinson after the brilliance of *Gaslight*. C. A. Lejeune in the *Observer* wrote:

> One of the worthiest and wordiest films you are likely to see for a long time . . . is *The Prime Minister*. Our Thorold Dickinson, who made such a good job of *Gaslight* last year, directed it. But apparently he couldn't stop it. It just goes on and on. . . . The film seems to me worthy to the point of being wearisome.

Moore Raymond in the *Sunday Dispatch* reported, 'It includes too much of Disraeli's long, exciting life. There are too many bits and pieces without a main theme. Still it's quite entertaining even if it isn't inspiring'.[8] George Pitman, in *Reynolds' News*, expressed disappointment:

> I came to praise and stayed to scoff. . . . The structure of the film suffers from diffuseness . . . and the ideology, if I may put it so, is all wishy-washy. . . . I'm the more sorry for director Thorold Dickinson, one of our grade A coming men, since he clearly has an entirely intractable proposition on his hands.[9]

Dilys Powell tried to find something to praise in the *Sunday Times*:

> It is foolish to pretend that Mr. Thorold Dickinson has not been driven to clichés in . . . *The Prime Minister*. But Mr. Dickinson . . . has been given an exceptionally difficult job; what is more he has not been helped by his scriptwriters, who have handed him all the familiar banalities of fluttering females, fruity old statesmen and raucous lower orders. He has however been helped by his actors. John Gielgud and Diana Wynyard give the narrative a continuity, which all its display of newspaper cuttings can never give it. . . . The film opens slowly but gathers speed and throughout its latter half moves into a rhythm and an emotional dignity for which Mr. Dickinson is owed much respect.[10]

The *Times*, however, conveys the impression that one still gets viewing the film today, when it declared that the film was

> too inclined to rely on a slow, plodding, unfolding of events by means of a screen which seems full of newspaper headlines, and all too seldom is character seen at its work of moulding these events to

Thorold Dickinson, the film director as intellectual

Dickinson directing Robert Adams and Eric Portman in *Men of Two Worlds*

Spanish *ABC* dramatized Dickinson's belief in the value of education

The High Command (with Lucie Mannheim) explored the secret life of an expatriate British colonial community

Man's inhumanity to man was explored in *Hill 24 Doesn't Answer*, for which Dickinson re-created the evacuation of Jerusalem during the First Arab-Israeli War

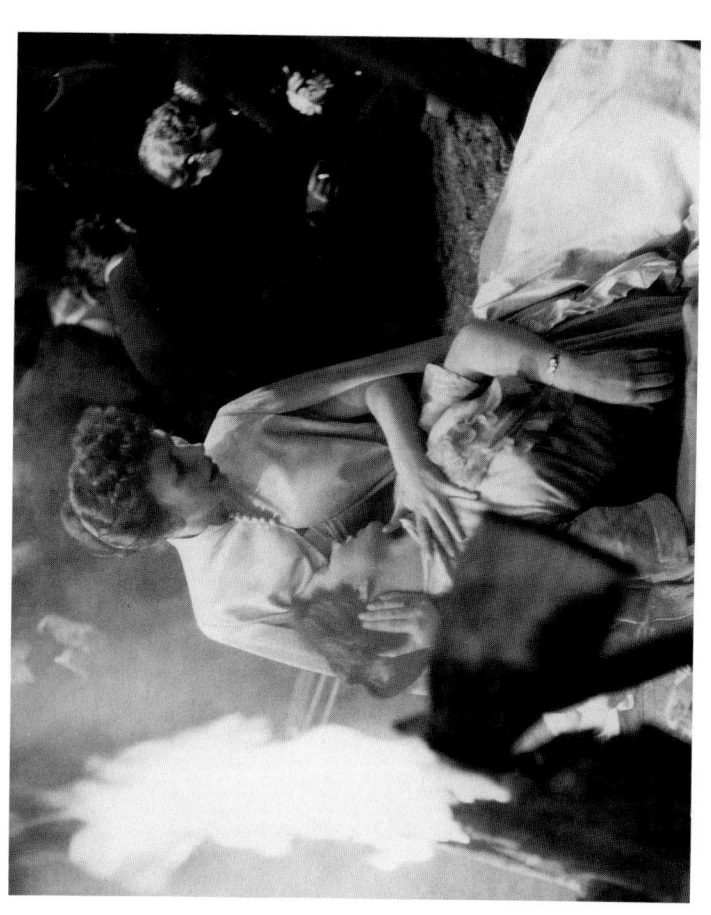

It also formed the basis of Secret People
(with Valentina Cortese) *about a terrorist gang*

Gaslight (with Anton Walbrook and Diana Wynyard) was an exposé of Victorian bourgeois patriarchal tyranny

Queen of Spades (with Anton Walbrook and Edith Evans) was a classic exposition of Dickinson's fascination with the inner man released at times of crisis

its will. Lack of inspiration in the direction, the slowness, the staginess, would be even more obvious than they are were it not for the acting of Mr. John Gielgud as Disraeli and of Miss Diana Wynyard as Mary Anne. . . . The scenes they share together have a warmth that lights up a film which keeps its dignity throughout but seldom flares into imagination.[11]

Unhampered by the patriotic considerations that may have inhibited some of the more critical comments made in Britain, the *New York Times* was scathing when the film opened in America:

Mr. Gielgud plays Disraeli when a young man as though he were a highly offensive and effeminate popinjay and then makes him out as an old man to be a doddering pickle-puss. . . . It is not alone that Mr. Gielgud atrociously overacts. The fault of his lumbering *Prime Minister* is that it lacks dramatic structure utterly. It is simply an hour and forty minutes of vignettes from Disraeli's life. . . . The core of a lukewarm love story occasionally come through but that is forever getting lost in the perplexities of English politics. Disraeli must have 'gone to the country'—or threatened to—more often than a vegetable truck. Mr. Gielgud is surrounded by a very distinguished cast of British actors. . . . But they too are horribly hobbled by a stiff and inadequate script.[12]

The film was not a box office success and seems to have made little impact, something that led Gielgud to complain in 1943 that *The Prime Minister* 'could have been exploited a good deal more than it has been from a wartime propaganda standpoint. He thought it was a golden opportunity missed'.[13]

Two of the continuing propaganda themes of World War II were the threat from a possible fifth column in Britain and the danger of careless talk. They were to be combined in Dickinson's next film, *The Next of Kin*. It originated from a request made in December 1940 by General John Hawkesworth, the War Office's director of military training, to Michael Balcon, head of Ealing Studios, for an instructional film on security. Initially, the War Office envisaged a twenty-five-minute short. But the number of different things that they wanted to get across made a feature film a more suitable format.

Dickinson was invited by Balcon to write and direct the film. It was to take about three months and was to be done as cheaply as possible without sacrificing quality. The War Office was putting up £20,000, the maximum they could allocate. But Ealing agreed to furnish the remainder of the finance, which eventually worked out at £50,000. It was agreed that the film would be commercially released in due course and that as soon as it started to earn a profit, Ealing would be repaid their investment plus a small percentage. The rest of the profits would go to the Crown.

It was clear that the War Office had no ideas about a story line, but they promised full support, access to army records, and the release of service personnel to work on the film. They secured Dickinson's release from his Warner Bros. contract, and they assigned as liaison officer on the project Captain Sir Basil Bartlett, BT. Baronet, who was himself a writer and agreed to help provide material for the screenplay.[14]

Dickinson set to work on the screenplay at Ealing Studios with the Ealing story supervisor, Angus MacPhail. Bartlett suggested using the organization of security at a major seaport like Liverpool as the mainspring of the story. Dickinson and MacPhail then worked for three weeks constructing a story along these lines, with the threatened German invasion of Britain as the background. But when they presented their treatment to the War Office, it was rejected. The German invasion background was vetoed and a combined operations assault on the Continent suggested as an alternative background. With advice from Lieutenant Colonel Ely of the Combined Operations Department, an outline was produced that satisfied the War Office. Since there was an urgent need to get on with it, John Dighton was drafted into the writing team to help prepare the shooting script. The film was to go into production under the working title *Security*, but eventually Dickinson devised the title *The Next of Kin*, a reference to the familiar wartime wireless announcement: 'The next of kin have been informed'.

Dickinson's involvement in the film was almost ended prematurely when, as he was in the process of investigating army records, it was discovered that he was technically a security risk. He had been classified as a 'premature anti-Fascist' because of his filmmaking activities in Republican Spain. But after some discussion, he was cleared to continue his work.

The shooting script was ready by May, and Dickinson, anxious to avoid well-known faces to make the impact of the story greater, handpicked a blend of army personnel and character actors. This had the additional advantage of keeping costs down because the service personnel were only getting their service pay. The film itself was shot between July 26 and October 24, 1941. The interiors were completed in seven weeks, even though Dickinson kept losing camera operators through call-ups. Eventually twenty-two worked on the film. But the studio began to complain when the schedule for shooting the final battle scenes overran. This delay was due partly to bad weather and partly to the unavailability of essential items of naval and military equipment.

To shoot the battle scenes, Dickinson received the use of a battalion of troops from the Royal Worcestershire Regiment, three naval landing craft and their crews, sixty officers and men of a commando unit, and the loan for three hours one afternoon of Royal Air Force (RAF) fighters and bombers. Dickinson and Basil Bartlett selected Mevagissey in Cornwall as their location, deeming it the nearest thing in Britain to a Breton port. They were given carte blanche to operate in and around the town by the district council so long as the consent of all property owners was obtained and damage was compensated for. Art director Tom Morahan set to work transforming the town into a Breton fishing port, while the strategy for the raid was worked out exactly like a real-life combined operation by Dickinson, Bartlett, production manager Cecil Dixon, and officers of the Worcesters. The actual filming was a fraught business, as Dickinson recalled in 1944:

> We discovered that the battalion was unaccustomed to landing operations and street fighting, so we set the various companies to work rehearsing, while we went from one to another with our view-finders choosing camera positions and eliminating military action which was ineffective on the screen. As all military action is specifically designed to be as invisible as possible by choice of uniform, camouflage, cover, night and dawn attacks and so forth, I had to spend much time compromising between the demands of the army and the demands of the cameraman Ernest Palmer. . . . All the time I was dictating notes to my continuity secretary against the time when we should want some semblance of a script. Besides trying to cover coherently a complex military operation, we had to thread our principal characters through the action and, bring them all to a nicely-rounded conclusion and a very sticky end. I insisted on them all living all the time in Mevagissey and being ready to come to any point at a moment's notice. This was the biggest charade in recent motion picture history and I wanted to take no chances. Incidentally, of course, we soon found that when the tides were right for landing at one point, the light was invariably wrong except for an hour or two in each cycle of tides, so we had to switch our schedule and leave one landing in the middle while we caught the tide at another landing. we worked inland between each cycle of tides. All this had to be exactly set in our call sheets which were distributed by dispatch rider at 4 p.m. on the day before. And alternatives had to be provided in case the weather was good for one situation and bad for another. What with that and the cliffs and one or two other problems, I lost a stone and a half [twenty-one pounds] in weight during those six weeks. . . . We had other excitements, timing explosions to represent bombing results, street-fighting, again with

timed explosions, and the day when German tanks were supposed to enter the town. We brought a fake light German tank into the narrow streets of the town, whereupon the military advisers decided that no tank would ever venture into such narrow streets, for it would be attacked from the upper floors of every building. What were we to do? We had diverted the bus service from the town, half the shops were isolated from their customers, the police were getting uneasy, the weather was perfect. And the major and I kept everyone waiting while we went to a café on the quay and worked out further action which would be equally spectacular yet feasible from a military point of view. . . . I shall never forget the afternoon of the air scenes. . . . The aircraft were due over the town in a quarter of an hour. As Palmer and I arrived at our principal longshot position, we were horrified to see hundreds of people around us on our cliff and fully four thousand on the cliff opposite. Any camera panning over and view of aircraft couldn't fail to take in masses of spectators. Just then an officer came up on a motor bicycle. He pointed at the people and asked: 'Shall I get the aerodrome on the phone and cancel the flying?' I said: 'No. The weather is perfect. Where are your company? 'Down in the town, watching' he said. 'Well', I said 'the only thing to do is to get them into their vehicles, drive up the cliff, fix bayonets and drive the civilians over the crest of the hill'. He went away without a word. When the aircraft flew in from the sea, there wasn't a civilian in sight.[15]

As bad weather slowed down shooting, the War Office withdrew half the battalion for other duties, and a vendetta developed between the commandos and the battalion that had to be calmed down. But eventually, Thorold Dickinson had 48,000 feet of film and 10,000 feet of soundtrack, which editor Ray Pitt assembled into a fifty-minute sequence. The whole was then edited down to a quarter of its length, and maps and headquarters dialogue scenes were inserted to explain the action and it was finished. The editing of this sequence took as long as the whole eighty minutes of the rest of the film. A score was provided by William Walton, and the film was ready for showing to service personnel by February 1942.

The film has neither a hero nor a conventional narrative thread. One of Dickinson's idols was Jean Renoir, and what he wrote admiringly of Renoir's *La Grande Illusion*—'The star of the film was an idea and the characters came and went as the subject required'—could be said also of *The Next of Kin*.[16] The film, in fact, was the dramatization of a slogan 'Careless talk costs lives', a mosaic of stories and incidents constructed around that single central idea. In a film that switches so freely back and forth from an English to a German view of the proceedings, it is the slogan which gives the film its dramatic unity. Everything dovetails into it. Several obvious and directly propagandist devices are used to set out the message. At various points during the film, the camera dollies into the posters and notices, bearing slogans such as 'Keep it under your hat'. The message is amplified by security officers in lectures to their men ('You are the real security men'). But it also informs every aspect of the story.

The film falls essentially into three parts. The first part shows how leaks of information occur. When the Army decides on a raid on the French coast, the 10th Chilterns are transferred to Watercombe on the Cumberland coast for training, and Major Richards (Reginald Tate) is assigned as security officer. Two sources of leaks are developed and interwoven, embracing both officers and other ranks. Both involve emotional entanglements, clearly seen as the greatest danger. A private, Johnny (Geoffrey Hibbert), gives away information at his meetings with his Dutch refugee girlfriend Beppie (Nova Pilbeam) and in his unauthorized letters to her, which he considers harmless. But this information is blackmailed out of Beppie by her employer Ned Barratt (Stephen Murray), a Nazi agent. Lieutenant Cummings, a callow young officer (Philip Friend), is led on by dancer Clare, similarly revealing vital information about troop movements and plans. But Clare, a drug addict supplied by a Nazi agent (Mary Clare), passes the information on, enabling the Germans to build up a picture of the regiment's activities. The Nazi dupes almost all meet unhappy ends: Clare and her control are arrested and will hang; Beppie kills Barratt and is herself killed by agent Davis (Mervyn Johns); Cummings is killed in the final raid;—the price of their witting or unwitting treachery. But the principal Nazi agent, Davis, survives with the important information that there are aerial photographs that are the key to the British plan.

The second part of the film shows the Nazi espionage network swinging into action, detailing the sinister chain reaching from Berlin into the heart of England. A respectable dentist, a genial Irish sailor, the mild-mannered 'Welsh' evacuee Davis, a collection of spies and fifth columnists,—all participate in the simple business of gaining the aerial photographs by switching briefcases with the careless wing commander, who is dining in a plush restaurant with a pretty girl, duplicating them, getting them out of England on a neutral ship to a neutral port and thence by plane to Berlin.

The third part of the film reveals the tragic consequences of this activity. The Germans identify Norville as the destination of the raid and move in extra troops. The British attack, and although they blow up vital installations, they suffer heavy losses, much heavier than they need have done, as a sombre narrator relates, because of the leak of information, 'The next of kin have been informed'.

Dickinson deploys three devices to put over the story—casualness, lightness, and realism, each of them making the message more grim. Apart from the monocled, heel-clicking, stereotyped Hun in the Berlin headquarters scene, Dickinson portrays his German spies for the most part as very ordinary, inoffensive, sympathetic figures, the least likely types to be involved in espionage and fifth column activities, and therefore the least likely to elicit suspicion. There is Barratt, the kindly, bespectacled, pipe-smoking, soft-spoken bookseller, who ruthlessly blackmails Beppie by threatening her family in Holland with concentration camp internment. There is Davis, the gentle, middle-aged Welsh evacuee, who murders Beppie and blows up an ammunition dump. There is Ma, the motherly, cheerful, cockney, theatrical dresser, who forces the drug-addicted Clare to get information by threatening to withhold her 'coke ration'.

When these figures have been established as spies, casual, apparently meaningless chatter in their hearing in pubs and at a dance takes on a sinister, and ultimately deadly, importance. This danger is the basis of an episode that takes place entirely on a train. Drunken soldiers chat in the railway buffet car, with a German spy in British army dress listening and pumping them. Another soldier becomes suspicious and reluctantly reports his suspicions to two officers, who equally reluctantly question the man, not wanting to make a fuss. Their suspicions aroused, they order him to strip, to see whether he has the strap marks of a parachute on his shoulders. He attempts to bolt and is caught and arrested. The point of the episode is not only the ease with which information can be leaked but the inbred reluctance of the British to make a fuss when they are suspicious, a reluctance that, the film suggests, must be overcome in the interests of national security. Even soldiers on duty are guilty of laxity in this regard, as Richards's arrival at the Watercombe headquarters is made to demonstrate. En route, one soldier gives him directions to the camp without ascertaining his identity, and another admits him without asking to see his pass. Both are reproved.

The simplicity and speed with which the Nazi spy chain gets the information to Berlin are conveyed by rapid cutting, movement, and pace. But this is reinforced by a grim light-heartedness, which Dickinson found paid dividends. Several times Davis makes jokes about spies and at one point in Barratt's shop is found ostentatiously reading a book entitled *I Am a Nazi Agent*. The gag ending of the film had Naunton Wayne and Basil Radford in a railway carriage, casually discussing secret plans. A man leans across to offer them a light and is revealed as Davis, still up to his nefarious activities. Similarly, the switching of briefcases is done against a background of high-key lighting, pretty girls and airy badinage between customers. Dickinson found that these were the scenes that frightened people most, reinforcing the impression of casualness and ease being fatal in wartime.

The absence of a central figure and the shifts in perspective that the film involved contribute to the overall concept of a 'paraphrase of reality', one of the descriptions Dickinson used to apply to his work. This sense of reality persists throughout the graphically shot and edited final battle scenes. Dickinson employs a mobile camera, though much of his camera movement is unobtrusive, and he tracks frequently on movement, so as not to make audiences camera-conscious. Close-ups are used sparingly, generally for emphasis and notably at moments of high drama, such as the use of intercut close-ups in the scenes in which Barratt blackmails Beppie and Clare wheedles information out of Cummings. There are long unbroken takes to get over essential information to the audience, in the discussion of the tactics of the Norville raid, in the questioning of the German parachutist on the train, and in the lectures and discussions on security.

But all is not straightforward realism. The opening sequence takes place in a church in Norville. The camera tracks in to two figures kneeling before the altar exchanging information in whispers. They are a Free French officer spying for England and a local woman. A priest enters the frame and nods significantly to the two. Cut to the doorway where a German soldier stands threateningly. Then from behind the statue of the Virgin Mary there is a high-angle shot of the kneeling French patriots, the German oppressor in the doorway, and behind him a statue of Christ suffering on the cross. The symbolism is clear. The camera tracks with the Frenchman as he leaves, and the shot dissolves to one of the Virgin Mary standing upright in a little boat, the seven symbolic stars of the sea forming a halo over her head. The composition of the scene and the visual symbols all contrive to invest the Allied cause with divine sanction and damn the Nazi regime as anti-Christian.

The result of Dickinson's efforts is a film that is not only a vivid illustration of the meaning of a wartime slogan but also a taut and exciting espionage thriller, with an extremely resourceful and gripping script, vividly staged action, and a first-rate cast, with Mervyn Johns outstanding as the ubiquitous German agent. Looking back, Balcon was to call it 'One of the most important films made in the life of Ealing'.[17] The Army was delighted with it, showed it widely to the armed forces and War Office personnel, and the general opinion was expressed that 'it had achieved more than one would hope to do in 12 months by talking, lectures, etc.' General Alexander later told Dickinson, 'That film was worth a division of troops to the British army'.[18]

It was decided to release it to the public as soon as possible. But before it could be released, it encountered several obstacles, which demonstrate the pitfalls of filmmakers in wartime. First, the film fell foul of the actual course of the war. The film went on originally at the Curzon Cinema, the armed forces' cinema in London, in February 1942. Then suddenly and mysteriously it was ordered by Churchill to be withdrawn. The reason became clear when the St. Nazaire raid took place on March 28, 1942. Had the raid failed, the film could have seriously harmed morale. But once the raid was successfully concluded, the film went on again and with the added advantage of topicality. Churchill, however, who had seen the film, said that he would like to see a few more dead Germans and fewer dead British. So Dickinson trimmed about twenty feet of film to meet the prime minister's objections.

But the film then fell foul of the Air Force, which objected to the depiction of the RAF wing commander carelessly giving away information that cost Army lives. A special showing was ordered for the air minister, the chief of air staff, and other top brass. Their objections were eventually overborn, in part by Churchill's support for the film. The MoI now took over the film from the War Office, and United Artists arranged to release it. Its premiere at the Carlton Cinema in London on May 15, 1942, was attended by the Army Council and representatives of the cabinet. It went on general release in June.

The attempts to prevent the film being shown provided admirable publicity. It was advertized as 'the most discussed film of the day'. The reviews were generally highly complimentary. The popular press pulled out all the stops. 'You must see the film, because you are the people the film is about', said the *Sunday Graphic*. 'A film that was worth waiting for. Fine entertainment', said the *Sunday Express*. 'Every man and woman, either in or out of the services, must see *The Next of Kin*', said the *Empire News*. 'One of the finest pictures ever made' said the *Sunday Chronicle*.[19]

The quality press shared the general enthusiasm. Dilys Powell of the *Sunday Times* called it

> a most enjoyable, exciting, ingenious and salutary film; a topical film which is not forced, a warning which isn't a throwaway. . . . A cautionary tale, in fact; but a tale told with authority and conviction. A caution which, however fantastic the possibilities presented, should seal our lips for the duration. The whole has been admirably directed by Thorold Dickinson, and the final sequences of the landing are rendered with an absence of heroics which is quite heartbreaking.[20]

C. A. Lejeune of the *Observer* concurred, calling it

> meticulously done in every department of writing, direction and acting. So many individual credits are deserved that I shall not attempt to distribute them. With nobody's eye on the box-office, everybody's mind has been on his work, and the result is a masterly team-job, slick, unselfconscious, and about as dull as dynamite. I expect *Next of Kin*, which was not made for the box-office, to be a box-office hit up and down the country.[21]

William Whitebait of the *New Statesman* set the film in the broader context of the change coming over the British cinema:

> *Next of Kin*, like *One of Our Aircraft is Missing*, is an admirable example of the new kind of English film, actual, thrilling and taking its tune from events. It compares well with the reconstructions of war incidents favoured by the Russians.[22]

The trade paper *Kinematograph Weekly* pronounced it 'excellent propaganda proposition, a box-office certainty for all classes'.[23]

The critics' prediction was fully borne out. United Artists reported in May 'that it is one of the best films they have handled from a box-office point of view'. They later reported that between June 1 and July 14 approximately three million people had seen the film in civilian cinemas, and box-office receipts totalled £47,000. By December 19, 1942, cash receipts had reached £89,000, of which 80 percent went to the Treasury and the rest to Ealing.[24] Dickinson estimated that eventually United Artists handed over £120,000 to the Treasury.

What was the effect of the film on the people who saw it? For the civilian audience, Mass Observation, a group devoted to applying techniques of anthropological research to modern civilised societies, did one of its spot checks on cinemagoers to assess the effect of the film. In this case, it interviewed about ninety people, just under half women and just over half men, as they left cinemas in central and north London. Sixty-five percent said that they liked it very much, 25 percent said that they liked it, and only 5 percent disliked it. Approval and disapproval was equal amongst both men and women. The report noted that 80 percent of those interviewed had got the message of the film, namely, that it was a warning against 'careless talk', and many people actually mentioned the slogan.[25]

But the effect on at least one member of an audience was far more dramatic than Dickinson had intended. He recalled:

It was then that I learned about the effect of film on the individual member of the audience —depending on the condition of the individual. The man running the Curzon—which was the armed forces cinema in London—had to indent for a case of brandy for bringing back people who had fainted. It really knocked people out. This one woman—he phoned me to my office across the road in Curzon St. House— he said: 'You've got to come over. I've got a case here I can't cope with.' Anybody with a security pass—civilians in the Civil Service —were all forced to go and see the film. Everybody was ordered to see it. This woman who was a woman of about fifty-something, with 2 sons overseas in the war. She was working in the Civil Service. She didn't faint and she wasn't distraught. But her mind refused to believe the end of the film was fiction. To her it was fact. It had really happened. But when I said to her, 'Well, how do you imagine we got our camera onto the German side as well as onto the British', she said: 'I don't care about that. That's not important. What I saw on the screen has really happened.' We had to get a psychiatrist to her. Her brain had been lifted out of the normal intelligence into a state. She said: 'I shan't sleep again for the rest of the war. This thing will haunt me. It was a wicked, wicked thing to have done —to put this on the screen.'

Once again Dickinson's experience of American distribution was to be disastrous. In April 1942, the U.S. Embassy in London was pressing for *The Next of Kin* to be shown in America. Sidney Bernstein of the MoI despatched a print to David Selznick, asking for his appraisal of the likely effect of the film in the United States. Selznick viewed the film with director Ernst Lubitsch and screenwriter Nunnally Johnson and cabled his reply to Bernstein in four typed pages:

> Release in this country of the film in anything like its present version would be a dreadful error from the standpoint of British-American relations. . . . All the English officers are portrayed as stupid, careless and derelict. . . . Calculated to increase the fears of Americans and mothers especially that the British are simply muddling along, and that their sons will die because of British incompetence. This is aggravated by contrast with portrayal of brilliance and complete efficiency of German intelligence. . . . The latter point is felt so strongly that all here believe the film could be more profitably run in Germany for home consumption and for building German morale . . . perhaps even worse is the portrayal of so many British civilians as informers and spies, giving the impression that England is overrun by traitors. . . . So strong

was the feeling that no attempt should be made even to salvage the film, that I had difficulty in forcing rational discussion.[26]

An attempt was made, however, to salvage the film. For its American release, thirty minutes was cut, leaving only the bare narrative skeleton and removing much of the textural detail so important to the film's effect. A foreword was added in which J. Edgar Hoover warned about the dangers of careless talk in the United States, and the film was distributed by Universal. The *New York Times* liked it:

> *Next of Kin* was put together to do something more important than entertain—a necessity which placed a rigid premium upon reality and credibility. Everyone connected with its production imported these virtues into it to an admirable degree. It is tightly and cleverly written, its incidents are dramatic yet always plausible. It was produced and directed expertly and is most impressively played.[27]

Dickinson, however, was appalled by the cutting, calling it 'A total numbing of a vital film'. This demonstrates very well the two-edged nature of the propaganda film and the wide gulf remaining in reaction to film between Britain and the United States, a reaction dictated by national circumstances, the wider propaganda context, national taste and character, and the very different traditions of filmmaking that were emerging in response to the war.

The by-product from Dickinson's point of view was an interesting development. While he was editing *The Next of Kin*, he was asked to organize a production unit for the Army Kinematograph Service (AKS). He was commissioned as a second lieutenant, rising rapidly to the rank of major, took over the old Fox Studios at Wembley, and assembled an expert team of filmmakers, including directors Carol Reed and Jay Lewis; writers Eric Ambler, Peter Ustinov, and Jack House; editor Reggie Mills; and cameraman Freddie Young. During their first year, the unit produced seventeen military training films.

Dickinson did not direct any of the films himself but controlled and coordinated production. His unit's greatest achievement was a forty-minute film, *The New Lot*, directed by Carol Reed from an Ambler-Ustinov script, featuring Bernard Miles, Peter Ustinov, John Laurie, and Raymond Huntley and aimed at explaining to new recruits the need for discipline and teamwork. Robert Donat made a guest appearance in a mock-film epic that the new recruits go to see at the cinema and laugh at for its fake heroics. It was so successful that the same team later remade it as a full-length feature film for Two Cities, *The Way Ahead*.[28]

Ustinov and Ambler wrote the script for another AKS production, which Carol Reed was to have directed and which Dickinson called later 'the greatest war film never made'. It was to be done for Lord Louis Mountbatten, ardent film fan and then chief of Combined Operations. It aimed to illustrate the planning and execution of a raid on the French coast, showing how each man had his part to play. It was to have been filmed in Scotland below Troon golf course in the autumn of 1942. But it was cancelled because the ships that would have been used to defend them while filming at sea were needed for North Africa.

Dickinson recalled that Ustinov devised a character that 'would have been immortal':

> We found that in all these landings the bulldozer was the essential implement and Ustinov invented this bulldozer driver who was absolutely dedicated to his bulldozer, but not interested in anything else, and no sense of humour, never read the newspapers or anything. So he went on exercises with this bulldozer. But the end of the film was the real thing happening and this bulldozer driver thought it was still an exercise. When the ammunition was firing in an exercise it was blanks but when live bullets came round him, he got furious, wanted to go back and report that they weren't using the proper stuff and people shouted at him: 'It's the real thing'. He said: 'Real thing. Nonsense. It's another exercise'. He never to the end of the film realized it was not an exercise.

In December 1942, Two Cities Films asked the Army for Dickinson's release to tackle a job of national importance, and he left the unit to be replaced as its head by Carol Reed. The work of national importance was *Men of Two Worlds*.

NOTES

1. Thorold Dickinson, *A Discovery of Cinema* (London: Oxford University Press, 1971), p. 77. For a detailed discussion of the film work of the Ministry of Information, see Anthony Aldgate and Jeffrey Richards, *Britain Can Take It: the British Cinema in the Second World War* (Edinburgh: Edinburgh University Press, 1994).
2. R. J. Minney, *'Puffin' Asquith* (London: Leslie Frewin, 1972), pp. 102-103.
3. Ronald Hayman, *John Gielgud* (London: Heinemann, 1971), pp. 131-132.
4. Ian McLaine, *Ministry of Morale* (London: George Allen and Unwin, 1979), p. 150.
5. Nigel Mace, 'British Historical Films in World War Two', paper given at Imperial War Museum Conference, 'Britain and the Cinema: The Second World War', March 27-29, 1985.
6. Lester D. Friedman, *Hollywood's Image of the Jew* (New York: Ungar, 1982), pp. 57-85. On continuing British anti-Semitism, see Angus Calder, *The People's War* (London: Panther, 1971), p. 575.
7. *Observer*, March 9, 1941.
8. *Sunday Dispatch*, March 9, 1941.
9. *Reynolds' News*, March 9, 1941.
10. *Sunday Times*, March 9, 1941.
11. *The Times*, March 5, 1941.
12. *New York Times*, February 4, 1942.
13. *Kinematograph Weekly*, July 24, 1941.
14. For a full account of *The Next of Kin* in the context of British wartime propaganda, see Aldgate and Richards, *Britain Can Take It*, pp. 96-114.
15. BFI, *Film Appreciation and Visual Education* (London: BFI, 1944), pp. 12-13.
16. Thorold Dickinson, *A Discovery of Cinema* (London: Oxford University Press, 1971), p. 72.
17. Michael Balcon, *Michael Balcon Presents . . . A Lifetime of Films* (London: Hutchinson, 1969), p. 134.
18. In a parliamentary debate on propaganda on July 7, 1942, Sir Patrick Hannon (Birmingham Moseley) referred to *The Next of Kin* as 'that stimulating, helpful and inspiring production', and

on July 14, 1942, there was parliamentary pressure for the film's early release in the United States (*H. C. Deb.* vol. 381, pp. 700, 1067-1067).
19. These comments were reported in *Kinematograph Weekly*, May 21, 1942.
20. *Sunday Times*, May 17, 1942.
21. *Observer*, May 17, 1942.
22. *New Statesman*, May 23, 1942.
23. *Kinematograph Weekly*, May 21, 1942.
24. The United Artists reaction and receipts information come from the War Office and Ministry of Information records (WO 165/96 and INF 1/199).
25. Mass-Observation File Report 1342 (May 1942).
26. Caroline Moorehead, *Sidney Bernstein* (London: Jonathan Cape, 1984), pp. 147-148.
27. *New York Times*, May 6, 1943.
28. On the work of the Army Kinematograph Film Unit, see Eric Ambler, *Here Lies Eric Ambler* (London: Weidenfeld and Nicolson, 1985), pp. 182-191 and Peter Ustinov, *Dear Me* (Harmondsworth: Penguin, 1978), pp. 149-154.

SIX

Emergent Africa:
Men of Two Worlds

At the time of the outbreak of war, comparatively little had been done by way of social and economic development to prepare the African colonies for the eventual independence that was always the stated aim of British colonial policy. This was due partly to economic restraint imposed by the Treasury and partly to the entrenched idea that nothing should be done that would interfere with the structures and practices of native life.[1]

But the situation changed rapidly and dramatically after 1939. It became necessary to counter German propaganda about Britain's 'cruel and exploitative Empire' by projecting the image of a beneficent and constructive Imperialism. Since this needed to be based on concrete reality, a positive programme of colonial development and welfare policy was initiated by the 1940 Colonial Development Act.

Even more pressing was the need to satisfy the Americans about the progress of the colonies towards independence. The war aims of the Allies, as embodied in the Atlantic Charter, included self-determination for all nations, and that view, coupled with America's ingrained hostility to British Imperialism, produced the attitude outlined by the American Undersecretary of State Sumner Welles in 1942; 'The age of Imperialism is dead. The right of people to their freedom must be recognised. The principles of the Atlantic Charter must be guaranteed'.[2]

The Colonial Office had to come to terms with the new imperatives and by mid-1942 had evolved the concept of 'partnership' to replace the old idea of 'trusteeship', equality rather than dependence, and this began to be used regularly in public pronouncements. In July 1943, the colonial secretary, Oliver Stanley, made a statement of colonial war aims in the Commons, containing a specific pledge 'to guide colonial peoples along the road to self government within the framework of the British Empire'.[3] It was the culmination of several years of planning and discussion, and it had the backing of the major political parties. So, as Lee and Petter remark, 'a comprehensive policy of "progress", recognising social, economic and political aspirations, and relating them to one another, was spelled out for the first time'.[4] Economic and social progress for the colonies became a theme of pamphlets, books, and speeches on the Right and the Left, though this had one particular side effect. 'The partnership doctrine sought to make dependence more palatable by portraying the colonial Empire as a system of cooperation animated by a desire for social and economic reform rather than a system of rule animated by a desire for good government'.[5]

The Colonial Office was aware of the need for positive propaganda to promote its new policy and commitment both at home and abroad. Noel Sabine was appointed public relations officer for the Colonial Office in 1940, though it was not until 1942 that he got a proper department and the rank of assistant secretary. His work was initially defensive and aimed at the maintenance of morale and solidarity at home and in the Empire, and he worked closely with the Ministry of Information to project a picture of the colonies and the mother country combining to defeat a common enemy. A Colonial Film Unit, established under the aegis of the MoI, produced documentary films for African audiences with the aim of promoting commitment to the war effort and support for continuing British rule.[6]

But by mid-1942, Sabine decided that a major commercial feature film was needed to project the newly evolved policies of 'partnership' and 'social and economic progress'. He contacted the MoI, and the journalist and novelist Mrs. E. Arnot Robertson, then working for the Films Division, prepared a short story called 'The White Ants' to dramatise the propaganda points required. It contains the essence of the story that became Dickinson's *Men of Two Worlds*. Set in East Africa, the story tells of the struggle by District Officer James Shearforth and educated black schoolteacher Lewis Hale to break the power of the local witch doctor, who is impeding the introduction of up-to-date scientific and medical methods, which would preserve the health and well-being of the villagers. Hale succumbs to the force of superstition when a spell is put on him and goes into a coma. But he rallies and recovers. Shearforth's involvement with his work puts stress on his marriage to Laura but the marriage survives.[7]

On August 6, 1942, Robertson sent the story to Sabine and also sent a memorandum to Jack Beddington, head of the Films Division, urging speed in getting it into production:

If we wait for the Colonial Office to send in their comments, you know how it will be—the two copies I sent will pass slowly from hand to hand while elderly District Officers gently decaying in Whitehall, argue for weeks as to whether the houseboy should speak Swahili or Kisukuma, whereas he'll obviously talk English in the film. And it is weeks before anything can be done.

She argued that production be initiated immediately and Colonial Office suggestions be incorporated at the script stage. Beddington wrote 'Rubbish' next to the comments about Colonial Office delays but approved the story ('I think this is delightful') and initiated MoI procedures for getting feature films made.[8]

After putting up the money for *49th Parallel*, the MoI had given up directly financing films but initiated feature films by preparing a package—a story with approved propaganda elements and the provision of official personnel and facilities in return for the right to approve the finished film. This was the procedure followed in the making of, for instance, *The Way Ahead* and *The Way to the Stars*. The producer to whom 'The White Ants' was offered was Filippo del Giudice, whose Two Cities Films was also to produce *The Way Ahead* and *The Way to the Stars*, and who was particularly cooperative. As he wrote to Beddington on March 7, 1942, 'it is the policy of this Company not to make any film whether on subjects connected directly with the war or not without the approval of the Ministry of Information'.[9]

Del Giudice agreed to pay £250 to the MoI for the film rights to the story and agreed to the appointment of an MoI official to advise on the production. On October 28, 1942, del Giudice suggested Thorold Dickinson as director of the project and requested the help of the MoI in securing his release from the A.K.S. Unit where he was director in charge of production. On November 10, Beddington wrote to Paul Kimberley, director of the Army Kinematograph Service, explaining that Robertson had prepared a story of British colonial administration that skilfully combined 'dramatic value with excellent Empire propaganda'. The Colonial Office and the MoI wanted to see it produced as soon as possible and in their opinion and that of Two Cities, only one British director was

> capable of shooting this film and capturing on the screen the atmosphere of the native village, with the sinister influence of the witch doctor at work beneath a surface of apparent order and calm of the subtle play of emotion in the relationship between the District Officer and his wife. That director as you may easily guess is Thorold Dickinson.

Chapter Six

He therefore requested Dickinson's release as 'he would . . . be doing work of great value in the national interest'.[10]

Kimberley replied to Beddington on November 12, 1942, to say that Dickinson was 'doing a good job of work for us and it will be a great sacrifice to lose his services'. But he had discussed it with Dickinson and left it to him to decide 'whether he could be rendering greater service to his country by directing a picture of this nature or carrying on with his present work'. Dickinson called on Beddington, discussed the situation, and took the script away. Beddington reported to Kimberley, 'He likes the story very much and realizes that it could be made into a very important film'.[11] Dickinson recalled his own enthusiasm for a film about East Africa that was 'not a spectacle of conquest or a documentary but an intimate dramatic story of the two races working side by side, photographed in the studio with a smattering of exterior local scenes'. His release from the A.K.S. Unit was arranged, and he was approved as director.[12]

On December 9, 1942, a production meeting was held at Two Cities' offices in Hanover Square, attended by Beddington, del Giudice, Arnot Robertson, Dickinson, and the other members of the production team: art director Tom Morahan, cameraman Desmond Dickinson, producer John Sutro, and production manager Richard Vernon. There was still no scriptwriter. Robertson did not want to turn her story into a script herself. It was decided to leave the choice to Dickinson and Sutro. It was also agreed that it was desirable to 'choose a native from Uganda for the part of the schoolmaster and bring him back to England'. It was arranged that Dickinson and the scriptwriter would leave for Tanganyika to do a preliminary survey in mid- to late January. The three remaining members of the first unit (Morahan, Dickinson, and Vernon) would follow three weeks later. The whole unit would spend some weeks making arrangements to begin shooting in July. Full Colonial Office and MoI cooperation was promised.[13]

Dickinson's first suggestion for a scriptwriter was Louis MacNeice, but the BBC refused to release him due to personnel shortage.[14] Joanna Dickinson went off to her favourite bookshop Bumpus's and came back with books and pamphlets about Africa. She drew Dickinson's attention to Joyce Cary's 'The Case for African Freedom', no. 11 in the Secker and Warburg Searchlight on Africa series. He read the pamphlet in a single sitting between 11 P.M. and 2 A.M. and decided that this was his man. Cary, Irish-born novelist, former colonial administrator in Nigeria, and a man of liberal-progressive ideas, was contacted by Dickinson and Sutro and agreed to take on the job.[15]

It was a five-man unit (Dickinson, Cary, Morahan, Vernon, and

Desmond Dickinson) that set sail on January 17, 1943, on the troopship *Duchess of Richmond* from Glasgow. Their destination was Lagos. But the convoy plans were changed in mid-ocean and they were put ashore at Freetown, Sierra Leone, where they were entertained by Graham Greene, then a security officer, while they waited for a plane. Eventually, with the help of the MoI, they got a plane to Lagos via Monrovia and from Lagos flew to Khartoum and then to Dar-es-Salaam, where Dickinson went down immediately with malaria. Vernon and Morahan were also to be ill during the trip. Quite apart from this setback, the ship carrying their movie camera and film stock was sunk, and they were left with just a stills camera. But they carried on. They scouted locations and settled on the village of Moshi near Mount Kilimanjaro. They collected props and artefacts, making contact with local chiefs through one of their assistants, a chief's son and a graduate of Makerere University. Dickinson noted later that their fictional district commissioner was far in advance of his real-life counterpart at Moshi:

> The D.C. who had been in charge for seven years at Moshi, which we made our base, said he had never found evidence of the practice of witchcraft in that area, yet our chief's son found one such doctor within ten minutes' drive of the town. He was an African herbalist of some skill, who, to build his power and influence, worked as much on the minds as on the bodies of his community. He worked to undermine their self-reliance, the weakness of which is the main adverse characteristic of the local character.[16]

After ten weeks, the unit flew home, armed with notes, sketches, and still photographs. Dickinson and Cary had been developing the script all the time, and now they completed their treatment, developing the characters and action from the original story. The district commissioner's wife was eliminated and replaced by a lady doctor, Catherine Munro. The African, renamed Kijana and later Kisenga, was made into a musician. Cary invented the characters of Magole the witch doctor and Mrs. Upjohn. Then a German refugee scriptwriter Herbert Victor was engaged, and he and Dickinson lodged in Oxford for several weeks, preparing the shooting script and dialogue. Cary went over it all, making emendations and improvements where he saw fit. Dickinson saw Victor's role as that of the audience, the layperson, who could prevent the script becoming too technical or esoteric. Victor, recalled Dickinson, was a man who 'knowing nothing of Africa, insisted on every point of the script being clear to the uninitiated, and on eliminating all points which could not be clarified in the two hour span of a motion picture'. They also engaged a psychiatrist, Dr. Felix Brown, to psychoanalyze the character of Kisenga. He vetted everything the writers prepared and suggested an important psychological motivation for Kisenga—a guilt complex following the death of his father. The hallucination scenes were based on Dickinson's own malarial hallucinations in Africa and incorporated symbolic elements, such as the white hands, suggested by Brown.

The script was completed and forwarded to the MoI, and immediate problems arose. Arnot Robertson disliked it:

> This seems to me an entirely unobjectionable but uninspired piece of committee work. The story sticks fairly closely to the original but the quality has gone; any character or force that may have been there have been worked out. Dialogue is pedestrian, and the music-theme introduced at the beginning and end is cheap and unconvincing. . . . There is hardly any effective conflict in this version and very little suspense —the Good White Man is so impeccably good that there is never any doubt that he will prevail over the evil forces which really haven't a fair chance. Possibly the photography will be exciting enough to stop the general effect of the film being laudable but dull. But it all lacks fire.[17]

The script and Robertson's comments were sent to various scriptwriters and anthropologist Gervas Huxley. Angus MacPhail, who had worked with Dickinson on *The Next of Kin*, pronounced the script

> immeasurably inferior to *White Ants*. . . . I think Thorold Dickinson is a first rate director, one of the very best in this country but I don't think he's a good writer. If he's summoned here to discuss the matter, I bet you he'll defend his script till the cows come home and no progress will be made by anybody. I'm glad Mrs. Arnot Robertson is indignant. She has every right to be.[18]

Ian Dalrymple, head of the Crown Film Unit, returned a detailed critique suggesting that it was unwise to make a Negro pianist the protagonist:

1. It is difficult to make a film both good and box-office about a negro.
2. It is difficult to make a film both good and box-office about an artist.

3. It is therefore doubly difficult to make a film both good and box-office about a negro artist.

He thought the story line pretentious and highbrow and the climax unsatisfactory. 'I really don't think that the final rescue of Kijana from mumbo-jumbo by music is either convincing or effective'. He concluded:

> In short while there is excellent material, I think the stage wants to be better set for the subsequent events. The events themselves want more dramatic unfolding; and personally I would concentrate on bringing out the struggle between the primitive and the westernized in Kijana, uncomplicated by his response to the music.

He also suggested incorporating a visit by one of the Colonial Film Unit vans: 'It would be interesting for the film-going public to see the use of film in this way; and might be an economical device to bring out the psychology and unexpected reactions of primitive folk'.[19]

The script, however, received more enthusiastic support from Gervas Huxley:

> I think that it should make a really interesting film of considerable propaganda value. I do not myself think that the white District Officer is too much of a plaster saint, but, as a matter of strict accuracy, I should doubt whether any East African native has yet progressed so far that he would be either a musician . . . or that his music would mean so much to him in psychological terms.[20]

There was also support from R. Nunn May, assistant director of the Film Division:

> The difference between this draft script and Arnot's original treatment is the difference between chalk and cheese. Arnot's treatment was a delightful little piece of literary camembert. What we have now is a whacking great hunk of feature film chalk. It is important, I think, that we should not judge the second by the standards appropriate to the first. . . . There is little to be gained by saying about this script all the things that, judging it by literary standards, can fairly be said of it—for instance, that it is obvious, crude, cheap and so forth. It is perhaps more important to appreciate that it has the makings of a rattling good film story, and that it shows British administration among primitive peoples through appropriately rosy spectacles. I think it not

unfair to say that the 'propaganda element' is clearer and more definite than it was in Arnot's sketch. . . . I think we should accept this draft script as the basis of the film and discuss it with the unit. From our point of view . . . there is a good deal to be said in its favour.[21]

The script was accepted, but changes were made in the light of the suggestions, for instance, incorporating the visit of a Colonial Film Unit van to the village. Arnot Robertson pronounced herself satisfied with the result: 'This seems a great improvement—a good workable treatment with the phoney features of the first treatment cut out'.[22]

The script was sent to the West African Students Union (WASU) by Jack Beddington with a request that they should recommend suitable African girls to act in the film. On July 28, 1943, he received a letter from Ladipo Solanke, secretary-general of WASU, saying that his executive committee had passed a resolution that

> the proposed film . . . should not be proceeded with owing to the fact that (a) the content and representation is contrary to African laws and customs (b) it casts a slur on the prestige of African peoples as a whole and is in no way suggestive of real cooperation between whites and blacks and (c) it prejudices future relations between the African peoples and the British Empire.

Four detailed pages of criticism were attached, suggesting that the script totally misrepresented African beliefs about healing and medicine, that it was a European view of witchcraft, and that Kijana was simply 'made to act as the British Imperial African Agency for purposes of establishing and prolonging British Imperialism among the African people'.[23]

Beddington passed on the letter to Sabine, who replied on August 31, saying that the script was being revised, not specially in response to the comments but in a way that would meet some of the objections. In addition, the secretary of state had 'received advice from several quarters including advice from certain Africans that the script represents a realistic and helpful treatment of the subject'.[24]

While on location, Dickinson had suggested to Two Cities that the film be made in Technicolor. Two Cities contacted the MoI, and Noel Sabine informed Beddington that the Colonial Office was strongly in favour.[25] The Ministry authorized the allocation of film stock in wartime, and it now approved the use of Technicolor for what would be only the sixteenth British Technicolor film since it was first used in 1936.[26] In October 1943, Dickinson set off again to shoot the location scenes. He, Desmond Dickinson, Morahan, Vernon, and assistant director Eric Davey flew to East Africa. The rest of the crew went by sea to South Africa and thence overland by rail, road, and river. The project took twelve weeks, during which much of the equipment was damaged due to the heat, damp, and mishandling en route. This necessitated on-the-spot repairs. But problems emerged all along the way, Dickinson recalled:

> Our first real trouble came when our manager, travelling with the unit and equipment, was interviewed on the South African radio in Cape Town. The Boer press bent their reports of his statement so as to belittle the subject of the film to stir up maximum hostility from the African population. The East African censor reported this to me, and I had to persuade the Governor of Tanganyika to suppress two weeks' issues of the South African press from the mails of Tanganyika, Kenya and Uganda to prevent if possible these lies from reaching the people with whom we were hoping to work whose cooperation was of paramount importance. This action in South Africa was typical of the virulent opposition of the Boers to Britain.[27]

The shooting of exteriors and back projection plates presented great difficulties:

> Our life was ruined by the positions of the sun. From 11 a.m. until 2 p.m. (the best hours for 'shooting' in Europe) the sun is right overhead, flattening out scenery and making human photography ugly. The eyes, for instance, disappear in their sockets. So it meant being ready to shoot from about an hour after sunrise (around 7 a.m.) until towards 11, and then knocking off for several hours to shoot again from between 2 and 5 p.m., when the setting sunlight becomes too yellow to give true colour value. The African peasant likes to work from dawn until 11 a.m. the rest of the day being too hot for regular work until the hour before sundown when he does a little gardening. We found the first part of the day pleasant to work in, but the afternoons under the blinding sunlight, when we were 'shooting' with the stifling bush around us, were cruel. 'Shooting' in the tropics is not a picnic, and it is not conducive to the calm thought and steady control which good picture-making demands.[28]

Scenes had to be improvised to accommodate changes in the weather, tracks for the camera had to be hacked out of the bush ('Even to get a simple four-seconds shot of a car travelling along a road we used to allow two hours of "artistic" hacking to make it possible for the single eye of the camera to receive an adequate impression of three-dimensional movement through the bush'), and shooting and travelling were impeded by wild animals. While Dickinson supervised the filming, Tom Morahan collected weapons, clothing, household utensils, and so forth, to ensure background authenticity, and Austrian-Jewish musicologist Hans Cory, who had been in Tanganyika since it was a German colony, travelled around making recordings of African dances and songs for use in the score. Cory was something of a character, and the refugee doctor in the film was based directly on him.[29]

But the final catastrophe befalling the unit related to the Technicolor film stock. Dickinson took with him monopack colour film that had been imported for the shooting of *Henry V*. But it was supposed to be used and processed within six weeks and was already stale when transported to Africa. To get it processed, something that could only be done in Hollywood, Two Cities arranged with the MoI to convey the film by road to Nairobi and then to fly it under refrigeration to the Gold Coast and by U.S. military aircraft to Florida and on to Hollywood. However, when the film arrived in Hollywood, the Technicolor laboratories were on strike, and by the time the film was processed the colour was running down the negative. Ninety percent of the film was unusable. Dickinson learned this a week before finishing shooting in Africa. The unit had covered themselves by taking the scenes also in black-and-white, and they salvaged some of these by including them in the film shown by the Film Unit van. But after all the effort expended on location, the bulk of the film had to be shot from scratch at Denham Studios, with the jungle and village reconstructed and glass-shot artist W. Percy Day providing painted backgrounds. All this considerably lengthened the shooting schedule and the cost. Shooting could not even begin until new Technicolor stock arrived from America. Work at Denham Studios finally began on February 26, 1945.

Shooting in Technicolor in the studio required considerable care and ingenuity. John Huntley described the filming, beginning with the tribal dance sequence:

> These festive dances . . . begin quite early by the light of a huge bonfire and go on all night. The moon rises at about 6 p.m. and is at its illuminating peak at midnight, at which time the fire is doused and dancing goes on by the light of the moon. To get the effect of the sudden transition from firelight to moonlight took a few rehearsals as the extinguishing of the orange arc lights on the gantries had to synch-

ronise with the dousing of the fire by water. When Thorold Dickinson and Desmond Dickinson were quite satisfied shooting proceeded and some most effective sequences resulted. The sudden complete contrast of glowing firelight and soft, brilliant moonlight, added to the colourful costumes make these sequences some of the finest of English Technicolor achievements. The longest tracking shot on this production was made on these sequences. Starting in the gloom—deepened by the glow of the fire in the middle distance—the camera tracked in for seventy-five feet right to the edge of the fire until a close shot of one of the leaping figures almost filled the screen. . . . Four dancers only are seen. . . . The light of the flames throws their weird, enlarged silhouettes on the surrounding vegetation and the whole effect is one of ominous portent. Tracking shots were used here to great effect. . . . For scenes in which the mental struggle between the educated African, Kisenga, and the African doctor Magole, rises to its climax, the story necessitated concentrating on a series of close-ups, one of the most intricate being in an involved tracking shot of only three feet in the confined space of Kisenga's hut. Kisenga is relating to the District Commissioner an ominous visit of Magole to his hut and the camera is recording a flash-back to the actual occurrence. Working with a 50 mm. lens in 800 ft. candle-power lighting, the camera started with Magole's face out of focus in the centre screen. As the latter begins to speak the camera tracks back a distance of only three feet and the face has to be in focus in this incredibly short space, with Kisenga's profile appearing at the side showing his reactions. This necessitated a number of movements, timed to a split second to ensure success, Robert Adams, as Kisenga, had to stand close to the camera ready for the Director's signal to sway into camera range a carefully measured distance in order to register his profile: the follow-focus assistant had to turn his salsen apparatus madly from the word 'action' in order to make 16 revolutions by the time the camera had tracked the short three feet, to ensure Magole being successfully in focus. Then, to put Magole out of focus again the whole process had to be followed in reverse. To add to the difficulties, all this was recorded in the confined space of a native hut.[30]

The shot was rehearsed for two and a half hours before it was taken. There were a number of difficult zip pan shots, which had to be equally carefully rehearsed, showing the terrified reactions of the natives to the arrival in the village of Magole. The reverse shots of Magole's departure after prophesying the death of Kisenga's father were taken with a 35-millimetre wide-angle lens, starting on a full head-

and-shoulders shot of Magole, to emphasize his mastery of the tribe. Crane shots, starting at a height of seventeen feet and tracking down to six feet, were used to record the departure of the tribe by lorry. Crane shots were also used to record the reactions of the natives to Kisenga's dramatic challenge to Magole to try to kill him. The scenes of the district commissioner driving out to see the ailing Kisenga also required ingenuity:

> The studios used the chassis of a V.8 with a platform slung specially low to accommodate the camera at a driver's viewpoint. Two 250 amp. arc took the place of headlights and the camera tracked round a circular path, picking up the vegetation caught momentarily in the glare of the headlights. Where it was necessary to show the actual car, an exact replica of the one used on location in Africa had to be specially built by a firm of coach-builders as it was found impossible to obtain one in England.[31]

Dickinson faced other problems, too, during the filming. One was the cast. All the time that he had been in Africa on his first reconnaissance trip, casting suggestions had been flying back and forth between him and Sutro by cable. On April 9, 1943, Dickinson cabled Sutro that 'casting now requires District Commissioner Leslie Howard type. Woman doctor Wendy Hiller.' They had been unable to find a suitable native in East Africa to play Kisenga and Dickinson suggested the black conductor Rudolph Dunbar. On April 12, Sutro cabled back, 'Leslie Howard out of question. Would you consider Leslie Banks?' Dickinson replied on April 28, 'Leslie Banks wrong age, suggest Ralph Richardson, Portman or even Redgrave, active, intelligent, not easily rattled type'. He also suggested the West Indian actor Robert Adams as Magole.

Eventually Adams was cast as Kisenga, Eric Portman as the district commissioner, and Phyllis Calvert as the doctor.[32] Dickinson later commented on the last two: 'They did their best but they had never visited East Africa and for the most part struggled against the usual stereotypes of white colonials'. He appreciated the performance of Orlando Martins as Magole, 'an experienced Nigerian actor who thoroughly enjoyed the villainy'. But there were major problems with Adams, who steadily lost confidence during the filming. The strain eventually became too much, and he disappeared. He was found by the police and returned, but by the end of the film Dickinson said 'his was less performance than behaviour'. The only genuine East African to play a major part was Eseza Makumbi, who was cast as Kisenga's sister. She had been discovered by Joyce Cary while Dickinson was ill and was pronounced a success by Dickinson.

Another problem was presented by the National Gallery. Dickinson wanted to film the opening sequence of Kisenga playing at a National Gallery lunchtime concert actually at the National Gallery. But Dame Myra Hess, who organised the concerts, refused permission. 'She had permitted no black man to play at any of the concerts, she said, and would not permit one to play for the film, even if it were for the government'. So the National Gallery had to be reconstructed in the studio.

The music and dance in the film, however, resulted in a much happier collaboration. To compose the score, Dickinson secured the services of Sir Arthur Bliss, who enjoyed working with Dickinson, calling him 'one of the nicest people I've even come across to work with'.[33] Sir Arthur utilized Cory's recordings for inspiration and came up with what John Huntley in his book on British film music called 'one of the finest film music works ever written'.[34] One of the most important elements of the score was the piano concerto *Baraza* (the Swahili word meaning a council meeting between an African chief and his headmen), which is Kisenga's composition. Consisting of three short movements and a cadenza, it was, wrote Huntley, 'bold, brazen, strident film scoring at its very best, a superb piece of movie music'.[35] Drum rhythms figured prominently over scenes of Magole plotting. But all the drumming sequences were made at Denham Studios. No location sound was used at all.

Bliss's music was also used to supply the necessary emotion for a reunion between Kisenga and his elderly parents, because the two East African natives playing the small roles were not professionals and could not produce the necessary feeling before the camera. The score was recorded by John Dennis, with Muir Mathieson conducting the National Symphony Orchestra and Eileen Joyce playing the concerto. In fact, *Baraza* was recorded before shooting began so that the visuals could be cut to the music.

The native dances were also re-created in the studio, based on filmed material from East Africa. Indeed, they were dances that the government was trying to suppress because the dancers took drugs to induce ecstatic states and the meaning of the dances was considered subversive. However, the reconstructions were so authentic that when the film was premiered in Dar-es-Salaam, the African mayor of the town said:

> I was particularly impressed by the complete accuracy of the *Kuanga* dances, in music, costumes, details of the ritual and atmosphere, and cannot understand how it is possible to film this which is one of the most secret ceremonies of the Africans.[36]

The dancers assembled for the film formed themselves into a professional troupe called *Les Ballets Nègres* and went out on tour.

On November 14, 1945, del Giudice was at last able to write to Jack Beddington at the MoI:

> *Men of Two Worlds* is now finished. . . . As soon as this film is ready it will be shown to you first and I am sure that you will be extremely pleased with the result of our work. This film will be a great tribute to your foresight for the idea came first from you and you remember the enthusiasm I showed when you first spoke of it. In my opinion Thorold Dickinson has done a masterpiece which will contribute highly to the better knowledge by audiences all over the world what the British Empire is doing in connection with the colonies and the speeding of civilization among the backward peoples.[37]

The film had gone through several changes of title before *Men of Two Worlds*, which effectively encapsulated the partnership idea in the story, was reached. *The White Ants*, the title of the original story, had given way to *Man of Two Worlds* then to *Threshold*, then briefly to *Gateway to the Sun* (which Dickinson thought sounded like a Fitzpatrick travel talk), then to *Kijana*, and finally to *Men of Two Worlds*.

But while Technicolor labs were preparing the print of the film, Dickinson was already plunged into his next project. Lord Wavell, viceroy of India, was anxious to improve the British image, and his public relations officer (PRO) had obtained a print of *The Next of Kin* for him and ran it. Wavell was impressed by Dickinson's way of explaining and justifying the work of the unpopular military security police. He wanted Dickinson to do a film story showing the beneficial side of the increasingly unpopular raj. So the PRO contacted Dickinson via the MoI. He recruited Joyce Cary, and with him and Joanna Dickinson, Thorold flew to India in January 1946.

After a lot of research, Cary and Dickinson came up with an exciting story based on British irrigation policy. The central idea was to show the creation of a reservoir by the persuasion of the Indians to flood a valley containing a Hindu temple in an area near Lahore. It was very much a parallel of the idea of moving the Litu tribe to avoid the tsetse fly in *Men of Two Worlds*, similarly charting the impact of progress on the natives and the efficacy of British colonial development policy.

But the project began inauspiciously. Dickinson was bitten by a dog and had to undergo a painful fourteen-day course of injections in case the dog was rabid. Joanna Dickinson was hospitalised with food poisoning. The central feature of the Hindu temple that they had chosen was a giant stone phallus, which might offend J. Arthur Rank, whose organization was to produce the film. But, most seriously, there was continual rioting and unrest in India. The Indian fleet mutinied while Dickinson was in the country and it was clear that conditions would not be propitious for filming. So after three months' research, the project was officially abandoned. The Dickinsons and Cary returned to England, where Dickinson was promptly hospitalized, but he was out in time for the premiere of *Men of Two Worlds* in July 1946.[38]

Peter Noble, in his history of blacks in film (published in 1947), hailed *Men of Two Worlds* as 'historic' and 'revolutionary', a landmark in the mature, unpatronizing depiction of blacks. Dickinson was reported as having believed that the film would be a 'potent weapon against discrimination'.[39] But the film is not really a race relations tract. There is no sign of white prejudice against Kisenga throughout the film. Any discrimination that he suffers comes from his own people. The film is much more obviously a potent vindication of British colonial policy, as indeed it was designed to be. It is in this that its historical interest lies rather than in the depiction of the blacks, who are imbued with that stiff tableau nobility that critics found in John Ford's *amende honorable* to the American Indian, *Cheyenne Autumn*. But credit should perhaps be given to Dickinson for an attempt to understand and take seriously African culture and the African mind at a time when prejudice was still rampant and deeply ingrained.

The basic theme of the film is the age-old conflict between backwardness reinforced by superstition and progress via education. The characters are simply types, representing the different black and white viewpoints. The action of the film centres on the government's wish to move the Litu tribe from their tsetse fly-infested tribal homeland to a new settlement area, part of a major resettlement programme aimed at eliminating sleeping sickness. The task of persuading the Litu to move is given to Kisenga, who after fifteen years in Europe as pianist and composer returns to East Africa as a teacher. He is opposed by the witch doctor Magole, who uses all his powers to block the move. The film details the battle of wills between them. Magole wills Kisenga's father to die when he falls ill, thus discrediting the English doctor

Catherine Munro who has treated him. Kisenga is shunned by the villagers, denounced by his sister and his mother, and ordered to leave by the chief. But he challenges Magole to kill him, and the resolution of the action comes when Kisenga survives the challenge, Magole's influence is destroyed, and the tribe is moved.

But more significant than this point is the fact that Kisenga only survives the conflict because of the intervention of District Commissioner Randall. Ill and depressed, haunted by guilt for his father's death, succumbing to superstitious fatalism, Kisenga is on the point of giving up the struggle ('What is fifteen years in England, compared with 10,000 years of Africa in my blood?'). Randall saves him. Randall, shrewd, wise, experienced, humane, is the white father figure, the classic embodiment of altruistic imperialism. He incarnates the sensible and forward-looking policy of the wartime Colonial Office. He is backed by Dr. Munro, good-hearted but impulsive, a newcomer who embodies the danger of proceeding too fast and too incautiously to implement a policy and with whom Randall has his own battles. Randall patiently explains the virtues of resettlement to the chieftains and tries to convince the Litu to move by argument and presentation of evidence. Munro, anxious to implement an obviously sensible policy as rapidly as possible, wants the Litu forcibly moved. She says angrily, 'I am surprised you stand such a lot of nonsense from people like the Litu', to which Randall replies, 'That's largely my job, isn't it?' Later Randall amplifies this: 'In our job one man has to take account of the native mind. That's the political job all over the world. Handling minds'. So he eschews the use of force, instead employing Kisenga to convince his people. This is not just expediency—Randall cannot himself challenge Magole. At one point he does so, but Magole slyly observes that his magic has no power over whites, only blacks. So it has to be Kisenga who challenges Magole, and for a while Magole's magic works against him. But in the end Randall uses the same means as Magole to win (i.e., willing Kisenga to live), in a scene ironically parallelling that in which Magole had willed Kisenga's father to die. To reinforce his point, he gets the children to sing Kisenga's chorale, and the battle is won. The obvious moral is that the whites have a vital role to play in Africa still, the white man's burden lives on, and Randall is really a latter-day Sanders of the River.

Just as Randall stands for education and progress on the white side, there is a white Magole too, the apostle of superstition and reaction—the travelling authoress Mrs. Upjohn, who in a devastating scene, written by Joyce Cary, is exposed to ridicule. She believes in racial purity—'The Soul of Africa'—and wants the natives to carry on living in ignorance and superstition, believing that culture and civilization contaminate their splendid primitive savagery. She demonstrates her ignorance of tribes and sects as she chatters offensively to Randall, who quietly and good-naturedly corrects her. Her views are ferociously denounced by Dr. Munro but dismissed with amused tolerance by Randall, allowing the film both the immediate 'gut' response and the civilized reply. The script is in fact somewhat toned down in the film version from the original text, in which Gollner, the Austrian refugee scientist, denounces the talk of the blood, race, and primitivism as 'mystic, escapist, fascist'. This is replaced in the film by a much lighter note, with Randall wryly observing, 'There'll always be an Upjohn'.

The film displays the classic white liberal faith in education. It is the educated native, Kisenga, backed by the other handful of educated natives (Aly the dispenser, Abram the schoolmaster), who carry out the enlightened policy of the educated whites (Randall, Munro). It is the ignorant and uneducated (Magole, Mrs. Upjohn), who oppose. The shared ideal is summed up the speech Kisenga makes when opening the new school:

> This is a great honour. To open a new school. And nothing gives me more happiness than to see new schools everywhere in the new settlement. I want my people to learn all that our white friends can teach. Knowledge is the only power that can fight against man's enemies, disease and superstition, and that worst enemy of all, fear. . . . Fear stands in the way of all progress; not only in Africa but in all the world. Fear of each other, fear of new things. But new things come by themselves—even in Africa, you cannot stop change. And people hate change. They hate because they fear and fear drives them to war. They fear because they don't understand the world or other people. Yes, they fear to learn, to know, to think. But children are not afraid, they are eager to learn. And so it is in the schools that we can fight with knowledge, with wisdom.

This is as much Dickinson's credo as it is Kisenga's.

Men of Two Worlds was Dickinson's most ambitious film, and it is perhaps his least successful. It is a difficult film to discuss, in part because the emergence of black Africa necessitates a double perspective in the critic, who needs to distance himself from the present and all that has happened since 1946 to assess the film's place in history and culture and to judge its contemporary impact. Curiously enough, the long-term verdict on the film is probably the one passed on it at the time by contemporary critics, who almost all saw it as a courageous, well-intentioned, historically interesting failure. William Whitebait in the *Spectator* said it was 'disappointing'. He thought the characters were types, village life was unconvincing, and the Technicolor was uneven. 'Only at rare moments does the drama come alive', he declared. But he praised Bliss's score.[40] Dilys Powell in the *Sunday Times* said, 'It is quite often dull. But *Men of Two Worlds* is on the right track: it has a subject, it is about something real, it is getting somewhere'.[41] Elspeth Grant in the *Daily Graphic* said: 'It is not without faults. It is repetitive. The colour is erratic. The crowd scenes are stiffly handled. But an interesting problem is presented and treated without a vestige of the smugness one fears in the discussion of racial differences'.[42] Frederic Mullally in *Tribune* thought it tedious and unoriginal though well meaning, and he praised the music, Tom Morahan's design, and the dream sequence.[44] The *Times* said, '*Men of Two Worlds* has its dull and inspired passages, but it is an honest film and has a subject of importance to illustrate'.[45] Campbell Dixon in the *Daily Telegraph* thought it well intentioned but poorly written and acted.[46]

The film fails for several reasons, not all of them the fault of Dickinson. Richard Winnington put his finger on one source of dissatisfaction when he wrote:

> This lengthy film on that old favourite superstition v. progress fails as a documentary to come within a thousand miles of *The Forgotten Village* and *Children of the Arctic North* because its settings being mostly fake, though amazingly good fake, are unable to compete with the excitement and beauty of the actual, and the story is not strong enough to compensate.[47]

Dickinson had made two lengthy trips to Tanganyika, which ensured a surface authenticity for the film in terms of music, costume, and artefacts, but only about ten minutes of film footage resulted that could be incorporated into the final version. But since Dickinson had settled for a realistic feel and style, the very fact of its almost total filming in the studio inevitably inspired this feeling of unconvincing artificiality.

It is instructive to compare Dickinson's failure in *Men of Two Worlds* with Powell and Pressburger's complete success in *Black Narcissus* (1947). Both films were shot in Technicolor at Denham Studios and drew on the expertise of Percy Day in process shooting. Both dealt with a conflict of cultures, between East and West in the Himalayas in *Black Narcissus*. But the Powell and Pressburger film is wholly and mesmerically successful because it was from the first designed totally out of the imagination. As Powell later said:

> The atmosphere carefully and meticulously built up from the first decision never to go to India, which was the most important decision. These films are nearly always pastiche or hotch-potch—you know, real Southern India in the studio—so I said: 'This won't do, such a delicate story, we've got to create a whole atmosphere here'.[48]

Black Narcissus is then wholly a designed and controlled creation of the imagination, in which the use of studio shooting and process shots, colour contrasts, and deliberately unreal effects blend to support and extend the central concept. It draws on melodrama, mysticism, and myth as its sources of inspiration and confronts the powerful drives of sex and religion. By contrast, Dickinson adopts a naturalistic and realistic mode to tell a semi-documentary propaganda story, and the very studio and process work that reinforces Powell's intention works strongly against Dickinson's. But the dominant mode of the production is so clear that when Dickinson introduces an imaginative hallucination sequence, it is so deliberately antirealistic that it jars and fails to convince, adding to the generally unconvincing atmosphere of the rest of the film.

Integral to the film, too, is music. This point can also be seen as a source of weakness, and it is something almost certainly traceable to Dickinson. In the original draft of the story, Kisenga was simply a student. It was Dickinson's idea to make him a pianist and composer, which made the musical elements crucial. He took this decision partly to help make the propaganda palatable. He may have noted the current vogue for concerto themes in films (the Warsaw Concerto in *Dangerous Moonlight*, the Cornish Rhapsody in *Love Story*, the use of Rachmaninov's Second Piano Concerto in *Brief Encounter*). He was also himself deeply fond of classical music. But serious reservations about this idea had already been raised in comments on the story treatment. Dickinson characteristically ignored them.

Once it was decided that Kisenga would be a pianist-composer, his music became a vital motif of the film, both visually and thematically. The film opens with Kisenga giving a performance of *Baraza* in the National Gallery before leaving for Africa to become a teacher. Later in Africa when Kisenga and Randall believe that they have made a breakthrough in their campaign to move the Litu, they sit down together and play the piano side by side. When Kisenga opens a new school, the native band plays 'Daisy, Daisy, give me your answer do'.

Finally, when Kisenga is dying, his hallucination sequence shows him torn between the tribal drums of his own people and the concert orchestra of his European sojourn. But he is saved when Randall decides to bring a children's choir to sing his chorale. Magole the witch doctor orders them away. But Saburi and Kisenga's other loyal friends take up the song. Kisenga revives and survives. The final message, then, is that music can heal and unify, something that lies behind the role of music throughout the film.

The performance of *Baraza*, a blend of African themes and idioms and European techniques, unites Kisenga and his white audience in the concert hall at the beginning. Music is used to demonstrate the close link between Kisenga and Randall, the representatives of different cultures, the men of two worlds working together. The hallucination scene separates the two elements in Kisenga's music, but the triumphant finale, using his chorale, reunites them.

The weakness of the film, however, perhaps lies partly in the fact that Kisenga is a composer at all rather than the student originally intended. As a composer rather than an ordinary black man, he is revered in white society and is also a character above and beyond the audience in status, thus not requiring them to question their attitudes to a black hero. He is also above his own people, remains for much of the film an outsider, and suffers far more from their prejudice than from that of the whites, who reveal nothing but sympathy. His distancing from black audiences is quite likely to have been similar to his distancing from white.

The music also dictates the form of two virtuoso sequences at the beginning and end of the film. The first sequence is that of the concert at the National Gallery. After an initial panning shot to establish locale and occasion (across Trafalgar Square to the National Gallery and down the pediment of the gallery to rest on an announcement of the concert), Dickinson uses his camera (a) to involve the audience and (b) to stress the unifying nature of music.

The camera follows some latecomers into the concert, which has already begun, panning with them through the galleries and craning up to watch them take their seats in the background. Then Dickinson uses cutting to stress the unifying spirit of music, establishing the rapport of audience and orchestra. First there is a long shot of the audience and orchestra together and then a close shot of the hands of the pianist, which are black. The camera pulls back rapidly, as if recoiling in surprise, to show that the pianist is a black African.

Having thus registered the presence of an outsider, Kisenga, Dickinson then proceeds to integrate him. There are a series of intercut close-shots of individual players in the orchestra looking from score to conductor, establishing the link between them, then we are shown pianist and audience in the same shot. Finally, after intercut close-ups of conductor, pianist, orchestra, and audience members, there is a comprehensive long shot, including all of them. Then, as the music ends, the audience relaxes and begins rising to its feet, the conductor beckons the pianist to rise, and there is a close-up of him beaming with pleasure. The construction thus carefully establishes the organic relationship of the members of the orchestra, the relationship between the orchestra and the audience, and finally the relationship of both with the black pianist.

At the end, there is the imaginative hallucination sequence, shot with a tilted camera and Vaselined lens to suggest disorientation. In constructing it, Dickinson drew on suggestions from a psychiatrist to get the right symbols to illustrate Kisenga's mental deterioration. But this in itself bespeaks a desire for realism, even in a fantasy sequence, and one that in the events jars with the rest of the film.

The sequence incorporates Kisenga's fears (Magole's magic) and guilt (responsibility for his father's death) and sets up a powerful conflict between the primitive beat of the tribal drums, representing his African heritage, and the sophisticated rhythms of the European orchestra, representing his European training. Kisenga lies in profile at the bottom of the frame line, his mother and father on each side of him, with Magole feeling his pulse. As he struggles, the camera tilts up to show mosquito netting towering far above him, again visually suggesting the distancing and alienating effects of his physical and mental decline. From the netting hangs the death symbol. Kisenga reaches out to touch it but cannot. His hand turns from black to white, indicating his confusion about his identity. He looks up at the symbol; it has disappeared. The African drummers fill the screen and Kisenga tries to reach them, but Magole bars his way. Beyond the drummers are the orchestra, whose conductor beckons Kisenga. Again Magole bars his way. But Kisenga makes his way to the piano, his father tries to stop him, and he throttles his father. As his father falls, he sits at the piano and plays the first chord, and then Magole stabs him in the arm with a knife. The camera lens is spattered with blood, and the picture goes sharply out of focus. In this sequence, the different musical forms represent the tensions, unlike the previous sequence in which Dickinson's cutting is done in time with the prerecorded musical score.

In general, apart from these two sequences, the shooting style is conventional: panning shots to establish locations, intercut close-ups for conflict, tracking on movement, medium two- or three-shots for discussions, though with the characteristically more extended Dickinson average shot length.

Perhaps the third element of weakness, and a recurrent one in Dickinson's work, is the film's didactic nature. It is in one sense a dramatized sermon, reminding one of Dickinson's Anglican clerical background, and very much of a piece with the element of preachment that is a continuing feature of his work (pro-Israel, pro-Spanish Republican, antiterrorist, antiracist). There is an almost total absence of the humour that had enlivened his earlier films. Apart from an early cameo of David Horne being annoyed at the National Gallery concert by a small boy eating a large sandwich next to him, the leavening of humour is missing. The characters are not fully developed but are spokespeople for points of view, and the stiffness of the African actors, with the exception of Orlando Martins, reinforces this feeling of minimal characterisation. Ironically, it is the villains that grab the attention of the uninvolved viewer, thanks to Orlando Martins and to a precise, assured character vignette from Cathleen Nesbitt as the reactionary Mrs. Upjohn. The film as a whole is too talky and schoolmasterish, only occasionally attaining moments of dramatic power, such as when Magole is seen drinking Kisenga's blood, photographed through a column of flame.

The film had taken three years of Dickinson's life and cost £600,000 to make, only to be greeted as a well-meaning bore. Looking back at the experience years later, Dickinson ruefully described it: 'the whole thing was a misery'.

NOTES

1. Stephen Constantine, *The Making of British Colonial Development Policy 1914-1940* (London: Frank Cass, 1984).
2. J. M. Lee and Martin Petter, *The Colonial Office, War and Development Policy* (London: Institute of Commonwealth Studies, 1982), p. 122.
3. Ibid., p. 244.
4. Ibid., p. 256.
5. Ibid., p. 150.
6. See Rosaleen Smyth, 'Movies and Mandarins: the Official Film and British Colonial Africa', J. Curran and V. Porter, eds., *British Cinema History* (London: Weidenfeld and Nicolson, 1983), pp. 129-143.
7. All the official documentation relating to the film is in INF 1/218. This includes a typescript of Arnot Robertson's original story.
8. Letter from E. Arnot Robertson to Noel Sabine, August 6, 1942; memorandum from Robertson to Jack Beddington (undated); Beddington's comment on the script, dated August 13, 1942; INF 1/218.
9. Letter from Filippo del Giudice to Jack Beddington, March 7, 1942, INF 1/224.
10. The proposals are in MoI minute dated October 23, 1942, and were agreed in a letter from del Giudice to E. L. Mercier of the Films Division, November 4, 1942; letter from del Giudice to Beddington, October 28, 1942; letter from Beddington to Paul Kimberley, November 19, 1942; INF 1/218.
11. Letter from Paul Kimberley to Beddington, November 12, 1942; letter from Beddington to Kimberley, November 16, 1942; INF 1/218.
12. Dickinson's own account of his involvement in the project is contained in his article 'Making a film in Tanganyika Territory' in ed., Peter Noble, *British Film Yearbook 1947-8* (London: Skelton Robinson, 1947), pp. 53-58, and his five-page unpublished account 'Men of Two Worlds' (March 1978), in the possession of the author.
13. Minutes of meeting at Two Cities office, Hanover Square, December 9, 1942; letter from Ivor Smith (Films Division) to A. W. Jenkins on travel arrangements, December 15, 1942; INF 1/218.

14. Memorandum from John Sutro to MoI, December 17, 1942, suggesting McNeice; memorandum from Ivor Smith to Beddington urging him to press the BBC for McNeice's release, December 21, 1942. There is a handwritten comment saying that Beddington would be unwilling to press the BBC too hard; letter from W. B. Woodburn, principal establishment officer of MoI, to W. St. J. Pym of BBC requesting McNeice's release, December 22, 1942; letter from J. G. Roberts of the BBC to W. G. Woodburn, refusing the request, December 24, 1942; INF 1/218.
15. Memorandum from Arnot Robertson to Beddington, December 30, 1942, reports that Dickinson is to discuss the script with Joyce Cary ('I think he's likely to be even better than McNeice'); Ivor Smith reports to John Sutro on the arrangements made for the reconnaissance party (including Joyce Cary), January 13, 1943. Cary's involvement is recounted in Malcolm Foster, *Joyce Cary* (London: Michael Joseph, 1968), pp. 344-345, 362-378.
16. Thorold Dickinson, 'Men of Two Worlds', p. 4.
17. Memorandum from Arnot Robertson, May 28, 1943, INF 1/218.
18. Letter from Angus MacPhail to Jack Beddington, May 31, 1943, ibid.
19. Letter from Ian Dalrymple to Jack Beddington, June 8, 1943, ibid.
20. Letter from Gervas Huxley to Jack Beddington, June 15, 1943, ibid.
21. Memorandum from R. Nunn May to Beddington, May 31, 1943, ibid.
22. Memorandum from Arnot Robertson, July 5, 1943, ibid.
23. Letter from Ladipo Solanke to Beddington, July 28, 1943, ibid.
24. Letter from Noel Sabine to Ladipo Solanke, August 31, 1943, ibid.
25. Letter from Sabine to Beddington, April 19, 1940.
26. An account of the involvement of Technicolor in the project is given by John Huntley, *British Technicolor Films* (London: Skelton Robinson, 1949), pp. 89-102.
27. Dickinson, 'Men of Two Worlds', p. 2.
28. Dickinson, 'Making a Film in Tanganyika Territory', p. 56.
29. On the music for the film, see Thorold Dickinson, 'Search for Music', *Penguin Film Review* 2 (1947), pp. 9-15.
30. Huntley, *British Technicolor Films*, pp. 97-98.

31. Ibid., p. 100.
32. Cable from Dickinson to Sutro, April 9, 1943; from Sutro to Dickinson, April 12, 1943; from Dickinson to Sutro, April 19, 1943; from Dickinson to Sutro, April 28, 1943; INF 1/218.
33. *Film Dope* 5 (July 1974), p. 3.
34. John Huntley, *British Film Music* (London: Skelton Robinson, 1948), p. 87.
35. Ibid., p. 86.
36. *Penguin Film Review* 2 (1947), p. 12.
37. Letter from del Giudice to Beddington, November 14, 1945, INF 1/218.
38. For an account of the Indian episode see Thorold Dickinson, 'Indian Spring', *Penguin Film Review* 5 (1948), pp. 62-72, and Foster, *Joyce Cary*, pp. 378-379, 394-399.
39. Peter Noble, *The Negro in Films* (London: Skelton Robinson, 1947), pp. 128-136.
40. *Spectator*, July 21, 1946.
41. *Sunday Times*, July 21, 1946.
42. *Daily Graphic*, July 19, 1946.
43. *Tribune*, July 20, 1946.
44. *News Chronicle*, July 20, 1946.
45. *Times*, July 18, 1946.
46. *Daily Telegraph*, July 22, 1946.
47. Richard Winnington, *Film Criticism and Caricatures 1943-53* (London: Paul Elek, 1975), pp. 52-53.
48. Ian Christie, ed., *Powell, Pressburger and Others* (London: BFI, 1978), p. 35.

SEVEN

Machiavellians and Mephistophelians: The Queen of Spades

After the failure of the Indian project, Dickinson began work with Joyce Cary developing the script of what would become *Secret People*, but this was put aside when Two Cities acquired the rights to Somerset Maugham's novel *Then and Now* and assigned Dickinson to film it. Dickinson worked with Simon Harcourt-Smith on a treatment, completed by March 1947, and by November 1947 they had completed a full script.[1]

The story was about Machiavelli and Cesare Borgia, and the basic idea was an interweaving of the events in Machiavelli's play *La Mandragola*, which in Maugham's story actually happened to Machiavelli himself (lodging in the house of a wealthy man and seducing his wife), with the efforts of Machiavelli, then secretary of the Florentine Council, to prevent Cesare Borgia taking over Florence. He does so by means of a combination of diplomatic intrigue, espionage, and sheer duplicity. It was in short a period tale of 'secret people'.

As was customary at Two Cities, the script was sent to various people for comment, in this case, Ernest Lindgren of the British Film Institute and experienced screenwriters Donald Bull and Marjorie Deans. They all replied with detailed critiques of treatment and characters, while expressing admiration for the overall job. They all agreed in particular that the political complexities were likely to prove too impenetrable for the average audience and that the ending was too abrupt.

Dickinson, however, was pleased with the script and delighted with the locations he discovered on a visit to Italy to select locales for the key sequences. He remembered with particular affection the ducal palace at Mantua:

We discovered in the ducal palace a whole set of apartments built for the ducal dwarfs, including a dwarf chapel served by a dwarf priest. We were going to use it in the film, because it was so difficult for tall people to move about in that it was there that Machiavelli was going to meet some enemy and fight him with a sword in this tiny constricted little place.

It was also on location that he saw a steep valley that gave him the idea for a marvellous opening for the film:

> One particular valley with a path coming down the middle and quite steep sides. Down this path was to come a mule with a peasant driving it. Across the back of the mule, a dead body. Then somebody came into the foreground, watched it coming and when it came right into closeup, the figure lifted up the head and cried 'Cesare Borgia'. Then the film went into flashback to tell the events leading up to this.

The costumes and sets were designed, and casting was underway—Trevor Howard to play Machiavelli, George Sanders Cesare Borgia—when a bombshell arrived from Hollywood. Two Cities were coproducing the film with the Hollywood based Regency Productions Company, run by Arnold Pressburger. Pressburger had submitted the script to the Motion Picture Association of America (MPAA), the Hollywood censors, and received back from them a letter dated December 22, 1947, casting serious doubt on the production's viability:

> In its present form a picture based on this material would be in violation of the Production Code and could not be approved by us. This basic unacceptability arises from the fact that the secondary theme of your picture is a story of seduction, adultery and illegitimacy, which are treated for romantic comedy. Such a portrayal of adultery is, of course, flatly in violation of the code and all it stands for. In addition to this basic difficulty, we set forth a number of detailed scenes which are also unacceptable. At the outset, we direct your particular attention to the need for the greatest possible care in the selection and photography of the dresses and costumes for your women. The Production Code makes it mandatory that the intimate parts of the body—specifically the breasts of women—be fully clothed at all times. Any compromise with this regulation will compel us to withhold approval of your picture.[2]

A list of thirty-seven specific objections followed.

Hasty meetings were arranged at Two Cities, and it was decided that the whole *Mandragola* subplot would have to go. Attempts were made to construct a new subplot from Molière's *L'École des Femmes*, based on the pathetic love of an elderly man for his ward. But they soon decided that the censorship code presented insuperable problems, and the whole project was abandoned. Soon afterwards personnel changes took place at Two Cities. Rank had taken over the company, and del Giudice's freedom was being limited. So Dickinson decided to leave the company. He took the *Secret People* project with him. But its development got no further because at short notice Dickinson was called on to take over the direction of *The Queen of Spades*.

This film had been fraught with difficulties. It had been scripted by Rodney Ackland and Arthur Boys for producer Anatole de Grunwald. Ackland had been signed to direct, and Boys was to be associate producer. But while Ackland was in America with his play *Crime and Punishment*, Boys and de Grunwald had quarrelled violently and Boys had resigned. Ackland returned to a chilly atmosphere, began shooting, and by his own account had shot the flashback sequence with Pauline Tennant, Edith Evans's first scene, and the scene of Yvonne Mitchell bursting into tears, and had then been dismissed.

There seem to have been several reasons. De Grunwald was apparently claiming a screenplay credit for some script revisions and both Boys and Ackland were resisting this. There seems also to have been some difficulty between Ackland and the star Anton Walbrook, with whom Ackland had quarrelled when he was doing some rewriting on the film *Dangerous Moonlight*. It was Walbrook's suggestion that Dickinson should be called on to take over *Queen of Spades*. According to Ackland, Dickinson pronounced the existing footage extraordinary and invited Ackland to stay on as codirector, and, initially, he rehearsed the actors while Dickinson directed the shooting. But he soon withdrew from the production completely, and Dickinson directed almost all of it himself.

There was a sequel to this drama, however. When the film was released, no separate screenplay credit was given, but the names of the screenwriters were printed in tiny letters on the same card as the title of the film. Putting this down to de Grunwald's vindictiveness, Ackland and Boys sued. The case was heard in the High Court on February 21, 1950, and judgement was found in favour of Ackland and Boys—namely, that they had been deprived of their due credit. The award was made against De Grunwald's company, World Screenplays. The company promptly went bankrupt, and Ackland and Boys never got the money they had been awarded.[3]

Whereas Dickinson had taken on *Gaslight* on three weeks' notice, he took on *The Queen of Spades* on only three days' notice. It was a production fraught with difficulties from the outset, and it is perhaps surprising that not only was the production completed but that it turned out to be a stunning masterwork and one of Dickinson's finest creations.

There is no sign in the assured and atmospheric handling of Pushkin's story of the frantic activity that went on behind the scenes. Dickinson was doing rewrite work on the script at night with the producer de Grunwald and keeping one step ahead of the shooting. The heavily annotated script in the Dickinson collection indicates just how much remodelling work was done. The prologue became a flashback, because it slowed things up in its original position. The dialogue was cut back and altered in some cases, Dickinson always preferring the visual to the verbal method of communicating information. Sequences were cut and transposed, frequently being shot with no real idea of what order they would finally be in.

The studios at Welwyn Garden City were out of date, cramped, and badly soundproofed. They were also situated next to the main railway line so that shooting had to be halted every time a train passed by. The lack of space in the studio presented problems for the countess's coach and horses. Designer Oliver Messel had insisted on designing a coach full-size and not to scale, so that it could not be moved more than ten feet in any direction.

The budget ran out before the film was completed, and Dickinson was forced to some daring improvisation because of the absence of sets, which were constantly being torn down and replaced. In addition, he was working with two actresses, Edith Evans and Yvonne Mitchell, who had not made films before and found it difficult to adjust to the demands of the camera after their experience of the stage. Evans, for instance, had been advised by Alec Guinness to let the camera do all the work, and so she underplayed drastically and had to be coaxed into expanding her performance. Mitchell tended to give her all in the first take and found herself unable to repeat her initial performance in subsequent takes.

So improvisation was the order of the day. The problems only served to spur Dickinson on to even greater heights of technical inventiveness and visual daring. The vertiginous high-angle shot of the arrival of the young countess at the palace of St. Germain was done because they could not afford to build the facade of the palace and so created the effect by putting up the corner of a wall with a gargoyle on it, directing lights to give the appearance of an open door and then shooting down onto the carriage. Similarly, the nocturnal vigil of Suvorin outside the countess's palace was done by projecting the character's shadow onto the ground marching relentlessly up and down. It was an effect inspired by *Farrebique* and necessitated by the fact that there were no sets for him to be seen with. Dickinson also shot down onto the bird market for scenes there because virtually no set existed for that, either. There were different reasons why Lisaveta's big scene, in which she breaks down after learning of the death of Countess Ranevskaya from Suvorin, was filmed in a single take, a medium two-shot of four minutes fifty-three seconds. One was because Yvonne Mitchell could not film the sequence bit by bit but needed to do it in one take.

Dickinson was helped considerably in all this by his production team. He had a strong and almost instinctive rapport with cameraman Otto Heller. The film crew were completely cooperative and prepared to work long hours to get the effects the director required. Anton Walbrook worked selflessly to help disguise the leading ladies' lack of camera experience.

Otto Heller used a variety of wide-angle lenses to suggest space and width where it did not exist, particularly in the ballroom sequence, where camera trickery was used to deceive the eye. Dickinson had to use a small ballroom set and only a handful of extras. So at the announcement of a mazurka, Heller changed to his widest lens and Dickinson began the scene by holding on a couple of dancers and then having a rapid reverse dolly shot to the back of the studio, making the ballroom seem enormous. Point-of-view dolly shots were used to suggest the movement of the immobile carriage, for instance, the camera dollying away from Suvorin standing outside the palace and away from Lisaveta as she sits in the departing coach. Chiaroscuro, angled shooting, and point-of-view shots were used constantly to disguise the fact that many of the sets were either small or half-built or in some cases nonexistent.

Dickinson paid tribute to others in the production team too:

> The film needed great care and experiment in the cutting room. Some dramatic values were revised and re-shaped during production and the final assembly of the film did not tally in all parts with the original conception. Anatole de Grunwald the producer and Hazel Wilkinson the editor contributed greatly to the final effect. The sound score was elaborate enough to need 3 recordists simultaneously to control the re-recording or mixing of the composite sound track, and some of the recordings they used were themselves blendings of other sources of sound. The final soundtrack . . . took almost as long to produce as the

shooting of the film in the studio. And . . . I cannot finish these notes without recalling the fine appropriateness of Georges Auric's score and its essentially Russian character, a quality which Auric tells me surprised him himself, when he came to play it through.[4]

Dickinson did not have the opportunity to preplan the film as he had *Gaslight*. But he was able to give it visual coherence by settling on a style early on, as he explained in 1950:

> One point about the style of the film. Many have remarked how unlike a British film, how continental, the picture seems. The subject itself is of a type unfamiliar in British films. And first attempts to bend the manner of the film to the British convention of the 'stiff upper lip' produced results which were quite meaningless in their lack of effect. After the first day I cast convention overboard and aimed in every scene at colourful, conscious contrast. I kept stillness, physical and mental, for an effect on its own, as in the cathedral for example. When the story went out of doors (the film was shot entirely indoors), there was always a wind blowing. Mist was dense, snow abundant, tobacco smoke almost impenetrable, artificial lighting by candles was always apparently from below unless chandeliers were visible. The tempest evoked by the ghost of the countess nearly blew the camera and its crew off their rostrum. Dust was thick as after a sandstorm, gems and silks glittered, rags and sores looked stinking. And Otto Heller's camera captured it all while his camera operator Gus Drisse traced camera movements of outlandish and intricate composition.[5]

Further internal coherence was provided by the employment of certain consistent stylistic devices. One is the constant placing of characters in the foreground of shots, dominating the screen in encounters and conversations. It happens so often that it gives the film a feeling of claustrophobia, concentrating the audience's attention on the characters. The first discussion between Suvorin and Andrey has each of them successively in the foreground of the shot, making its use clearly a visual motif. The second device is the use of mirrors, whose prominence is a reflection of the 'secret people' theme. Not only do characters look at themselves in mirrors at crucial points (Suvorin after his decision to go after the secret of the cards, Lisaveta when she realises that she is falling in love with Suvorin), but also they and their actions are frequently seen reflected in mirrors.

Such devices provide a visual unity to the film, which plays creatively off the movement and angle of the camerawork. As in *Gaslight*,

Dickinson employs a mobile camera and long takes. But his changes of camera angle and direction, the pace and variety of camera movement, are dictated not as in *Gaslight* by preplanning but by a desire to keep the audience on the edge of their seats. There is method within the diversity, however, in that to get over information, such as in Suvorin's visits to the bookseller and the notary, Dickinson uses rapid intercutting between the actors, with an average shot length of five seconds. But he uses much longer uninterrupted takes for nonverbal scenes and for the creation of mood, the camera prowling restlessly to lend an appropriately feverish and hallucinatory tone to the proceedings. This is demonstrated in the very first sequence, in which the film opens on a hand of cards and then the camera pulls back to reveal the onlookers at the card game and then dollies around the table, picking up the gamesters, the cards, and the piles of money, conveying to the audience simply by camera movement the flickering excitement of the game.

In several ways, *The Queen of Spades* is an extension of the ideas explored in *Gaslight*. The plot is similar. In this film, Suvorin, a penniless engineering officer, learns that Countess Ranevskaya, who has reputedly sold her soul to the Devil, possesses the secret of victory at cards. So he sets out to seduce her niece Lisaveta to gain access to the old lady. The countess dies when he confronts her, but her ghost delivers up the secret. Suvorin wagers all on a card game, loses, and goes insane. As in *Gaslight*, we have an innocent, trusting, deceived woman and a heartless, cold, obsessive antihero, motivated by greed to use the woman. The use of Anton Walbrook both as Mallen and Suvorin emphasizes the similarity of the characters. 'I am not interested in problems of good and evil. To me they are beside the point', says Suvorin early in the film. The point is his desire for wealth, acclaim, and position, and it is the end he ruthlessly strives for.

Also as in *Gaslight*, repression is a theme. Lisaveta, the brow-beaten niece and ward, discovers love for the first time in Suvorin's courtship, and she blossoms. Suvorin, forced by his lack of status and money to save rather than spend, longs to break out and indulge in the free and easy life of wealthier officers. This attitude gives an added psychological dimension to his greed. It also permits Dickinson to use dance to suggest abandon.

The can-can in *Gaslight* had been used to suggest the sexuality of the relationship between Mallen and Nancy. In the opening sequence of *The Queen of Spades*, Dickinson uses the gypsy dance for a similar purpose. Dickinson evokes scenes of wild revelry in the gambling hall—singing, dancing, drinking, hand clapping, caressing—its joyous abandon conveyed by rapid cutting, pulsating music, and movement within the frame of the actors. At the centre of this is the wild gypsy dance. At one point, the dancer's swirling dress fills the top half of the screen and her bare legs the bottom half. Eventually she bends over backwards in a gesture of lubricious submission and is carried off by the officers. Dickinson cross-cuts between this and Suvorin, standing motionless, silent, black-clad, apparently thoroughly disapproving. But as we later learn, this image symbolizes all that he secretly wants: women, drink, gambling. When he returns to gamble at the end, the gypsy, knowing of his disapproval, cheekily offers him a drink. He seizes it and downs it, preparing for the plunge into sexuality and licence that will never come.

Similar to *Gaslight*, too, is the use of religious symbolism. In *Gaslight* it had been religious rituals (church service, morning prayers) counterpointed to Mallen's evil plot to drive Bella insane. Here it is much more basically the symbolism of good as opposed to evil. Countess Ranevskaya, on her visit to St. Germain, pointedly takes and wears a crucifix. But having got the secret of the cards and sold her soul to the Devil, she uses it in the card game. She flings the crucifix on top of a transparent table, so that, with the camera shooting up from a low angle, it dominates the frame. Returning home a rich woman, she kneels before an icon of the Virgin Mary, praying for forgiveness, and, in a powerful moment, a gust of wind blows out the candles and the face of the icon goes black, as God symbolically turns his face away from this disciple of the Devil. The same icon, mutely disapproving, stands in the background of the scenes in which Suvorin seeks to get the secret from the countess and in which having got it, he tries to persuade Lisaveta to marry him.

Ritual becomes prominent too in the funeral scene, when Suvorin leans over the open coffin of the countess, and her eyes suddenly open, an unholy terror given added chill by occurring in the ornate Russian cathedral, an imposing setting of candles, painted frescoes, chanting, and black drapes.

The major difference from *Gaslight*, however, is the presence of the supernatural. *The Queen of Spades* is—and this is what attracted Dickinson to it—a ghost story, a Faustian tale of bargains with the Devil and supernatural apparitions. This theme adds a whole new dimension, missing from *Gaslight*, that enables Dickinson to use the power of suggestion and his talent at evoking atmosphere to play on the nerves of his audience.

In terms of horror and suspense, Dickinson creates some superb sequences, in which he uses suggestion to create terror. The visit of the countess to the palace of the Count of St. Germain is worthy of Whale at his best. After an introductory model shot of the palace facade, the camera tracks through cobwebby corridors, along a bench of flasks and alembics to hands moulding a wax figurine of the countess. The figure dissolves to a ball, where the count's sinister servant invites the countess to visit his master. After her lover has rifled her strongbox and fled, she decides to visit St. Germain. She arrives at the palace, in the high-angle shot already described. Dickinson cuts from this to ornate doors, which close behind her as she enters, apparently of their own accord. The camera dollies in to a skull on the engraved door knocker. Cowled figures bearing candles lead her through shadowy corridors, until they arrive at a closed door. In a stunning point-of-view shot, the camera tracks in to the door, which opens, revealing a gaping blackness beyond. There are a shrill scream of terror and a dissolve to the frightened horses, whinnying and rearing outside. The camera tracks along the line of bottles, containing the wax figures of those who have sold their souls to the devil. The hands of the still unseen count add the figure of the countess to them. By leaving unseen what is beyond the door, Dickinson brings into play the already heightened imagination of the audience.

He does the same for the appearance of the countess's ghost. Suvorin, alone in his room, hears a noise outside. He opens the door, but nothing is there. Then he hears the tapping of the cane and the swish of the heavy silk gowns, which always heralded the approach of the countess. Suddenly there is a gust of wind, and in a rapidly edited succession of images, the lamp blows over, the table is knocked over, papers are blown around the room, and a curtain envelops the camera. The camera tracks slowly into Suvorin's face, as we hear the ghostly voice whispering the values of the three winning cards. Then the camera pulls back from close-up to reveal the room in order and with no sign of the previous disarray. The ghost then is not seen by the audience, removing any danger of bathos, but is left instead to the imagination. The use of sound to indicate the countess's approach is extremely effective and parallels the loud ticking of the clock in the countess's room as Suvorin confronts her and the sudden stopping of the clock as the countess dies.

There is a long wordless passage of pure atmosphere in which Suvorin slips into the palace after the countess and Lisaveta have gone to the ball. In a superb, heavily shadowed sequence, the camera tracks Suvorin round the palace interior, the lines of balustrades bisecting the screen, doorways framing him, the clock ticking loudly and oppressively. This contrasts sharply with the immediately succeeding sequence, with its high-key lighting and high-angle shooting of a brilliantly danced mazurka at the ball.

Dickinson uses rapid camera movement to convey horror. For instance, after the death of the countess, when Suvorin flees out into the street, the camera cranes up as far as it can to reveal him isolated in a snow-filled square. After a dissolve to a close-up of the dead eyes of the countess, he runs through the streets, tracked by the camera, and the flight sequence ends with the camera again craning up and away to show him lost and lonely in the maze of streets.

Similarly, when Suvorin visits the cathedral and bends over the body of the countess, there is a dolly-in to a full close-up of her dead face. The eyes suddenly open, and the cameras pulls back rapidly as Suvorin screams and recoils in horror. In the scene in which Suvorin goes mad, Dickinson begins with a distorted montage of cards, money, faces, and voices, to give visual expression to Suvorin's mental turmoil, and then dollies rapidly into a full close-up of his face as he screams. Then his head falls on one side, like a doll with its neck broken, and he is led away, muttering the names of the three cards, as the camera pans down to the queen of spades, the cause of his downfall, on the floor.

The lighting of the film adds considerably to the atmosphere. It is predominantly low-key, creating some marvellous chiaroscuro effects. Dickinson maintained that this was not a fundamental departure from the 'realism' of the lighting of his previous films because in the early nineteenth century, all lighting was candlelight and inevitably cast long shadows. Nevertheless, the lighting as a whole has an undeniable and virtuoso Expressionist feel, which evokes comparisons with Murnau's *Faust* and the much-filmed *Student of Prague*, in the third version of which Anton Walbrook himself had played the leading role.

Stylistically, Dickinson continued with longer takes and a mobile camera. He also utilized montage and symbolism, a legacy of his immersement in silent films during his Film Society days. Visual symbolism, common in silent cinema, had gone out of fashion with the coming of sound, but here Dickinson used it to enhance the atmosphere and underline the supernatural menace. He superimposes the grinning death's head of the fatal book's title page over Suvorin's own face and also superimposes a crawling spider in its web over the face of Lisaveta, as she lies in bed fondling the false love letters from Suvorin. There is symbolic significance, too, in the release of the caged birds at the end (Lisaveta's gaining of her freedom) and in the young countess's flinging of the cross on the transparent tabletop (loss of her soul to the Devil).

Dickinson gives full rein to his sardonic sense of humour in the Dickensian gallery of grotesques who people the sidelines of the story: the bibulous notary, the fierce, beetle-browed bookseller, the decrepit old general who pays court to the countess, and the toothless old servant who creeps cackling into the countess's bedroom to steal a sweetmeat. The film is in fact very well served by its cast, particularly by Anton Walbrook, whose Suvorin is a masterly study of obsession and spiralling insanity. His eyes burn with greed and ambition, as one character remarks, 'like the eyes of Satan' as the icy self-control gradually crumbles and finally vanishes altogether. The primal shriek of joy when he realises that he has gained the secret of the cards, the pleading with and hectoring of the countess, the tense excitement of the final card game, and the eventual precipitation into madness are screen acting of a very high order. He is given admirable support by Edith Evans as the tyrannical, demanding, eccentric, and haunted countess and by Yvonne Mitchell as her sheltered, vulnerable niece.

In its extravagance of style and setting, in its exuberantly fluid camera style and Expressionist lighting, in its mastery of the mechanics of suspense and suggestion, *The Queen of Spades* is a triumph of pure imagination and one of the classics of that era of high ambition and grand achievement in British filmmaking. It was widely praised by the critics. Dilys Powell in the *Sunday Times* declared:

> *The Queen of Spades* is something rare in this country; a successful essay in romantic period, something so rare . . . that I can think of no other example. . . . *Queen of Spades* belongs, what is more, not simply to romantic period, but to *the* romantic period, historically speaking: here is the solitary, self-sufficient figure, here is the sense of darkness and diabolism, which is the combination of the late 18th and early 19th century Gothic. . . . [T]his is one of the best scripts we have had in England for years. And Oliver Messel's settings and costumes are among the most beautiful I can remember seeing on the English screen. Direction and playing are on a high level.[6]

The *Daily Telegraph* called it 'a little masterpiece in the high Romantic tradition'.[7] The *Daily Worker* thought it 'the most successfully stylish of any British costume film yet made'. The *Star* called it a 'film of haunting beauty and macabre power. . . . As an artistic conception, harmoniously composed and completely satisfying in every detail, the film offers something new in British achievement'.[9] The *Daily Mail* thought it 'tasteful and highly imaginative'.[10] Several reviews called attention to the film's un-Englishness. The *Daily Graphic* noted, 'The great advantage that *The Queen of Spades* has over most British films is that it doesn't look in the least British. And, of course, it shouldn't'.[11] The *Manchester Guardian* found it 'full of recollections (witting or unwitting) of Cocteau, of Eisenstein and of several German directors, but especially Galeen, the man who made *The Student of Prague*'.[12] The *Daily Herald* thought it 'full of atmosphere, brilliantly photographed in the imaginative German style of the best silent film days'.[13] Few reviewers dissented from the general praise.

Chapter Seven

NOTES

1. The script is preserved in the Dickinson Papers.
2. Letter from Stephen Jackson of the MPAA to Arnold Pressburger, December 22, 1947, Dickinson Papers.
3. Rodney Ackland's account is in Rodney Ackland and Elspeth Grant, *The Celluloid Mistress* (London: Allan Wingate, 1954), pp. 193-228.
4. Thorold Dickinson in 'A Symposium on the Queen of Spades', *The Cinema 1950,* ed., Roger Manvell (Harmondsworth: Penguin, 1950), p. 46.
5. Ibid.
6. *Sunday Times*, March 20, 1949.
7. *Daily Telegraph*, March 21, 1949.
8. *Daily Worker*, March 19, 1949.
9. *Star*, March 18, 1949.
10. *Daily Mail*, March 18, 1949.
11. *Daily Graphic*, March 18, 1949.
12. *Manchester Guardian*, March 19, 1949.
13. *Daily Herald*, March 18, 1949.

EIGHT

'Films of Value to Humanity': *Secret People, Hill 24 Doesn't Answer, Power among Men*

Secret People, Dickinson's next film after *The Queen of Spades*, was the crystallization of his thematic and ideological ideas and his philosophy of cinema. It was to be his great bid to make a film of ideas for discriminating audiences, an 'art house' film for Britain, that would equal the European standard that he so much admired and point British cinema in a different direction from slavish imitation of Hollywood. It was also to prove his downfall.

The original story had been told to Dickinson by a Liverpool police inspector while he was doing research there for *The Next of Kin* and involved the Irish Republican Army (IRA):

> At the outbreak of war in 1939, this political group began using explosives in London and Liverpool. And this married woman and her husband, both Catholics, were involved; at the last meeting of the group on a named assassination she pleaded with those there to stop this horrible killing. She was ignored. She was in an agonizing position. If she did nothing the killing would take place; if she went to the police both she and her husband, of whom she was very fond, would certainly be killed themselves; due to her stand at the final meeting it would be clear who had tipped off the police, and although her husband did not agree with her stand it would be assumed that they were both implicated. She made her decision to go to the police. They caught everybody just as we show on the screen. Now as the woman was now in danger, to save her life the police had to remodel her face, invent a new identity for her and send her out of England.[1]

Chapter Eight

The story fascinated Dickinson as a vehicle both for discussing the ethics of terrorism and for exploring his now familiar theme of 'secret people'. He discussed the story with Joyce Cary as they sailed for Africa to film *Men of Two Worlds*. While on the voyage, Cary sketched out a ten-page outline of a story called *The Quick and the Dead*, based on the idea and their discussions around it. He set it in 1914 and incorporated a situation based on the siege of Sidney Street. The basic elements of what later became *Secret People* were all there in the first draft of the story.

It centres on Mary Brant, a singer with a pierrot show, married to an older man, Frank Sayler. Sayler works for an international revolutionary group, using his job as a warehouseman to import arms and explosives from abroad. Mary's father and mother believe in peaceful change and the brotherhood of people, and she is torn between their philosophy and that of her husband. She is eventually persuaded by her husband and his friend Kelman, the leader of the revolutionary group in London, that some must die for the good of the many. Kelman plans to murder a visiting foreign minister at a country house garden party, where Mary will be performing with her pierrot troupe. Frank, working as a waiter, places a bomb, which goes off killing an innocent waitress and spattering Mary with blood. Appalled, she denounces their schemes. Kelman decides that she must be eliminated. When two detectives question Mary about Frank, she denounces Kelman to them. But the detectives are gunned down as they leave, and the police surround the revolutionary gang in their headquarters in Sussex Street. After a short siege, it is burned down. Frank's body is recovered from the ruins, and Kelman is also believed to be among those who perished. The police announce that Mary is dead, to protect her from revenge by the revolutionaries. Five years after the end of the war, Mary is running a nightclub in Morocco when Kelman arrives with Mary's daughter Nora, who is now committed to both him and the revolutionary cause. She pleads with Nora to leave him, but Nora refuses. So she threatens to denounce Kelman unless he gives up Nora. Kelman refuses, stabbing Mary to death as the police close in to arrest him. Nora is left weeping over her mother's body.

After the abortive Indian project, Dickinson interested Two Cities in *Secret People*, as it was now called, and it was announced as a forthcoming production. Dickinson and Cary prepared a script, completing it by December 1946. They eliminated the husband Frank and the siege of Sidney Street idea and instead focused on the relationship between Maria Brent and Louis Kelman. But the rest of the plot remained much the same. Maria, meeting Kelman while on a trip to

Paris, becomes involved in his plot to assassinate the foreign minister of a European dictator. The waitress is killed and Maria denounces the use of violence, but the revolutionary gang try to persuade her of its validity. She betrays them to the police but is injured by a bomb as they try to escape. Recovered, she changes her name to Lena Martin and leaves the country. The finale with her encountering Kelman and Nora takes places in the Middle East, where 'Lena' is working as a nurse in a military hospital.

However, at short notice Dickinson was switched to *Then and Now*, and when that project was cancelled, he left Two Cities, taking the script with him. After *The Queen of Spades*, he returned to the idea, reworking the script with Wolfgang Wilhelm in 1949. The principal changes now were to make Maria and Nora sisters and to set the final encounter in Dublin. Kelman became Maria's former fiancé and the chief disciple of her liberal peace-loving father who is gradually corrupted by violence until he becomes a conscienceless assassin.

Dickinson and Wilhelm had particular difficulty with the opening, trying and discarding several. In one version, they began with events in the home country of Kelman and Maria before their arrival in England; in another, café proprietor Anselmo recounted the story to a group of students in his café arguing about the rights and wrongs of political assassination. But they all took too long to get into the story proper, so Dickinson and Wilhelm decided eventually to begin the story with the arrival of Maria and Nora as exiles in England. It was decided to set the story in the 1930s because Dickinson feared that if it were set in the present, it was in danger of being overtaken by contemporary events. So he chose the most recent prewar period.[2]

But work on the script was once again set on one side when Associated British Pictures, impressed with Dickinson's work on *The Queen of Spades*, offered him a prestige project, the job of scripting and filming Thomas Hardy's *The Mayor of Casterbridge*, which was to be produced with a major star in the lead for the Festival of Britain year. The story was a classic 'secret people' project, and Dickinson set to work with Wolfgang Wilhelm in 1949 to prepare a script. Their final version, completed by January 1950, followed Hardy's story fairly closely except for the end. Theirs had Michael Henchard departing alone from Casterbridge rather than actually dying as he did in the book.

The script began with drunken hay trusser Michael Henchard selling his wife and daughter to a sailor for five guineas. The consequences of that act were to return to haunt him. Twenty years later, he is a successful businessman and mayor of Casterbridge. His wife returns, believing the sailor dead, and he remarries her. She brings her daughter Elizabeth Jane with her, and Henchard believes she is his own daughter. Henchard quarrels with his assistant Donald Farfrae, who sets up in business in competition with him. Mrs. Henchard dies and Farfrae marries Lucetta Templeman, whom Henchard hoped to marry. Henchard's business is ruined, the story of his sale of his wife is revealed, and he takes to drink. Henchard's only comfort is his daughter, but then her real father, the sailor, returns to claim her, and after Lucetta's death, Farfrae marries her. Henchard leaves Casterbridge, ruined and desolate.

The script was completed, the set designs drawn up, and casting was about to begin when Associated British abruptly cancelled the project. They had decided that the cost would be too great for them to recoup from the British market, particularly since there was no guarantee of an American release for so intrinsically British a subject.[3] So Dickinson once again turned back to *Secret People*. He approached Sir Michael Balcon about the possibility of producing it at Ealing Studios. Balcon held Dickinson's work in high regard:

> Although I had worked with him only rarely, I had watched his work closely, and it seemed to me that he had been given little opportunity to do himself—and the British film industry— justice. All too often he had been given scripts not of his own choosing, scripts not worthy of his great ability. In *Secret People* he at last had a script of his own making, something essentially of the cinema and not adapted from a novel or a play, something in which both emotionally and intellectually he was very much involved; in fact a subject to which he could bring full enthusiasm as well as his usual skill. It seemed to me it would be a tragic loss if he were not able to go ahead.[4]

So Balcon agreed to produce it at Ealing. It was the first production to be brought in from outside rather than originated at the studio, and it received the overall credit 'A Thorold Dickinson production'. But an Ealing producer was assigned to work on it, and it was, at Dickinson's request, his old friend Sidney Cole. Dickinson moved onto the Ealing lot in October 1950 to begin preproduction of the film.

Dickinson also arranged for every aspect of the filming to be charted by Lindsay Anderson for a book later published under the title *Making a Film*. Anderson had met Dickinson while he was at Oxford and involved in running the film society there:

> The first time I ever met Thorold, we were at Oxford, myself and Peter Ericsson, the film society, we invited Thorold down to speak to the film society and he came and was extremely friendly and inter-

ested in ideas in a way that was exceptional for a British film-maker and he did like to be taken seriously and there weren't all that number of people who could take you seriously in those days. That's how we got to know Thorold.[5]

A group of the young Oxford cineastes, Anderson and Ericsson amongst them, launched *Sequence* magazine, a lively and stimulating quarterly devoted to the cinema, which contained the earliest critical writings of such future luminaries as Karel Reisz, Gavin Lambert, and Anderson himself. The magazine praised *The Queen of Spades* and was to come to Dickinson's defence in the filmwright controversy which he launched in the pages of *Sight and Sound*. It was to Anderson then that Dickinson turned to record the process of the making of what he hoped would be his finest film.

Dickinson was insistent that the two leading roles should be played by continental actors. He had first in mind Lea Padovani and François Perier, but neither was available, and he eventually chose Valentina Cortesa, an Italian actress recently working in Hollywood, and Serge Reggiani, the French actor, who had starred in Carné's *Les Portes de la Nuit*. Dickinson also cast the chief supporting roles, which were played by Charles Goldner, Megs Jenkins, Reginald Tate, and Geoffrey Hibbert, the last two of whom had been in *The Next of Kin*. He also selected Audrey Hepburn for her first important film role, as Nora.[6]

The first shooting script was ready by January 1951. But it was revised partly for budgetary reasons. Paris location shooting was vetoed because of the expense, and the twelve-week shooting schedule was cut to eleven weeks. The Dublin locations were reduced to the absolute minimum. Balcon had some reservations about the script, suggesting an introductory sequence in Maria's home country to set up the characters and background and worrying that the death of Maria at the end would leave audiences with the feeling that the secret organization carried on undefeated. He wanted to see Louis being killed as well. But Dickinson held out against any suggested alterations and succeeded in filming the script more or less as it stood. Christianna Brand was brought in to write some additional dialogue for Maria in her scenes with Louis, to suggest the romantic relationship between them, and shooting began on March 15, 1951, being completed eleven weeks later. Dickinson was delighted with the result. He thought Reggiani was perfect ('a fallen angel, an idealist degraded'), was delighted with Cortesa, and felt that he had succeeded in doing what he had set out to do.

He was to have a rude awakening. The film was put on at the Odeon, Leicester Square, where performances were disrupted by Communist demonstrators, who, believing that the dictator in the film was intended to be a Fascist (Franco or Mussolini), interpreted the film as an attack on the Communist opponents of Fascism. But more seriously, the reviews were almost without exception utterly damning. The *Observer*'s C. A. Lejeune thought *Secret People*

> muddled, inadequate and often inaudible. . . . [T]he direction is shrewd over details if weak in large effects. . . . I'm pretty sure there is a good film somewhere in connection with *Secret People* either in the director's mind or on the cutting room floor. Such a pity it isn't at the Odeon.[7]

The *News Chronicle*, drawing attention to Anderson's book, declared:

> That *Secret People*, after all the creative agonies recorded by Mr. Anderson, should turn out to be a confused spy thriller concealing a tentative message deep down below some strained effects of style is another tragedy of British film hopes.[8]

The *Daily Herald* announced, 'It was all such an embarrassing mixture of pretentiousness and naivety I felt ashamed and wanted to look away'.[9] The *Manchester Guardian* felt it was

> admirable in its intention, and in many of its details, but on the whole mismanaged. . . . On the one hand it tries to treat its serious theme seriously: on the other, its story is infused with a lot of melodrama—and some of this melodrama is much too full of coincidence and implausibility.[10]

The *Daily Express* reported 'it claims to be a message picture but don't ask me what the message is'. The *Evening Standard* called it 'a mausoleum of good intentions'; The *Daily Graphic*, 'jumbled and incoherent'; The *Daily Telegraph*, 'bitty and uneven'; The *Spectator*, 'the most boring film I have ever seen in my life'. Only the *New Statesman* lightened the gloom by pronouncing it 'stylish, thoughtful and just a little disappointing'.[11]

There can be little doubt that the film is a considerable disappointment after the splendours of *The Queen of Spades*, for reasons that were pointed out both at the time and subsequently. The film opens in 1930 with Maria and Nora, daughters of Pietro Brentano, liberal opponent of dictator General Galbern, arriving in London and café owner Anselmo taking them into his home as his wards. They are naturalized as British subjects under the name of Brent in 1937. They visit the Paris Exposition, and there Maria sees again her former boyfriend, Louis

Balan. She is unaware that he is there to assassinate Galbern. The Brents return to London, and Nora, who is a ballet dancer, is engaged to dance at a reception for Galbern, thanks to Louis's intervention. Louis persuades Maria to take a bomb into the house where the reception is being held. Later she returns, spattered with blood, to tell Louis that she delivered the bomb. It went off, killing not Galbern but an innocent waitress, who died in her arms. Police arrest her, and she confesses. The police arrange to trap Louis and the others as they visit her at the café. But one of the terrorists throws a bomb, and Maria is injured. Police announce that she is dead, change her face and her identity, and plan to send her to America for safety. She agrees to go, if she can take one last look at Nora. In Dublin, she sees Nora dance but also sees the terrorist cell leader. Police uncover plans to assassinate Galbern's son. Maria discovers that Nora is being used by Louis, meets them in the park, denounces Louis as a ruthless murderer, is stabbed to death by Louis's associate Steenie, and dies in Nora's arms. Louis and Steenie are arrested.

The film is basically a dramatized debate about the ethics of terrorism in which Dickinson comes down firmly against political assassination. 'We must love one another or die—in our heart we know this to be true' are the final words heard, the words of Maria's father, an opponent of political violence, who believes that the pen is mightier than the sword. It is a view that Louis has dismissed as outdated. When Maria visits Louis in his lodgings, he tells her that she talks a lot about her father's work but does nothing about it. She gives Louis her father's pen and reminds him that her father always called it 'his sword'. Louis calls it 'a relic from another world'.

Louis attends a meeting of the terrorists at which they discuss the assassination of Galbern. Interestingly, the English member is against on the grounds of public opinion but the rest convince him and the vote for the murder is unanimous. Louis is also influential in persuading Maria to carry the bomb to the reception for Galbern ('Resistance to tyrants is obedience to God'). But after the waitress's death, she is taken to meet the group, and they dismiss her talk of conscience and the loss of innocent lives ('sheer sentimentality'). The scene is shot to emphasize the evil and menace of the terrorists, in low angle, with Maria dominated by the group, whose faces are in shadow. Similarly, the terrorist leader's face is never seen. He is identified by his shoes, cane, and voice only. The image of a sinister shadowy, immoral force is thus visually confirmed.

The visual style of the film is on the whole sombre and low-key, in keeping with the theme. But like Dickinson's previous films, it shows strong traces of the continental influence. The scene early in the film with Anselmo, the café owner, lying bloated on his bed, listening to a gramophone record, recalls a similar scene at the start of Pabst's *Love of Jeanne Ney*. The encounter between Louis and Maria in his lodgings with an open window overlooking the Great Western main line into London was modelled directly on a scene in Renoir's *La Bête Humaine*. But perhaps most of all the film is Dickinson's hommage to *Hôtel du Nord*. For not only does he employ the characteristic long takes of Carné's film, but he also effectively reworks elements of the plot of the French film: the doomed love affair, the change of identity, a girl injured and rushed to hospital, the details of café life, with Serge Reggiani taking on some of the characteristics of Louis Jouvet and Valentina Cortesa of Annabella in the original film.

There are, as one would expect from Dickinson, a number of bravura visual sequences. The Paris Exposition is represented by a vigorous montage of fountains, fireworks, champagne corks popping, stormtroopers outside the German pavilion, and top-hatted officials outside the British. There is an impressive point-of-view sequence of Maria being rushed to hospital after the explosion, the camera going in and out of focus, faces peering down at her, fragments of what is going on around her as seen through her eyes. The film also contains what Dickinson called 'the most eloquent shot I ever made'. Maria, about to leave for a new life in a new country, sees her younger sister for the last time as she is dancing on the stage of a Dublin theatre. The camera tracks back from Maria's box, down the aisle and up onto the stage, reversing so that when the curtain falls, separating the two sisters, it gives us Nora's eye view of the audience.

A number of typical and welcome Dickinson comic vignettes appear: the jaunty old lady who auditions Nora, an ex-actress chucklingly recalling that she had no moral support when she went on the stage; the startled little man in a bowler hat who bolts out of the prostitute's room when the police call; the flustered British official at the Exposition who is informed that the British Pavilion must be closed for ten minutes to allow General Galbern to have a private view.

But none of this is enough to save the film, which must be seen in the end as a resounding failure. The dramatic structure is ramshackle, the tension is not maintained, and neither Cortesa nor Reggiani is able to excite much interest or sympathy in the audience. The principal weakness of the film was in fact pinpointed in July 1947 by Nigel Balchin, who, having been sent the script to read, wrote back to Dickinson that it should either be done as a thriller in the manner of Hitchcock or John Buchan or as a philosophical drama:

My blunt criticism is that the script as it stands falls between two stools. If it is about the Hidden Hand and Bombs then there aren't enough bombs. If it is about the Philosophy of Extremism, then there isn't enough philosophy. I am sorry to be so destructive. I am sure there is a good film to be made about international espionage and sabotage. But I am pretty sure that it would have to be a commentary on the contemporary international scene and not, as this tends to be, a mere use of Europe in the 30's as a setting.[12]

But Dickinson failed to heed the criticism as he seems to have failed to heed all criticism of this script, in which he had invested so much emotional and intellectual commitment.

Ironically, a film had already been made that tackled the subject of sabotage, the politics of extremism, and the dilemma of conscience in 1930s Britain, and that was *Sabotage* (1937), Alfred Hitchcock's film of Joseph Conrad's 'The Secret Agent'. It has several features in common with *Secret People*: a terrorist ring operating in London, a woman innocently involved with one of their agents, a bomb outrage that kills a harmless boy. It was infinitely more cohesive, involving, disturbing, and successful as an exploration of moral ambiguity, innocence, guilt, and extremism within the thriller format than *Secret People*. Ironically it was actually projected during preproduction of *Secret People* to allow costume designer Anthony Mendleson to get a feel of the 1930s dress and atmosphere. But Dickinson seems not to have learned from it.

In retrospect, Sidney Cole agreed with Balchin's criticism of the script.[13] Lindsay Anderson also felt that there were great problems with the script, considering it 'half-baked'. But Dickinson was unwilling to listen to any suggestions that he might make about it ('You had to play it his way'). He felt that Balcon should have pressed him more firmly on the script. But Balcon, whose invitation to Dickinson to film *Secret People* at Ealing was 'a very disinterested act', was 'too respectful—the return of this senior eminence to Ealing to be given every opportunity to complete his film'.[14]

Even Raymond Durgnat, who saw quality and value in the film, expressed reservations about the period and the setting:

> At least as far as the wider public was concerned it was perhaps unfortunate that the film was set in the thirties. Had the Fascist General suggested pre-war Spain, and the assassins Stalinists, the story's ethical balance might well have been very sharp. But the thirties suggested to most people, Hitler and Mussolini. By that association, the film, in

postulating the bomb and the pen as alternatives, seemed to be reducing the liberal conscience to a scrupulous, pacifistic ineffectiveness. Confronted with a Hitler, a Mussolini or a Franco, there's little doubt that, if the pen is mightier than the sword, it's only because it can lead to the unsheathing of so many swords that the potential aggressor prefers to replace his own in its scabbard. Yet another area of reference might have offered an Eastern European régime as the dictatorship and a band of aristocratic emigrés as the terrorists. . . . Sensitive though the film is, one may feel oneself, quietly, fighting its argument, even, withdrawing from it, as it goes.[15]

Dickinson was understandably deeply disappointed by the film's failure:

We never disguised the fact that *Secret People* was what you would call an art house subject, not for the general public so much as for a smaller audience. That was why we cast two players, one from Italy, one from France, both firmly established in their own countries, so that we could have an entry into both these markets; it wasn't supposed to be a film that would get all its money back here. But when the film failed in England, they didn't in fact try to sell it in Europe at all.[16]

Dickinson was always to blame the Communist demonstrations for the failure of the film. He said that Ealing took fright at them, cut the film, and sent it out as a second feature, never bothering to seek to promote it effectively. But it seems clear that it was killed by the reviews and by the problems of the film itself, in terms of subject, structure, and approach. It certainly put an end to Dickinson's concept of a British art cinema and in a very real sense to Dickinson's British film career too.

But *Secret People* was to return to Dickinson's life during his retirement when he was enraged by references to it in an article on Ealing by John Ellis published in *Screen* magazine in 1975. Ellis, referring to the early 1950s wrote, 'There was an acute suspicion of the left as somehow dehumanized (the product of Stalinism), which led Dickinson to make *Secret People*, viciously condemning a group which attempts to assassinate a fascist dictator'.[17] Dickinson wrote a short, angry rebuttal to *Screen* and a longer, equally angry letter to Stuart Hall, director of the Centre for Contemporary Studies at Birmingham University, where Ellis had obtained a master's degree for a thesis on Ealing that formed the basis of the *Screen* article. Dickinson declared that Ellis's statement was untrue and verged on the libelous:

There is nothing in the film to suggest whether the dictator is fascist or communist, nor is the point of the film the attempt to kill him. I developed the subject, with help from liberal Irish novelist Joyce Cary, from an incident which occured in Liverpool in the autumn of 1939 from the activities of an IRA group which became callous to the sacrifice of humane life. Heavily disguised at the request of the police, the story condemns this callousness, with the theme Violence breeds Violence. The group fails to kill the dictator, murdering a waitress instead. Further deaths inevitably follow. No sane or sensitive person, who has seen the film can agree with Ellis' interpretation, which I find contemptible.[18]

Ellis himself replied to Dickinson in a carefully argued four-page letter, in which he correctly pointed out that the visual and aural evidence of the film pointed to the dictator being a Fascist and argued that because of the narrative structure of the film, he took the central message to be 'one of the corrupting effect of militant action against Fascism'.[19] But he did not retract his statement.

The whole controversy highlighted the original problems of the *Secret People* script to which Durgnat had already drawn attention. But it also highlighted the differences between an old-fashioned liberal and the New Left, between the old *Sight and Sound* consensus and the new *Screen* caucus, and demonstrated just how far behind Dickinson, the educator and cineaste, had been left by the politicization and radicalisation of film studies. As James Leahy recalled:

> Thorold was personally very hurt. It was one word 'vicious'. It was partly a romantic naiveté about the integrity of the artist. He had not wanted to do what he was accused of doing and had worked against doing what he was accused of doing yet he hadn't totally succeeded.[20]

However, when it comes to the crunch, Dickinson's heart was in the right place. His primary concern was with the innocent waitress who had died; Ellis's concern seems to have been with the 'militant action against Fascism'. That is the measure of the difference between liberal humanism and the New Left. There can be no meeting of minds under those circumstances. At this point film criticism becomes irrelevant, and it is a matter of political choice and basic morality. At that point, I stand with Dickinson.

Dickinson swallowed the failure of *Secret People* and threw himself into a new project in 1952. The Central Office of Information came up with the idea of a film about the wartime cooperation of the three armed services, and since this had occurred notably in Malta, there was an opportunity for a tribute to the George Cross Island. A company (Theta) was set up to produce the film, and Dickinson was recruited as director, Peter de Sarigny as producer, and William Fairchild as scriptwriter. As it happened, they represented the three services: Fairchild having been a naval commander; De Sarigny, an Air Force wing commander; and Dickinson, an Army major. The three of them flew to Malta to gather material, and Dickinson decided that the documentary information they had gathered was so good that they should do it as a neorealist film in the Italian manner, with the people involved playing themselves. Dickinson was clearly still clinging to his 'art house' ideas.

Together with Fairchild, Dickinson prepared a script called *The Bright Flame*, from President Roosevelt's reference in 1943 to Malta as 'one tiny bright flame in defiance of the darkness'. The script interwove the actual events of the siege of Malta with a personal story centred on Flight Lieutenant Peter Ross. He has a romance with Maltese girl Maria, whose brother Giuseppe returns to the island as an Italian spy and is hanged.[21]

But Rank, who were financing and releasing the film, raised objections both to the script and to the budget, and Dickinson was removed from the project. Dickinson believed that it was because they regarded him as uncommercial after the failure of *Secret People*. But it is much more likely that they did not like the neorealist concept and wanted a more straightforward war film. Brian Desmond Hurst was brought in as director, and Nigel Balchin was assigned to work on the script. The resulting film, *The Malta Story* (1953), retained elements of Dickinson's conception, but with the addition of a story line emphasizing the loneliness and stress of command and a star cast headed by Alec Guinness, Jack Hawkins, Anthony Steel, and Flora Robson, it fitted rather more obviously into the genre of celebratory war films that the British cinema was currently producing.

Frustrated and angry at the failure of his ideas and his career, Dickinson accepted an offer of work from Israel. It resulted from a summer school he organized as chairman of the British Film Academy in 1953. He lectured on the making of military training films, and an Israeli woman involved in the planning of a feature film about the Arab-Israeli war of 1948 attended it. She was so impressed by Dickinson's lecture that she arranged for him to be invited to Israel to advise on the making of the film, the first to be produced in Israel. He and Joanna left for Israel in July 1953, and it was not long before he was asked to actually direct the film, *Hill 24 Doesn't Answer*.

Before embarking on *Hill 24*, Dickinson was asked by the Israeli Defence Ministry to make a short propaganda film to create greater sympathy for the army in an indifferent public. The result was an effective short film, *The Red Ground*, shot in the Judaean Hills in December 1953. Dickinson told the story entirely in pictures because he could not understand the Hebrew commentary that was to go with it. It opens with a long tracking shot through the streets of Tel Aviv and then suddenly freezes a frame on a soldier, David, crossing the road. David is the central figure of the film. We see an operation being performed on him in hospital, and the film flashes back to tell how he got injured. He and his troop were going out on patrol, and we see them bivouacking for the night, rising early in the morning and setting off on trucks. David, as he rides along, recalls in another flashback his last leave. He and other soldiers hitching a lift are ignored by civilian drivers and eventually picked up by fellow soldiers. In town, they are ignored. Family and friends are busy with their own lives and their own affairs. When David tries to get into a cinema, he finds that the queue is too long, and a tout tries to sell him an overpriced ticket. There is a general air of indifference to the soldiery.

The flashback ends, and the patrol discovers a burning car and a dying man, the result of an Arab attack. As the patrol investigates the area, they are attacked by Arabs and David is injured and rescued. The ambush is done with many changes of camera angle, point-of-view shots, and whip pans, and the result is graphic and moving. Dickinson cuts to David in his hospital bed. He is released, limps away, and then gradually the limp gives way to a proud marching gait, and shots of David's feet dissolve to the marching feet of the Israeli army. He is one of the many fighting and dying in defence of Israel.

Dickinson was back again in the milieu in which he had so notably flourished—wartime. The film recalls in both its vivid documentary immediacy and its emotional commitment the shorts and the feature that Dickinson made in support of the British war effort. The film is given added poignancy by the fact that the soldier chosen to play the lead role of David was himself killed two weeks after the film was finished while on patrol in the area where *The Red Ground* had been shot.

Hill 24 Doesn't Answer was shot in Israel between April and September 1954. Dickinson had taken with him to Israel his wife Joanna, the cameraman Gerald Gibbs, the sound man Ben Brightwell, and the actor Edward Mulhare. The rest of the cast and crew were recruited locally. Dickinson began shooting from the already prepared script by Zvi Kolitz and Peter Frye. He started with the desert episode about a captured Nazi and found it so melodramatic and extreme that he closed down the production and set about rewriting the script with Joanna. It was originally five hours long, but they cut it down to less than two hours. They gathered the reminiscences of the capture of Jerusalem from Israeli veterans and re-created it as exactly as possible from these memories, to the extent that when the veterans saw the film they were bowled over by its authenticity. Dickinson also arranged with the British ambassador to have the script flown back to the Foreign Office in London for their comments. Their response was 'We're delighted that an Englishman is making this film because otherwise it might be very embarrassing, and we strongly approve of the script'.

Sixty percent of the film was shot on location, in the Negev desert, in Haifa and at Acre. The Jerusalem street scenes were filmed at Acre, and the Zion Gate was reconstructed to scale for the attack. The interiors were shot in a converted nail factory on the road from Haifa to Jerusalem. The factory was a haunt of birds, and a revolver had to be fired before each scene was filmed to disperse them. The actors did their dialogue scenes between midnight and 3 A.M. when there was no traffic on the road outside.

With his usual concern about music, Dickinson listened to the work of the leading Jewish composers at Israel Radio and selected Paul Ben-Haim to score the film. He was initially unwilling to be involved but was persuaded, and he provided the themes that Dickinson could use while he was filming and then completed the full score. But he insisted on a full-scale choral finale. The producers backed him, and although Dickinson thought it was 'pure Warner Bros.' and prolonged the ending of the film, he accepted it. He was already back in England editing the film when the problem arose, so he cabled his assistant in Israel to shoot enough footage of the desert, tanks, and so on, to cover the music and edited it together, adding as a final caption the words 'The Beginning'. Once again, for good or ill, it was Dickinson's work. For he effectively wrote, directed, and edited it with Joanna's assistance. It was to be his last film, and in many ways his most emotional.

The film centres on 'the secret people' idea. In this case, the inner person is revealed by the confrontation with the need to fight for the Jewish homeland. But there is a strong propaganda element, and the film is punctuated by speeches about the Jews' right to their homeland and the need to fight for it. It opens with shots of four dead Israeli soldiers, James Finnegan, Allan Goodman, Esther Hadassi, and David Amiram. Their names are called, and we see them being briefed to hold Hill 24 until it is claimed for Israel when the UN apportions the territory after the expiration of the British mandate and the fighting of the Arab-Israeli war in 1948. Then in flashback we see what has led each of the three men to their involvement in the war.

James Finnegan is an Irishman serving with the Palestine British-controlled Police in 1946, though nothing is made in the script of his being an Irishman serving with an occupying force. He participates in an operation to arrest illegal immigrants. In a sequence of rapid cutting, boats come ashore, lights flash on, and lines of soldiers advance to round up the immigrants. Finnegan finds two of them, Yehuda Berger and Miriam Mizrachi, huddling under a rock and quixotically gives them a flask of brandy before leaving them. The Jewish underground blow up a radar station, and the police search for the terrorists. At a road block, Berger is spotted by Finnegan and pursued. In an excitingly shot chase sequence, he is pursued through the night-time streets of Haifa. He vanishes, but Finnegan, searching a suspect house, encounters Miriam again and takes her in for questioning. Berger is also brought in, having been picked up by a British patrol, and he denounces the British for being in Palestine, defending his right to fight for his homeland. He is removed to jail and Miriam is released, but Finnegan is ordered to watch her. He begins to talk with her and soon falls in love with her. She articulates the Jewish case, and he comes to support it. When she is again arrested, he returns to England and resigns his commission. He hurries back to Israel as the war breaks out, resumes his courtship of Miriam, and joins up.

Allan Goodman is an American tourist, who, inspired by romantic dreams of freeing the Holy Land, joins the Israeli army and takes part in the attack on Jerusalem. In the vividly staged street fighting, Allan sees things that horrify him—an old man shot, another blinded by gunfire, a third blown up. He is himself blown up while trying to warn a detachment of Israeli troops who are walking into an ambush. He comes to in a hospital where he is tended by nurse Esther Hadassi but where there are no drugs and little water. Allan gives way to disillusionment and asks a rabbi why God has allowed so many Jews to die both in Palestine and in Europe. The rabbi replies that those who believe in God, as the Jews do, are in the front line of the battle of good against evil, and those in the front line suffer the most casualties. The rabbi then recites the Twenty-third Psalm to him.

But news arrives that they have been forced to surrender to the Arabs to avoid further casualties. In a deeply moving scene, in which the camera eloquently pans round the ward, the injured and the staff defiantly sing a Jewish hymn as the Arab soldiers enter. The singing swells to a chorus of triumph, even though in a tragic procession the Jews evacuate the old city, the rabbi holding Allan's hand. Once he is recovered, Allan rejoins the fight.

David Amiram's story recalls *The Red Ground*. He leads a scouting patrol in the Negev, chaffing an eager, inexperienced rookie Issachar, who is promptly killed. The Israeli patrol engages an enemy detachment holding a ruined fort and drives them off. Amiram captures one of the enemy and drags him into a cave to escape the enemy barrage. There he discovers that his prisoner is a wounded Nazi mercenary fighting for the Arabs. He pleads for his life ('We couldn't help ourselves'), apologises, and then, increasingly delirious, denounces the Jews, rants about Deutschland, tries unsuccessfully to provoke Amiram to shoot him, and finally drops dead doing the Nazi salute. The Israeli air force and tanks advance into the area, having been alerted by Amiram's patrol, and he watches joyously as they sweep across the desert.

The flashback ends, as the four soldiers arrive at Hill 24 and scramble up to hold it for the night. The next morning a UN truce supervision group arrives with an Arab and an Israeli officer. There is no sign of the soldiers. Each side claims the hill. But on investigating, they discover all four dead and, in Esther's hand, the Israeli flag. The UN official pronounces the hill Israeli, the camera cranes up and then, over aerial shots of the Holy Land, appear the words 'The Beginning'.

The film is throughout vividly and excitingly made. The photography of Gerald Gibbs is superb, sharply defined black and white, making the most of photogenic locations. The battle scenes are extremely effective. The Dutch Army was to be so impressed by them that it purchased copies of the film to instruct its soldiers in street fighting. It has a strong pro-Israeli propaganda content, but there are several genuinely moving scenes, particularly in the second flashback sequence. The film's principal weakness is the third episode, which, despite Dickinson's rewriting, remains gratuitous and crude. The acting is also no more than competent, though it was from this film that William Wyler selected Haya Harareet, who played Miriam, to star in his film of *Ben-Hur*.

Hill 24 is notable in being unquestionably Dickinson's most emotional film. It may have been in part the subject, the use of participants' memories, the recent date of the events, but it showed him responding with full-hearted commitment to both the film and the cause it depicted. Thematically, it is mainstream Dickinson with each of the three principal participants—Finnegan, Goodman and Amiram—facing a crisis in which the 'secret person' within them, an Israeli patriot, emerges. Finnegan discovers that his love for Miriam and her arrest open his eyes to the worth of the Israeli cause, Goodman's faith is restored by the experience of the evacuation and the words of the rabbi, and Amiram refrains from exacting personal vengeance and retains his dignity at the height of the battle. Visually, Dickinson was able, by the use of genuine locations, amateur actors, and reconstructed real-life events, to approach his new ideal of neorealism.

The film was premiered in Jerusalem in 1955 and attended by the Israeli prime minister, the British ambassador, and other members of the diplomatic corps. When it was shown at the Cannes Film Festival in the same year, Haya Harareet received the homage of the jury. It was acclaimed by the French press. *Le Monde* called it 'a work of quality, noble in its inspiration, impeccable in its execution'. *Les Lettres Françaises* said it was 'the best film of Dickinson's that we have seen, a work that is generous, full of variety and sincere, exceedingly interesting'. *Combat* declared it 'overwhelming in its telling, its preciseness, its dominant lyricism . . . overwhelming also in its honesty'. *France Observateur* noted 'the profound emotion provoked by the film is also of a rare quality'.[22]

When it was released in Britain in 1955, the critics were rather less encomiastic, though always generous in applauding Dickinson's intentions, achievements, and some of his effects. In the *Observer*, Gavin Lambert pronounced the makeshift conditions of production justified by 'the director's open response to the material, by a sense of place and immediacy that could never have been obtained under more orthodox conditions'. But he complained:

> Enclosed in a complex flashback structure, these stories with their rather summary characterisation and continual shots of emphasis detract from a scene that demands the clear, sweeping dramatic line. The love story is also marred by insipid dialogue and a clumsy performance from Edward Mulhare. It is only at the climax of the second episode—the siege of Jerusalem and its evacuation—that the director's grasp really imposes itself and adds a new vital dimension to the film. With the sequences of street fighting at night and the sad exodus in the morning, *Hill 24* achieves a fierce realism and an impressive grandeur. . . . Dickinson captures the tensions and turbulence of the birthpangs of a nation, the confusion of loyalties and hatreds, the terrible repetition of deaths. The feeling persists for the rest of the film and carries it through to the final ironic climax. Technically, too, the achievement is remarkable. Restrictive conditions have not cramped the long atmospheric camera movements, the elaborately planned sound-track, the strong, cumulative cutting style that mark this director's work.[23]

The *Times*'s verdict was as follows:

> Mr. Thorold Dickinson's first concern on *Hill 24 Doesn't Answer* has understandably been to show something of the fire and the passion, the suffering and the discipline, the faith and the courage that to-

gether brought about the state of Israel. It is a subject that makes an obvious appeal to the imagination and of the generosity of Mr. Dickinson's response there is no question. The pity is that he and his Jewish collaborators have been no more than half successful in what they set out to do. In everything which touches the individual and shows him talking and in relationship to others, the film fails abysmally. The dialogue is deplorable and the actors do not give the impression of believing a word of it . . . But in conveying the sense of a people sure of their destiny and willing to die to bring it about *Hill 24 Doesn't Answer* soars to something approaching the heights. The scenes of street fighting in Jerusalem are brilliantly managed and throughout the camera gives a vivid impression of the harsh nature of the country, a country which demands and receives the extremes of emotion.[24]

The *Manchester Guardian* noted that Dickinson

made it evidently with much sincerity and—in certain scenes in Jerusalem—with effective dramatic pathos. It is certainly not to be counted against this film that it is a work of Zionist propaganda, but it would have done its job of propaganda much better had it been less crude . . . and had its conclusion preached a less horrid sermon about the expendability of human life in national causes. It is an exceptional film in its mixture of silliness and honesty, and indeed, nobility.[25]

The British consensus is a just verdict on the film. But it was once again an art house subject, made little box-office impact, and confirmed for the industry that Dickinson had become hopelessly uncommercial. But the film opened up another and unexpected avenue of endeavour. *Hill 24* was seen and liked at the United Nations, and in 1956 Dickinson was offered and accepted an appointment as chief of Film Services of the Radio and Visual Services Division of the UN Department of Public Information. Dickinson told the *Evening News*, 'I shall be in New York for at least two years. I am not quite clear what my job will be'.[26]

It was a decisive move for Dickinson, for he had turned his back on the commercial film industry and on fictional feature filmmaking and committed himself full-time to the documentary movement, which had hitherto been a minor and comparatively unimportant part of his career. He was in a sense being driven in that direction by his increasing commitment to uncommercial projects and by the absence in Britain of any body like the wartime Ministry of Information that had provided a congenial milieu for his maverick talent.

Films of Value to Humanity

During his four years in New York, Dickinson's principal work was the feature-length documentary *Power among Men*, which he produced and coedited and which won prizes at the Venice and Moscow Film Festivals and the Selznick Golden Laurel Award in 1959. It was a four-episode film describing the encounters between men and women of different nationalities and their successful cooperation in different projects. A *New Yorker* reporter, interviewing Dickinson in 1959, remarked that it seemed to be a composition of associated ideas rather than a conventional narrative film. Dickinson replied:

> Exactly. I think it's a kind of musical arrangement more than a visual one. That makes the whole thing hard to describe, because I can't recall any very close precedent. The film isn't a fiction feature because it's factual, but then it isn't a documentary either or even a propaganda piece. You see, I've never found out exactly why they asked me, a commercial entertainment man, to come over here and take on what is an information job, but I've proceeded on the assumption that it was to put some emotion into information— or at least to prevent all the intrinsic emotion draining out.

The idea for *Power among Men* came from the undersecretary in the Department of Public Information, Professor Ahmed Bokhari:

> He said he wanted a political film, a film of ideas—such as the idea that ordinary people are capable of learning to survive in the atomic age, and that one needn't be terrified of nuclear power as such but there is indeed a grave human dilemma and that it is advisable for the audience to be vigilant. Professor Bokhari agreed with me that our one reelers amounted only to so many little wavelets lapping a vast shore and that it would be well to make one big movie—a tidal wave to wash right over that shore and sweep away its accumulated debris of indifference if you don't mind the figure. People asked us about the script but Professor Bokhari answered that a script would be no use - we would have to go to the countries that seemed likely to offer some expression of our ideas, talk things over with the people there and let them act it out.[27]

The actual production of the film began when Julien Bryan of the International Film Foundation heard of the project and let Dickinson look at a short documentary that he and Victor Vicas had shot in 1946 and never released. It was about a group of bombed-out peasants returning to the ruins of their village in Southern Italy and receiving United Nations Relief and Rehabilitation Administration (UNRRA) aid to rebuild it. Dickinson decided that this should be followed by a 'twelve years after' sequence and sent Gian-Luigi Polidoro to Italy to film it in September 1957. Alexander Hammid, the Czech director, was sent to British Columbia to film a sequence about the building of a hydroelectric project. Dickinson himself visited Haiti in January 1958 to supervise the filming of a sequence about the reclamation of wilderness into farm land and Oslo to shoot the story of the battle between a beekeeper and a nuclear research establishment. This was the only sequence in which an actor was used, the actual beekeeper being too shy to appear before the cameras. By August 1958 Dickinson was back in New York, editing the final film. Virgil Thompson, a neighbour of Dickinson's, wrote the score. The cost of the film was 'exceedingly small'.

Dickinson had a multinational team of directors under his control, and they regularly produced short documentaries highlighting aspects of UN work. There was only one that Dickinson himself devised, and this showed him harking back again to the old Film Society days. It was *Overture*, a nine-minute visual interpretation of Beethoven's *Egmont* overture. Directed by G. L. Polidoro and edited by Krishna Singh, it was nominated for an Oscar. It was the film Dickinson was proudest of from his UN period:

> In *Overture*, Beethoven's nine-minute *Egmont* Overture provided the track along which we strung images evoking a simple impression of the United Nations idea. With main titles in five languages and no word spoken, we found the reel was accepted all over the world: four hundred copies circulated in India alone. We projected some 250,000 feet of film from many sources to find the five minutes (450 feet) of film which we inset into *Overture*. That is the most difficult of all forms of compilation work, to illustrate ideas with significant shots which march with the rhythm of a fixed musical composition. We must have made sixty or more versions of the film before we got it right. For one thing, the music rejected all scenes of violent action and dictated its need for after effects and steady movement. For another thing, a vast majority of shots good enough to be preserved from newsreels were clipped far too short—usually a statutory four seconds—for the tempo of the music. To use such shots we had to tighten the cutting rhythm ahead of them to make them register.[28]

The film actually made money for the UN because Dickinson persuaded Columbia Pictures to distribute it with a Brigitte Bardot film

Love Is My Profession. But all his experiences at the UN were not so joyous as *Overture*. *Blue Vanguard* (1957), a film about the UN emergency force along the Suez Canal, could not be shown because of objections from France, Britain, and Israel ('That was the real trouble at the United Nations, that unless everybody agreed that the film was all right, it couldn't be shown').

Dickinson's final directorial ventures came about by accident. The UN Television Service put out a series of half-hour programmes called *Dateline* about the work of the organization. Being short of two for the series, they asked Dickinson to provide them, and he agreed to direct, write, and present them himself. He worked at high speed to do them. *Geneva Round the Clock*, about the work of the Palais des Nations in Geneva, was put together with the help of a crew of French documentarists under Alain Tanner. *Paris*, an account of the work of UNESCO, was filmed with the unwilling cooperation of the strongly nationalist and anti-UN French television service, ORTF. They provided inferior equipment and constantly changed the technical staff. But Dickinson managed to complete the filming on schedule. The two films are mainly sets of interviews, interspersed with footage of the UN buildings and some crisply cut library footage of their activities in the field.

But by 1960 Dickinson had become disenchanted with the UN and refused an offer to renew his contract. As he wrote in 1962:

> Most films other than fictions for commerce are made for one or more sponsors, who rarely know much about the craft of cinema or of the effects of films on audiences. By the end of 1960, United Nations publications had some five hundred national sponsors, plus the influence of a dozen or more specialised groups and agencies. By the time any material has been scathed by the pressures from all these entities, its vitality has been bled white. Facts or half facts are still presented with the utmost tact, but the spark to fire the brain through the emotions of the viewer or reader simply is not there, and only the converted can be expected to appreciate the material. If the United Nations dares to comment, it cannot avoid some measure of controversy. This it dare not do. Only the converted layman can break this circle of ineffectuality. And he must have the courage to be unpopular and the patience to persist.[29]

Dickinson had since 1950 been engaged upon 'films of value to humanity', in his denunciation of the politics of violence (*Secret People*), his account of the birth pangs of a nation (*Hill 24 Doesn't Answer*), and his paean to the spirit of international cooperation (*Power among Men*). But he ended the decade alienated both from the commercial sector of filmmaking and from the sponsored sector. He could no longer make feature films, and he felt unable to persist with documentaries. The resolution of his dilemma came with an offer to enter full-time education and to devote himself to the creation of that intelligent and visually aware audience that he was making his films for.

NOTES

1. *Film Dope* 11 (January 1977), p. 15.
2. All the various versions of the script together with Cary's original story are in the Dickinson Papers.
3. The scripts and designs of *The Mayor of Casterbridge* are in the Dickinson Papers. A selection of John Howell's designs was published with an article by Thorold Dickinson, 'The Mayor of Casterbridge—some notes', *Sight and Sound* (January 1951), pp. 363-371.
4. Lindsay Anderson, *Making a Film: The Story of Secret People* (London: George Allen and Unwin, 1952), p. 14.
5. Author's interview with Lindsay Anderson.
6. Anderson's book contains a detailed account of the production.
7. *Observer*, February 10, 1952.
8. *News Chronicle*, February 9, 1952.
9. *Daily Herald*, February 9, 1952.
10. *Manchester Guardian*, February 8, 1952.
11. *Daily Express*, February 11, 1952; *Evening Standard*, February 7, 1952; *Daily Graphic*, February 11, 1952; *Daily Telegraph*, February 11, 1952; *Spectator*, February 8, 1952; *New Statesman*, February 10, 1952.
12. Letter from Nigel Balchin to Thorold Dickinson, December 29, 1947, Dickinson Papers.
13. Author's interview with Sidney Cole, May 15, 1985.
14. Author's interview with Lindsay Anderson, September 16, 1985.
15. Raymond Durgnat, *A Mirror for England* (London: Faber, 1970), p. 231.
16. *Film Dope* 11, (January 1977), p. 15.
17. John Ellis, 'Made in Ealing', *Screen* 16 (Spring 1975), p. 120.
18. Letter from Thorold Dickinson to Stuart Hall, June 2, 1975, Dickinson Papers.
19. Letter from John Ellis to Thorold Dickinson, June 6, 1975, Dickinson Papers.
20. Author's interview with James Leahy, September 9, 1985.
21. The script is in the Dickinson Collection.
22. BFI microfiche, *Hill 24 Doesn't Answer*.
23. *Observer*, November 13, 1955.
24. *Times*, November 10, 1955.
25. *Manchester Guardian*, November 12, 1955.

26. *Evening News*, September 27, 1956.
27. *New Yorker*, March 14, 1959.
28. *A.I.D. News* 3 (November 1972), p. 6.
29. Thorold Dickinson, 'Films to Unite the Nations', in *Film Book 2: Films of Peace and War*, ed., Robert Hughes (New York: Grove Press, 1962), p. 147.

NINE

Dickinson and Film Education

In 1960, frustrated by his inability to do more with the UN documentary programme, Dickinson returned to England to take up a newly established Senior Lectureship in Film at the Slade School of Fine Art in University College, London. It had been inaugurated by the British Film Institute, which had arranged finance from University College, the British Film Producers' Association, J. Arthur Rank Group Charities, and Associated British Picture Corporation, and it was the first post of its kind in Britain. The aim of the department, which Dickinson proceeded to set up, was to turn out film students who would go into production, teaching, or criticism. In 1965 the hitherto experimental Film Department came onto the strength of University College, London, and in 1967 Dickinson became the first professor of film in Britain. The *Times* announced, 'The appointment and a postgraduate diploma course in film studies which will follow should finally put the seal of acceptance on cinema as a university subject in this country'.[1] The department eventually ran a two-year postgraduate diploma course and a research programme of master's and Ph.D. students. It also ran weekly seminars in cinema for undergraduate bachelor's in fine arts students. All these activities were based around public screenings of films in the college open to all.

So Dickinson had finally achieved full-time what at one level he had always been—a teacher. His first two students were Raymond Durgnat and Don Levy. In 1985, Durgnat recalled the experience of being taught by Dickinson:

> Not only was Thorold's stature imposing, but his spirit was too: a mixture of clergyman loftiness, high culture grandness and leonine

energy. He could be kindly, rude and horizon-scanning in marvellous alternation. Like many film directors, he was thoroughly physical, and many of our discussions happened with him stalking along the Slade's grey corridors, with his big silvery head and shoulders filling them, and me trotting along beside him and stepping sharply back at all the basement's blind corners. He kept up a pace just like his films, you could see where they got their swiftly prowling dolly-shots and quick-pivot pans around fast-moving people. My thesis subject fascinated but rather frustrated him, as it did me. The idea was to give movie analysis some roots in industry and market pressure, public taste in particular, and it sounds easy, but the big problem was how to square it with all the prejudices built into high culture finessing. Thorold thoroughly understood the size of the problem, but was impatient with theoretical small print and slightly bristled from my Freudian components. His turn of mind was typically 30's English, and so was his left-liberal humanism, something between Anglicanism and Marxism, but neither. It was idealistic but energetically pragmatic, not so far from '30's logical empiricism, like Ayer, or Coldstream's love of earthy detail. Thorold greatly respected Gracie Fields culture and warm audience emotion, and we both thought in terms of concrete examples. I'd try a hypothesis and he'd roll that big silver head around and scan the horizon for a usefully awkward example. His style with me was slightly majestic but conversational, but I must say his broad formulations really straightened out some of my tangles and put my trajectory through some right-angle turns. Or prevented pseudo-problems from arising. His was the sort of film director's intellect that I really admire: sensitive but decisive, nuanced by experience, but as bold and healthy as instinct swiftly applied to the choice at issue and the job in hand.[2]

The programme of films that Dickinson showed at the Slade directly reflected his philosophy of film history, featuring those nonconformist artists (mainly continental) whose contribution to film art he deemed central: Griffith, Stroheim, Renoir, Eisenstein, Antonioni, Bresson, Fellini, Resnais, Buñuel, and Godard. It was the intellectual and ideological legacy of the Film Society. More recent developments in film criticism passed him by. The exciting, pioneering work of *Movie* in the 1960s, which, in the wake of *Cahiers du Cinéma*, accepted Hollywood films as art and devoted serious and respectful critical attention to the likes of Minnelli, Preminger, and Nicholas Ray, made no impression on him. *Citizen Kane* was the only Hollywood film to be included in his Slade programme. He was positively hostile to the linguistics-based criticism of the 1970s, describing it as a 'heresy' and impatiently dismissing it in a footnote of *A Discovery of Cinema*.[3]

He remained a product of the distinctive British film culture of the 1920s and 1930s analysed by Peter Stead. In his seminal article on British responses to Hollywood, Stead defined the indigenous British film culture as 'a national film institute, a network of film societies, a number of intellectual film journals, a whole tradition of documentary film-making, and close links between those interested in film and educationalists, especially those engaged in adult education'.[4] Their standpoint was one of nostalgia for the silent cinema and a marked preference for continental and particularly Soviet films, both feelings dictated by the belief that there was an 'intelligent audience' waiting to be discovered, which wanted more intellectually demanding and artistically complex films. Inevitably these cinematic intellectuals detested Hollywood, believing that its commercialism stifled Art, that its films were artificial and eschewed the realism they sought in their films, that its movie moguls manipulated the mass audience unscrupulously, and that its product failed to fulfil cinema's role as educator.

Dickinson stands four-square in this tradition. But as a heroic individualist, he did not subscribe to every one of its tenets. He did not, for instance, believe that silent films were superior to sound films. He was also not particularly enamoured of the documentary movement. Nevertheless, he was all his life active in many branches of the film culture. He was from the first involved in the British Film Institute: 'I used to go to meetings, selecting films for the archive, suggesting which ones they ought to ask for. And then the educational work began and I used to advise them. I was in and out of the place all the time'.[5] He was in fact a member of the National Film Archive Committee from 1950 to 1956 and of the committee of the BFI Experimental Production Fund from 1952 to 1956. Furthermore, he was one of the pioneers of the British Film Academy (BFA), set up to confer intellectual respectability and artistic standing on cinema, and was its chairman in 1952-53. In 1952 he also joined the organizing committee of Political and Economic Planning (PEP), which prepared the report on the British film industry.

He was deeply involved in the film society movement, seeing film societies as one of the crucial means of educating people cinematically. He was a member of the council of the Film Society from 1932 to 1939 and president of the International Federation of Film Societies from 1958 to 1966. In his later years, he was a regular member of prestigious Film Festival Juries, acting as chairman of the Venice Film Festival Documentary Jury in 1959 and 1964, chairman of the Feature and Short Jury of the Berlin Film Festival in 1967, and chairman of the Jury of the Guadalajara Festival in 1972.

Dickinson sought constantly to widen popular appreciation of how film worked, how films were made, and what constituted film art. He returned regularly to these themes in articles written for *Sight and Sound*, *Penguin Film Review*, *University Vision*, and the *Ciné-Technician*. The philosophy he articulated over the years received its grand synthesis in his *A Discovery of Cinema* (1971). He had already contributed the section on silent film to *Soviet Cinema* (1948), cowritten with Catherine de la Roche, and had written with Roger Manvell a six-part series for BBC Radio called *A Film Is Made* (subsequently published in the Pelican book *The Cinema*) in 1951. Similarly, he had cooperated fully with Lindsay Anderson in his account of the filming of *Secret People*, published as *Making a Film*. He was also chairman of the committee of the BFA, which supervised the writing of *The Technique of Film Editing* by Karel Reisz, published in 1953. There were fifteen editions of the first version, and it was translated into Spanish, Czech, Polish, and Russian. An enlarged edition with a new section added by Gavin Millar was published in 1958. It was a book that showed Dickinson's imprint very strongly, down to the endorsement of directorial auteurism, the disparaging comments about Hollywood, the attitude to Griffith, Pudovkin, and Eisenstein, and the explanation for the decline in quality in Carné's work.

In 1968, Dickinson inaugurated the Slade Film History Register, a project whose origins he described in an article in 1972:

> In co-ordinating for university students programmes of films illustrating the development of the film since 1895, it became obvious to me that here was a record, sometimes conscious, largely unconscious, rarely self-conscious, of the look and behaviour of the world since the turn of the century, an asset that no previous century had produced. It was neither possible nor desirable to keep film as an art detached from film as a record of the other arts as well as sociology, history and politics: we felt that the whole field was surely the job of university film studies. Some students became interested and I showed them several programmes on the 1930's. Then eighty hours of films on North American history were tested on audiences of interested students, of which fifteen hours were selected, copied and shared co-operatively among a dozen history departments under the UCOLFILM scheme, financed by a grant from the Calouste Gulbenkian Foundation. Programmes were also assembled to illustrate the background of the lectures which Mr. A. J. P. Taylor gives annually in University

College London. In April 1968 we called a conference of modern historians and film and television executives and producers under Mr. Taylor's chairmanship which resulted in setting up the University Historians' Film Committee, sponsored by the British Universities' Film Council, which also published a transcript of the conference. In September 1969 a second conference developed the inspiration generated at the earlier one. . . . The increasing liability is the control of the whereabouts of the existing footage. . . . To cope with the problem, it occurred to me that a national register of film of historical and sociological importance which is preserved in this country together with a record of sources of such films in other countries would be appropriate. Three years ago we obtained from the Social Science Research Council, a Government appointed body, a contract to compile a national register on the lines of my proposal. . . . We appointed Frances Thorpe, an experienced librarian and researcher, to direct the project. The aim was to work towards a new kind of film, uncompromisingly historical, which would make no concessions to entertainment and would cater for adults who wanted to enrich their historical knowledge by studying its sight and its sound.[6]

Five major film archives (the National Film Archive, the Imperial War Museum, British Movietone News, Pathé Film Library, and Visnews) together with a number of smaller collections were involved with the work of the Register. Frances Thorpe writes of this work:

The Register concentrated on pre-1963 material held by these archives because of the existence of the British National Film Catalogue which started publication in 1963. There were three strands to the Register's work-copying the issue sheets of the major newsreels to show what had been seen by cinema audiences e.g. Gaumont British News; selectively indexing and classifying news stories from these newsreels and listing and viewing major films and television programmes which had used actuality footage and were considered to be useful for teaching about twentieth-century history. Between 1969 and 1973 the Slade Film History register helped to co-ordinate and inspire a significant number of scholars and researchers both in the UK and abroad. Several national and international meetings were held, productions including *Double-Headed Eagle* (Lutz Becker 1973) and *The World at War* (Thames TC 1973), used the records compiled by the Register, universities such as Leeds incorporated film into their courses and the Open University course 'War and Society' introduced film as a primary source of historical evidence under Professor A.

Marwick and Lisa Pontecorvo. Articles and books appeared on various aspects of the subject and in all these activities Thorold Dickinson's experience guided those working at the Register and encouraged its further development. In 1973 the SSRC funds were exhausted and despite Thorold Dickinson's efforts further funding could not be found at this difficult time in university development. The Register continued with a much reduced programme supported by University College, London and the British Universities Film Council. In 1975 all the records and one remaining member of staff were transferred to the BUFC where some of the work was able to be continued. The inspiration for creating such a project was an example of the breadth of Thorold Dickinson's vision of the role of film and its value as a means of communication and understanding.[7]

In 1971, Dickinson retired from teaching and was made professor emeritus and awarded a Ph.D. of London University. He was succeeded as head of the Film Department by James Leahy, who held the rank of senior lecturer. Speaking in 1985, Leahy assessed his predecessor's position:

> I think it would be fair to say that what he had always conceived of was a kind of two-pronged attack-films being studied as a historian might study a manuscript for its explicit meanings but also to some extent for the society which produced it and what was going on around it and why its meaning at one particular moment might have been different from meanings that subsequently came up.[8]

Leahy believes that this derived from Dickinson's experience of showing the Nazi film *Baptism of Fire* to various people in the government during the war and finding that they were totally depressed by it because it presented such an overwhelming picture of the invincibility of the Nazi war machine through the organisation of the visual material that they accepted it as reality:

> Although he did not perhaps explicitly theoreticize it, there was always this great concern to see the film on the screen clearly and understand its visual organization and visual articulations. His idea was that visual understanding was as important to our modern age as literacy but also to see the kind of context that gave it an impact at its historical moment and the way in which this impact might change. This was one thrust—he wanted film to come to the attention of historians. Another aspect of his concern was that a filmically articulate

academic world would be able to use film and he had a conception of something which was not a University audio-visual department and not a television network but which had the academic expertise of the University department but some of the creative skills of a television production department. He did have a hope and belief that top class academic documentaries from a University Film Department was possible and he was very proud of the film that Mirek Dohnal . . . a Czech refugee made—a very nice film for the Papyrology Department of University College, which won an award at the Venice Film Festival. . . . His vision then was to get academic teachers to use film (a) as an aspect of their research (b) as an aspect of their teaching (c) as an aspect of the interlock between their research and their teaching (d) also to try to get academics to use film to communicate their ideas more generally. . . . Also there was the desire not just to educate academics but also with students, an engagement with the history of cinema and the kind of thing which is clearly stated in his book.

Leahy shared many of Dickinson's ideals and aspirations for the Film Department. But he believes that Dickinson had his limitations ('It was very much the traditional pre-*Movie Sight and Sound* position'). He did not believe that much of any value came out of Hollywood and was resistant to the new theories from France, which involved Marxism, structuralism, and semiotics. Leahy introduced all these elements into the teaching at the Slade.

Dickinson had been engaged in a constant uphill struggle to gain acceptance for film in the academic world and ended up, as he had with the United Nations, somewhat disillusioned. According to Leahy:

> Thorold had almost an ivory tower conception of the academic profession as people who were interested in truth and evidence and scholarship and he did really believe that if you showed people something and explained it they would understand it, and he just did find some of the things which went on very very upsetting. . . . Thorold did once say to me that he was horrified about the academic profession, that there was more back-biting and hypocrisy and double-dealing and treachery than he had ever encountered in the film industry. . . . University College was always so busy talking about its place in the history of British higher education that it was difficult to get things through. He became very disillusioned with academics. He found them (a) narrow-minded and (b) political in the smaller sense and untrustworthy. On the other hand he did have some very successful achievements.

> His theory about how to win an academic argument was to wheel on a big name and if you can get for instance Mountbatten to turn up at the right moment, then you win the argument. He did play the academics at their own game but I think they rather resented being beaten by these kinds of weapons.

Throughout his retirement Dickinson remained totally supportive of Leahy's regime at the Slade and never interfered. But the department ran into difficulties. Outside funds originally pledged for a specific period to launch the department dried up. There were changes of academic priorities at the national level and a shift of emphasis from postgraduate to undergraduate teaching, leading to a reduction in the number of bursaries available for the Film Department. There was a polarisation in the film critical world in the wake of the advent of semiology and considerable intellectual friction. On top of all this, the educational cutbacks of successive governments began. The film screenings, which were open to all University College students, became, with the reduction in film student numbers, more specialized, more expensive, and less generally attractive. Eventually, the postgraduate diploma was abandoned, the department's activities were scaled down, and the staff progressively took voluntary redundancy. The Film Department finally ceased to exist in 1984. What was its legacy? James Leahy recalled:

> The department was very much conceived on the very real English conception of the authority of prestige. It was a kind of trickle-down idea, that if a major university was doing it, then it would trickle down and other universities would do it, polytechnics would do it, schools would start to do it. In some sense that conception has succeeded even though University College has gone. For example when Bulmershe [College, Reading] started up, it was helpful that I was somebody at University College who could be their first external examiner and that's a very important course and probably operates with greater academic rigour than for one reason or another we were able to operate at University College. Thorold did a lot of work for the C.N.A.A. [Council for National Academic Awards] and then I did a lot of work after him. . . . Certainly the B.F.I. Lectureship scheme [Film lectureships established at the Universities of Warwick, Kent, and East Anglia] was helped by the existence of University College and again that was a grant-giving committee that I served on for many, many years, and so there was a bit of a 'trickle-down' effect. It did work. It would have worked much more if the fat years had continued and it had continued to be an era of affluence and expansion.

Dickinson's dedication to the promotion of a film culture was recognised in the honours and awards showered on him in retirement. He was appointed a Commander of the Order of the British Empire in 1973 and was visiting professor of film at the University of Surrey, Guildford, from 1975 to 1977, receiving that university's honorary doctorate in 1976. He received honorary life membership of the Association of Cinematograph, Television and Allied Technicians (ACTT), the British Universities Film Council, and the International Association for Audio-Visual Media in Historical Research and Education (IAMHIST). He was made a fellow of the British Film Institute. His eightieth birthday was commemorated by a season of his films at the National Film Theatre and both Channel 4 and BBC-2 announced their intention of showing *The Queen of Spades* as a tribute. In the event Channel 4 showed it, and BBC-2 hastily substituted *The Spanish Gardener*.

Dickinson lived in retirement in Lambourn, Berkshire, but his last years were darkened by failing eyesight, increasing ill health, and in 1979 the shattering blow of the death of his wife Joanna, to whom he had been devoted and who had been his companion, helpmate, and supporter for fifty years. He was wholly out of sympathy with the new critical orthodoxies and felt anger and frustration at the undermining of his life's work by a new generation of 'Young Turks'. As he told *Film Dope* in 1976:

> I'm sure that anybody who dabbled in film study should be practical as well as theoretical, that the theory derives from the practice. And the people who run, for instance, things like the Society for Education in Film and Technology, many of them have no practical knowledge at all, so they have to put something in its place, and in the case of SEFT, they're putting in politics of one particular, rather narrow kind. And I find this a betrayal of the whole subject because film should be studied as a whole, and then used in whatever application you see fit. Not confined to the preachment of left wing or right wing or whatever wing politics.

Thorold Dickinson died on April 14, 1984, at Oxford. At his funeral Sidney Cole spoke the eulogy, ending with these words:

> All deaths are sad, of course, but what counts are the lives that preceded them. I have tried to indicate how good a life Thorold's was for his colleagues, his students, his friends. And to say 'thank you' to him for his talent, for his help and encouragement, for his understanding and his generosity. In short— for the legacy of a good and memorable human being.

Chapter Nine
NOTES

1. *Times*, May 27, 1967.
2. Letter from Raymond Durgnat to author, July 12, 1985.
3. Thorold Dickinson, *A Discovery of Cinema*, (London: Oxford University Press, 1971), p. 20.
4. Peter Stead, 'Hollywood's Message for the World: The British Response in the 1930's', *Historical Journal of Film, Radio and Television 1* (1981), pp. 19-32.
5. *Film Dope* 11, p. 21.
6. *A.I.D. News* 3 (November 1972), pp. 6-7.
7. Letter from Frances Thorpe to author, December 28, 1985.
8. This and subsequent quotations come from author's interview with James Leahy, September 9, 1985.

CONCLUSION

In its obituary, the *Guardian* described Dickinson as 'one of Britain's most distinguished film directors'.[1] He was certainly that, but he was also one of Britain's most neglected film directors. Where his contemporaries like Michael Powell and David Lean have been the subject of in-depth critical studies, Dickinson has attracted comparatively little attention.

What work has been done has accorded Dickinson his deserved meed of respect. Raymond Durgnat was the first to discuss his oeuvre in five characteristically perceptive and allusive pages in *A Mirror for England* (1970), describing him as a 'philosophical stylist' and an 'English moralist', a liberal of a radical tinge and an internationalist perspective. It was a description that, when pressed, Dickinson was willing to accept.[2]

Roy Armes interestingly compared Dickinson with Michael Powell in a chapter in his *Critical History of the British Cinema* (1978), rightly seeing them both as individualists who faced all the problems that individualism posed in the context of the British film industry. He contrasts Powell the extrovert and arch-romantic with Dickinson the introvert and a 'moralist of sensitive and compelling insight'. But he sees them both as united by a rejection of a naturalist aesthetic.

Neither the contrast nor the comparison quite fit the facts, however. For one thing, it is clear that both theoretically and practically Dickinson often aimed for naturalism and latterly neorealism. The contrast between Powell and Dickinson that Armes posits can be profitably applied to *Black Narcissus* and *Men of Two Worlds*, where a clash of cultures (East versus West, Africa versus Europe) is examined. The contrast between the two is further informed by the use of studio-created artifice as against location-dictated naturalism. But there were occasions when Powell and Dickinson drew close together. If, for instance, one compares Powell's *49th Parallel*, charting the progress of a party of stranded German submariners across Canada, with Dickinson's *The Next of Kin*, with its account of Nazi spies and fifth columnists in Britain, we can see the two directors directly addressing the very real wartime threat of the enemy within and depicting it in similar hard-hitting and realistic style. But if we compare Powell's *The Red Shoes* with Dickinson's *The Queen of Spades* (both of them starring Anton Walbrook), we are in a world of primal Romantic myth, face to face with the timeless artistic preoccupations of obsession, madness and death.

The links between Powell and Dickinson are in some respects stronger than the contrasts. What is common to them is that they emerged as fully fledged artists during World War II and these two pairs of films reflect two sides of the wartime experience—on the one hand, greater realism in style and content and, on the other, a liberation of the imagination, which caused one of the richest flowerings of talent in British film history.

Another product of the British wartime film revival with whom a productive comparison can be made is Robert Hamer. He strongly resembles Dickinson in his civilized sensibility, sardonic wit, visual sophistication, and strong Gallic influence. Their choice of projects also shows some interesting similarities, as they explore the tyranny of the Victorian *pater familias* (Dickinson's *Gaslight* and Hamer's *Pink String and Sealing Wax*) and the nature of British colonialism (Dickinson's *Men of Two Worlds* and Hamer's *His Excellency*, both starring Eric Portman), and both tackle ghost stories (*The Queen of Spades, Dead of Night*). Dickinson and Hamer testify more strongly than any other directors to the stylistic influence of the classic French cinema on some British cineastes. But beneath this similarity lies a fundamental distinction that ultimately separates them. For Dickinson's intrinsic English moralism is distinctly at odds with Hamer's cheerful Gallic amoralism, as most tellingly revealed in *Kind Hearts and Coronets*. Further comparisons need to be made to properly relate Dickinson to his contemporaries, but they seem unlikely to modify the view that in sum Dickinson's films have a continental feel, an English moral tone, and a 1930s liberal intellectual bent.

If Dickinson has been neglected in Britain, he has been almost unknown in the United States. This is because of a consistent and tragic record of the mutilation or outright suppression of his films. It began with his first film *The High Command*. When the film was released in America, it was sold on the name of James Mason, who played a supporting role but who subsequently became an internationally famous star. To emphasize Mason's role, some fifteen minutes were cut from the middle of the film, simply because he did not appear in them and despite the fact that they included vital dramatic confrontations involving the actual star of the film, Lionel Atwill. In this truncated form, the film played for years in cinemas and later on television. Ironically, it may well be the most widely seen of all Dickinson's films.

The most serious fate, of course, overtook *Gaslight*, suppressed for years to make way for MGM's Hollywood remake. But *The Next of Kin* was shorn of thirty minutes, which caused in Dickinson's words 'a total numbing of a vital film'. *Men of Two Worlds* was not released until 1952 because of its subject and then not widely shown. Twenty minutes were cut from *Secret People*, including the whole of the section including Maria Brent's transformation into Lena Martin, her trip to Dublin, and her death. *Hill 24 Doesn't Answer* was shown complete in American cinemas but shortened by thirty minutes on television. It is a record that makes dismal reading.

But there are some signs that a discovery of Dickinson may be under way. The Boston Museum of Fine Arts staged a complete retrospective of his major films in 1977, and the audiences who saw them were bowled over. Deac Rossell, the Museum Film Coordinator, wrote to Dickinson, 'The British should recognise you as a national treasure. You have been so many places, touched so many lives, accomplished so many things'.[4] Dickinson films have also been included in the Museum of Modern Art British Cinema retrospective, which ran from 1984 to 1985, in New York.

By any definition, Dickinson was an undoubted auteur, his primary concern being with the working of his characters' minds and their underlying psychological development. In particular, he was drawn to those 'secret people', divided beings whose inner selves emerged at a moment of crisis. This very much reflected his own divided allegiance, the desire for art and education, to entertain and enlighten, to expand and to uplift.

It was not just thematically but visually, too, that Dickinson was an auteur. For in his philosophy the two were inseparable. His style had its own distinctive signature: the long takes, the mobile camera, the sparing use of close-ups, the conscious musical form. Sidney Cole, who edited two of his feature films, saw his particular qualities as 'a sense of style, rhythm, an instinctive sense of where to place the camera, an appreciation of compositional values. . . . Thorold wanted to make films that had purpose and significance, that were entertainment of course but were more than just entertainment'. He saw Dickinson as 'a man of principle aesthetically and socially'.[5]

Lindsay Anderson, who had studied his films and who saw him at work at close quarters on *Secret People*, saw his strengths as

> a combination of editing style and camera style, a style of film-making that is difficult to exactly analyze because it is a kind of elegance. In an almost abstract way you can enjoy the movement and look of his best films as you would enjoy music. It has that musical quality. That is

why *Gaslight* and *Queen of Spades* are his best films. There is a particular kind of taste and style like listening to a bit of Ravel and enjoying the orchestration. The musical and choreographic and rhythmic principles of ballet—these are qualities which have to an alarming degree been lost and for instance rhythm as a very satisfactory aesthetic basis to film is something that is practically unheard of today, and that is why Thorold's best work is not appreciated today for what it is because people don't know how to look at it.[6]

The aesthetic legacy of the Film Society was unmistakable with successive continental influences observed, absorbed, and endorsed: Eisensteinian montage, German Expressionist lighting, Carné's poetic realism, Renoir's penchant for location shooting, Italian neorealism. The silent classics imbued Dickinson with a fondness for visual symbolism that as often as not underlines his moralism. This can be seen in the recurrent use of mirrors to read the souls of his protagonists at moments of crisis (*Gaslight, The Queen of Spades, Secret People*) and in the use of dance as the image of sensuality and evil (Clare's dance in *The Next of Kin*, the can-can in *Gaslight*, the tribal dances in *Men of Two Worlds*, the gypsy dance in *Queen of Spades*).

Intellectually, Dickinson was a product of the interwar intelligentsia. Lindsay Anderson believes that

> Thorold's most lively period perhaps, the period that influenced him most, was before the war, when it was exciting and good fun, and you were a pioneer with the Film Society and there was a left wing you could identify yourself with without being embarrassed by Communism, and he was editing films and they were having fun and doing the best they could and laughing at getting away with it.

There is much truth in this statement. But Dickinson was always his own man and never unthinkingly endorsed left-wing ideas en masse. He developed an interest in African independence and a dislike of British expatriate snobbism, but he retained considerable respect for the achievements of the British Empire, as is clearly evidenced by *Men of Two Worlds* and his proposal for a film on the suppression of the slave trade. He was a patriot when many 1930s intellectuals notoriously were not, and not only his willingness to work for various government departments but also his insistence on getting Foreign Office approval for the script of *Hill 24 Doesn't Answer* confirm this. He was basically an old-fashioned liberal with the characteristic paternalism that made him in many ways a natural teacher. He retained a

Conclusion

romantic faith in education and in particular in the creation of an intelligent, articulate, and cultured film audience, the sort of audience who would appreciate the sort of films he wanted to make—films of ideas. It was this didactic side which made him such a natural and effective propagandist for causes in which he believed (Republicanism in Spain, the Allied cause in World War II, Israel, the United Nations). His commitment to all these causes stemmed from a basic belief in justice, truth, and humanity.

As a romantic and an idealist, and in pursuit of his dream of a British 'art house' cinema on the continental model, Dickinson threw himself successively into commercial cinema, sponsored cinema and full-time education, and ended life, as idealists often do, disillusioned and disappointed with all of them. He had from the first insisted on full directorial control at a time of great producer power, and just as the logic of his intellectual position eventually drove him out of the commercial film industry, so too did his practical demands. By the 1950s, Lindsay Anderson believes,

> [h]e found it difficult to get work under the conditions which by then were the only conditions he would accept and they were the conditions of being his own producer and being responsible for his own script and casting and all the things you can say looking at his films he was not strong at. Thorold was really a very stylish film-maker and he was an excellent camera director and his good films have a unique and individual style and for that reason are very pleasurable. He was not very mature in his ideas and he was not at all sophisticated. Indeed at times he was rather childish. So although he was given a hard time after *Secret People*, it is also that he gave himself a hard time. He wouldn't accept subservience.

Perhaps the happiest and most fulfilled period of his creative life therefore was during the war when, under the benign wing of the Ministry of Information, he was able to commit himself to work that could simultaneously entertain, educate, and enlighten, work that could advance a cause he believed in and that would at the same time raise the qualitative level of the British cinema. Once the war was over, the ministry disbanded and the commercial free-for-all returned; the higher and nobler objectives tended to be neglected by the industry in the pursuit of profit.

For all his desire to articulate and to argue logically, for all the intellectual arrogance, the stubborn pursuit of his philosophic ends, the inability to suffer fools gladly, which Dickinson manifested from time to time, he was at heart a Romantic, fired by the nineteenth-century idea of the artist as individual creator. He had, along with the 1930s intellectuality, the idealism, naiveté, and burning enthusiasm of the Romantic artist. This is betrayed in his belief in the filmic artist's *instinctive* rejection of colour in favour of black and white and in his *instinctive* rapport with Otto Heller.

So to the end he remained a man of two worlds, the world of intellect and of instinct, of the head and of the heart. So he could be both generous and outgoing, wilful and intransigent. But it is significant that his best films were those of the heart (*Gaslight, The Queen of Spades, The Next of Kin, Hill 24*) rather than those of the head (*Men of Two Worlds, Secret People*)

Overall, Dickinson's career is an object lesson in the perils and pitfalls of an artist at large in a commercial works. He left behind him a small but precious corpus of work, three undisputed masterworks (*The Queen of Spades, Gaslight, The Next of Kin*), and ten others, long and short, all of which contain passages of real merit. His life was lived in pursuit of a not ignoble dream, to which he devoted his intellectual and emotional energies and which in the end eluded him. But his career and his presence can be said to have enriched the British film culture, and that is a legacy to be proud of.

NOTES

1. *Guardian,* April 14, 1984.
2. Raymond Durgnat, *A Mirror for England* (London: Faber, 1970), pp. 229-234.
3. Roy Armes, *A Critical History of the British Cinema* (London: Secker and Warburg, 1978), pp. 216-233.
4. Letter from Deac Rossell to Dickinson, March 24, 1977, in author's possession.
5. Author's interview with Sidney Cole, May 15, 1985.
6. This and subsequent quotations are from author's interview with Lindsay Anderson, September 16, 1985.

Filmography

As Coeditor
1927 *Huntingtower* (George Pearson)
1928 *Love's Option* (George Pearson)
1939 *Auld Lang Syne* (George Pearson)

As Editor
1928 *Oxford* (Charles Calvert) (uncompleted documentary)
1930 *The School for Scandal* (Maurice Elvey)
1931 *The Sport of Kings* (Victor Saville)
1931 *Contraband Love* (Sidney Morgan)
1931 *Going Gay* (U.S.: *Kiss me Goodbye*) (Carmine Gallone)
1931 *For Love of You* (Carmine Gallone)
1931 *Other People's Sins* (Sinclair Hill)
1931 *The Great Gay Road* (Sinclair Hill)
1931 *Lloyd of the C.I.D.* (U.S.: *Detective Lloyd*) (Henry Macrae) (serial)
1932 *The First Mrs. Fraser* (Sinclair Hill)
1932 *Karma* (Himansu Rai)
1932 *Perfect Understanding* (Cyril Gardner)
1932 *Java Head* (J. Walter Ruben)
1933 *Loyalties* (Basil Dean)
1934 *Sing As We Go* (Basil Dean)
1935 *The Silent Passenger* (Reginald Denham)
1936 *Whom the Gods Love* (U.S.: *Mozart*) (Basil Dean)
1936 *Calling the Tune* (Reginald Denham)
1936 *The House of the Spaniard* (Reginald Denham)

As Director
1936 *The High Command* (Fanfare/Associated British) Producer: Gordon Wellesley; screenplay: Katherine Strueby (from the novel by Lewis Robinson); dialogue: Val Valentine, Walter Meade; photography: Otto Heller, Jimmy Rogers; editor: Sidney Cole; music: Ernest Irving; art director: R. Holmes Paul; cast: Lionel

Atwill (General Sir John Sangye), Lucie Mannheim (Diana Cloam), Steven Geray (Martin Cloam), James Mason (Major Jimmy Heverill), Allan Jeayes (Sergeant Crawford), Kathleen Gibson (Belinda), Henry Hewitt (Defence Counsel), and Leslie Perrins (Carson)

1938 *Spanish ABC* (P.F.I.) Producer: Ivor Montagu; directed and edited by Thorold Dickinson and Sidney Cole

1939 *The Arsenal Stadium Mystery* (G. and S. Films/W. and F. Films) Producer: Josef Somlo; screenplay: Patrick Kirwan and Donald Bull (from a story by Leonard Gribble); adaptation: Thorold Dickinson and Alan Hayman; photographer: Desmond Dickinson; art director: Ralph Brinton; editor: Sidney Stone; cast: Leslie Banks (Inspector Slade), Greta Gynt (Gwen Lee), Esmond Knight (Raille), Ian Maclean (Sergeant Clinton), Liane Linden (Inga), Brian Worth (Philip Morring), Anthony Bushell (Jack Doyce), Richard Norris (Setchley), Wyndham Goldie (Kindilett), Maire O'Neill (Mrs. Kirwan), E. V. H. Emmett, George Allison, and the Arsenal team

1940 *Gaslight* (British National) (U.S.: *Angel Street*) Producer: John Corfield; screenplay: Bridget Boland and A. R. Rawlinson (from the play by Patrick Hamilton); photographer: Bernard Knowles; art director: Duncan Sutherland; editor: Sidney Cole; music: Richard Addinsell; cast: Anton Walbrook (Paul Mallen), Diana Wynyard (Bella Mallen), Frank Pettingell (Rough), Robert Newton (Vincent Ullswater), Catherine Cordell (Nancy), Jimmy Hanley (Cobb), Minnie Rayner (Elizabeth), Mary Hinton (Lady Winterbourne), and Marie Wright (Alice Barlow)

1940 *Westward Ho!— 1940* (MoI) Screenplay: Donald Bull, photographer: Desmond Dickinson; editor: Sidney Cole

1940 *Yesterday Is Over Your Shoulder* (MoI) Screenplay: Donald Bull; photographer: Desmond Dickinson; editor: Sidney Cole

1941 *The Prime Minister* (Warner Bros.) Producer: Max Milder; screenplay: Michael Hogan and Brock Williams; photographer: Basil Emmott; art director: Norman Arnold; editor: Leslie Norman; cast: John Gielgud (Benjamin Disraeli), Diana Wynyard (Mary Anne Wyndham-Lewis), Stephen Murray (W. E. Gladstone), Owen Nares (Lord Derby), Fay Compton (Queen Victoria), Lyn Harding (Bismarck), Pamela Standish (The young Queen Victoria), Leslie Perrins (Lord Salisbury), Kynaston Reeves (Lord Stanley), Glynis Johns (Miss Sheridan), Irene Browne (Lady Londonderry), Will Fyffe (Agitator), Frederick Leister (Lord Melbourne), Nicholas Hannen (Sir Robert Peel),

Barbara Everest (Baroness Lehzen), Gordon McLeod (John Brown), and Vera Bogetta (Lady Blessington)

1942 *The Next of Kin* (Ealing/United Artists) Producer: Michael Balcon; screenplay: Basil Bartlett, Thorold Dickinson, Angus MacPhail, and John Dighton; photographer: Ernest Palmer; art director: Tom Morahan; editor: Ray Pitt; music: William Walton; cast: Mervyn Johns (Arthur Davis), Nova Pilbeam (Beppie Leemans), Stephen Murray (Ned Barratt), Reginald Tate (Major Richards), Geoffrey Hibbert (Johnny), Philip Friend (Lieutenant Tommy Cummins), Phyllis Stanley (Clare), Mary Clare (Ma Webster), Joss Ambler (Mr. Vernon), Basil Sydney (Naval Captain), Brefni O'Rourke (Brigadier), Alexander Field (Durnford), Jack Hawkins (Major Harcourt), Torin Thatcher (German General), David Hutcheson (Security Officer), Frederick Leister (Colonel), Charles Victor (Seaman), Frank Allenby (Wing Commander Kenton), and Thora Hird (ATS Girl)

1946 *Men of Two Worlds* (Two Cities/G.F.D.) (U.S.: *Kisenga: Man of Africa*) Producer: John Sutro; photographer: Desmond Dickinson (in Technicolor); art director: Tom Morahan; editor: Alan Jaggs; screenplay: Thorold Dickinson, Herbert Victor, and Joyce Cary (from a story by E. Arnot Robertson); music: Arthur Bliss; cast: Eric Portman (Commissioner Randall), Phyllis Calvert (Dr. Catherine Munro), Robert Adams (Kisenga), Orlando Martins (Magole), Arnold Marle (Professor Gollner), Cathleen Nesbitt (Mrs. Upjohn), David Horne (Agent), Cyril Raymond (Education Officer), Sam Blake (Rafi), Uriel Porter (Saidi), and Eseza Makumbi (Saburi)

1949 *The Queen of Spades* (World Screenplays/ Associated British) Producer: Anatole de Grunwald; screenplay: Rodney Ackland and Arthur Boys (from the story by Alexander Pushkin); photographer: Otto Heller; designer: Oliver Messel; art director: William Kellner; editor: Hazel Wilkinson; music: Georges Auric; cast: Anton Walbrook (Herman Suvorin), Edith Evans (Countess Ranevskaya), Ronald Howard (Andrei), Yvonne Mitchell (Lisaveta), Mary Jerrold (Vavarushka), Anthony Dawson (Fyodor), Pauline Tennant (Young Countess), Miles Malleson (Tchybukin), Athene Seyler (Princess Ivashin), Michael Medwin (Ilovaisky), Ivor Barnard (Bookseller), Gibb McLaughlin (Birdseller), and Valentine Dyall (Messenger)

1952 *Secret People* (Ealing/G.F.D.) Producer: Sidney Cole; screenplay: Thorold Dickinson and Wolfgang Wilhelm (from a story by Thorold Dickinson and Joyce Cary); photographer: Gordon

Dines; art director: William Kellner; editor: Peter Tanner; music: Roberto Gerhard; additional dialogue: Christianna Brand; cast: Valentina Cortesa (Maria Brent), Serge Reggiani (Louis Balan), Audrey Hepburn (Nora Brent), Charles Goldner (Anselmo), Megs Jenkins (Penny), Irene Worth (Miss Jackson), Reginald Tate (Inspector Eliot), Geoffrey Hibbert (Steenie), Michael Shepley (Manager), Athene Seyler (Mrs. Kellick), Sydney Tafler (Syd Barnett), John Chandos (John), Norman Williams (Sgt. Newcombe), and Michael Allan (Rodd)

1953 *The Red Ground* (Israeli Defence Forces) Director-screenplay-editor: Thorold Dickinson

1955 *Hill 24 Doesn't Answer* (Sik'or/Eros) Executive producers: Zvi Kolitz and Jack Padwa; producers: Thorold Dickinson and Peter Frye (from a story by Zvi Kolitz); shooting script and editing: Thorold and Joanna Dickinson; photographer: Gerald Gibbs; art director: Joseph Carl; music: Paul Ben-Haim; cast: Edward Mulhare (James Finnegan), Michael Wager (Allan Goodman), Haya Harareet (Miriam Mizrachi), Arie Lavi (David Amiram), Michael Shilo (Yehuda Berger), Zalman Lebiush (The Rabbi), Margalit Oved (Esther Hadassi), Azaria Rappoport (Nazi Officer), and Yosef Yadin (Jerusalem Commander)

As Producer/Supervisor of Films for the United Nations

1957 *Question in Togoland* (Brett Porter) (short); *Out* (Lionel Rogosin) (short); *Blue Vanguard* (Ian McNeill); *Three of Our Children* (Nicholas Reed/Ramon Estelle) (short)

1958 *Overture* (Gian-Luigi Polidoro) (short); *Exposure* (Robert Hughes) (short); *Pablo Casals Breaks his Journey* (V. R. Sarma) (short); *Big Day in Bogo* (Nicholas Reed) (short); *Power Among Men* (Alexander Hammid/Gian-Luigi Polidoro/V. R. Sarma) (Dickinson also coedited)

1959 *In Our Hands* (V. R. Sarma) (short); *A Scary Time* (Shirley Clarke) (short); *Workshop for peace* (Alexander Hammid) (short)

1960 *The Farmer of Fermathe* (Gian-Luigi Polidoro) (short)

Other Work

1926 *The Little People* (cowriter)
1935 *Midshipman Easy* (production supervisor)
1939 *The Mikado* (second unit director)
1940 *Miss Grant Goes to the Door* (cowriter) (short)
1953 *The Malta Story* (cowriter of original story)

Select Bibliography

Unpublished Sources
British Board of Film Censors, Scenario Reports, British Film Institute.
Thorold Dickinson Papers, British Film Institute.
Thorold Dickinson, 'Men of Two Worlds' (1978), unpublished paper.
Mass-Observation File reports, Sussex University Library.
Ministry of Information Records, Public Record Office.
Mace, Nigel. 'British Historical Films in World War Two', Imperial War Museum Conference Paper, 1985.
Todd, Michael J. 'Thorold Dickinson: A Framework for a Working Life', master's thesis, University of East Anglia, 1984.

Interviews
Lindsay Anderson (author) September 16, 1985.
Sir Arthur Bliss (Peter Griffiths, David J. Badder), *Film Dope* 5 (1974), pp. 2-5.
Sidney Cole (author), May 15, 1985.
Thorold Dickinson (author), April 8-12, 1976.
Thorold Dickinson (David J. Badder, Bob Baker), *Film Dope* 11 (1977), pp. 1-21.
Thorold Dickinson (K. R. M. Short), April 15, 1981.
James Leahy (author), September 9, 1985.

Published Sources
Ackland, Rodney, and Grant, Elspeth. *The Celluloid Mistress* (London: Allan Wingate, 1954).
Aldgate, Anthony, and Richards, Jeffrey. *Britain Can Take It: The British Cinema in the Second World War* (Edinburgh: Edinburgh University Press, 1994).
Ambler, Eric. *Here Lies Eric Ambler* (London: Weidenfeld and Nicolson, 1985).
Anderson, Lindsay. 'The Director's Cinema'. *Sequence* 12 (Autumn 1950), pp. 6-11, 37.
———. *Making a Film: The Story of Secret People* (London: George Allen and Unwin, 1952).
Balcon, Michael. *Michael Balcon Presents . . . A Lifetime of Films* (London: Hutchinson, 1969).
Barr, Charles. *Ealing Studios* (London: Studio Vista, 1993).

Baxter, John. *The Cinema of Josef von Sternberg* (London: Zwenmer, 1971).
Bliss, Sir Arthur. *As I Remember* (London: Faber, 1970).
British Film Institute. *Film Appreciation and Visual Education* (London: BFI, 1944).
Brunel, Adrian. *Nice Work* (London: Forbes Robertson, 1949).
Butler, Ivan. *To Encourage the Art of the Film: The Story of the British Film Institute* (London: Robert Hale, 1971).
Calder, Angus. *The People's War* (London: Panther, 1971).
Christie, Ian, ed. *Powell, Pressburger and Others* (London: BFI, 1978).
Clarens, Carlos. *George Cukor* (London: Secker and Warburg, 1976).
Cole, Sidney. 'Shooting in Spain', *Ciné-Technician* 4 (1938), pp. 1-2.
_____'A Studio Passes', *Ciné-Technician* 4 (1938), pp. 117-118.
Constantine, Stephen. *The Making of Colonial Development Policy 1914-1940* (London: Frank Cass, 1984).
Denham, Reginald. *Stars in My Hair* (London: T. Werner Laurie, 1958).
Dickinson, Margaret, and Street, Sarah. *Cinema and State: the Film Industry and the Government 1927-84* (London: BFI, 1985).
Dickinson, Thorold. 'Concerning a National Register of Films of Historical and Social Importance', *A.I.D. News* 3 (November 1972), pp. 6-7, 19.
_____*A Discovery of Cinema* (London: Oxford University Press, 1971).
_____'Experiences in the Spanish Civil War', *Historical Journal of Film, Radio and Television* 4 (1984), pp. 189-193.
_____'Films to Unite the Nations', *Film Book 2: Films of Peace and War*, ed. Robert Hughes (New York: Grove Press, 1962), pp. 147-150.
_____'The Filmwright and the Audience', *Sight and Sound* (March 1950), pp. 20-25.
_____'Griffith and the Development of Silent Film', *Sight and Sound* (October-November 1951), pp. 84-86, 94.
_____'Has the Cinema Grown Up?' *Films and Filming* (July 1964), pp. 44-47.
_____'Indian Spring', *Penguin Film Review* 6 (1948), pp. 66-72.
_____'Mad Dogs and Location Units', *Ciné-Technician* 3 (1937), pp. 56-57.
_____'Making a Film in Tanganyika', *British Film Yearbook 1947-48*, ed. Peter Noble (London: Skelton Robinson, 1947), pp. 53-58.
_____'The Mayor of Casterbridge: Some Notes', *Sight and Sound* (January 1951), pp. 363-371.
_____'PBI (Films)', *Ciné-Technician* 11 (1945), p. 102.

_____'Search for Music', *Penguin Film Review* 2 (1947), pp. 9-15.
_____'Secret People', ed. Roger Manvell, *The Cinema 1952* (Harmondsworth: Penguin, 1952), pp. 88-99.
_____'Some Practical Problems of Film Study', *University Vision* 12 (December 1974), pp. 508.
_____'Spanish ABC', *Sight and Sound* (Spring 1938), p. 30.
_____'The Third Eye', *Diversion* ed. John Sutro, (London: Max Parrish, 1950), pp. 170-177.
_____'Why Not a National Film Society?' *Sight and Sound* (Summer 1938), pp. 75-77.
_____'The Work of Sir Michael Balcon at Ealing Studios', *The Year's Work in Films 1950*, ed. Roger Manvell (London: 1951), pp. 8-17.
_____'Working with Pearson', *Silent Picture* 2 (Spring 1969), pp. 5-7.
Dickinson, Thorold, et al. 'Round Table on British Films', *Sight and Sound* (May 1950), pp. 114-122.
Dickinson, Thorold, et al. 'A Symposium on the Queen of Spades', *The Cinema 1950*, ed. R. Manvell (Harmondsworth: Penguin, 1950), pp. 46-77.
Dickinson, Thorold, and de La Roche, Catherine. *Soviet Cinema* (London: Falcon Press, 1948).
Dickinson, Thorold, and Lawson, Alan. 'Film in the USSR—1937', *Ciné-Technician* 3 (1937) pp. 95-111.
Dickinson, Thorold, and Manvell, Roger. 'A Film is Made', *The Cinema 1951*, ed. R. Manvell and R. K. Neilson Baxter (Harmondsworth: Penguin, 1951), pp. 9-56.
Durgnat, Raymond. *A Mirror for England* (London: Faber, 1970).
Ellis, John. 'Made in Ealing', *Screen* 16 (Spring 1975), pp. 78-127.
Foster, Malcolm. *Joyce Cary* (London: Michael Joseph, 1968).
Friedman, Lester D. *Hollywood's Image of the Jew* (New York: Ungar, 1982).
Grantley, Lord, Richard Norton. *Silver Spoon* (London: Hutchinson, 1954).
Greene, Graham. *The Pleasure Dome* (London: Secker and Warburg, 1972).
Hayman, Ronald. *John Gielgud* (London: Heinemann, 1971).
Huntley, John. *British Film Music* (London: Skelton Robinson, 1948).
_____*British Technicolor Films* (London: Skelton Robinson, 1949).
Koch, Howard. 'A Playwright Looks at the Filmwright', *Sight and Sound* (July 1950), pp. 210-214.
Lee, J. M., and Petter, Martin. *The Colonial Office, War and Development Policy* (London: Institute of Commonwealth Studies, 1982).

Low, Rachael. *Film-making in 1930's Britain* (London: George Allen and Unwin, 1985).

———. *Films of Comment and Persuasion of the 1930's* (London: George Allen and Unwin, 1979).

Macfadyen, Joanna. 'Gracie's Artistry Reflects the Psychology of the Masses', *World Film News* 1 (June 1936), p. 5.

McLaine, Ian. *Ministry of Morale* (London: George Allen and Unwin, 1979).

Minney, R. J. *'Puffin' Asquith* (London: Leslie Frewin, 1973).

Montagu, Ivor. *The Youngest Son* (London: Lawrence and Wishart, 1970).

Moorehead, Caroline. *Sidney Bernstein* (London: Jonathan Cape, 1984).

Neill-Brown, J. 'Pioneers', *Ciné-Technician* 4 (1938), pp. 48-49.

Noble, Peter. *The Negro in Films* (London: Skelton Robinson, 1947).

Oakley, Charles. *Where We Came In* (London: George Allen and Unwin, 1964).

Pearson, George. *Flashback* (London: George Allen and Unwin, 1957).

Perry, George. *The Great British Picture Show* (London: Paladin, 1975).

Reisz, Karel. *The Technique of Film Editing* (London: Focal Press, 1958).

Richards, Jeffrey. *Age of the Dream Palace: Cinema and Society in Britain 1930-39* (London: Routledge, 1984).

———. 'Death at Broadcasting House', *Focus on Film* 26 (1977), pp. 46-47.

Sainsbury, Frank. 'Closeup—Thorold Dickinson', *Ciné-Technician* 6 (1940), pp. 66-68.

Salt, Barry. *Film Style and Technology: History and Analysis* (London: Starword, 1983).

Sarris, Andrew. 'Two or Three Things I Know about Gaslight', *Film Comment* 12 (May-June 1976), pp. 23-25.

Smyth, Rosaleen. 'Movies and Mandarins: The Official Film and British Colonial Africa', *British Cinema History*, ed. J. Curran and V. Porter (London: Weidenfeld and Nicolson, 1983), pp. 129-143.

Stead, Peter. 'Hollywood's Message to the World: The British Response in the 1930's', *Historical Journal of Film, Radio and Television* 1 (1981), pp. 19-32.

Thorpe, Frances, and Pronay, Nicholas, with Coultass, Clive. *British Official Films in the Second World War* (Oxford: Clio Press, 1980).

Ustinov, Peter. *Dear Me* (Harmondsworth: Penguin, 1978).

Winnington, Richard. *Film Criticism and Caricatures 1943-5* (London: Paul Elek, 1975).

Index of Film Titles

Another Dawn, 42
The Arsenal Stadium Mystery, 52–58, 63
Auld Lang Syne, 24

Baptism of Fire, 164;
Battleship Potemkin, 32
BBC-the Voice of Britain, 36
Behind Spanish Lines, 51,
La Belle et la Bête, 19
Ben-Hur, 150
La Bête Humaine, 142
Black Narcissus, 114–15, 169
Blackmail, 68
Blue Vanguard, 155
Brief Encounter, 115

Cabinet of Dr. Caligari, 32
Calling the Tune, 29
Caravan, 64
Un Carnet de Bal, 37
Cheyenne Autumn, 111
Children of the Arctic North, 114

Citizen Kane, 3, 160
Contraband Love, 25

Dangerous Moonlight, 115, 124
Dead of Night, 170
Death at Broadcasting House, 29
The Double-Headed Eagle, 163
Drifters, 37

Earth, 32
Ecstase, 41

Farrebique, 126

Faust, 131
Fire over England, 41
The First Mrs. Fraser, 26–28
For Love of You, 25
The Forgotten Village, 114
Forty-Ninth Parallel, 99, 169

Gaslight (1940), 1, 2, 3, 4, 17, 18, 19, 30, 31, 33, 58, 60–73, 76, 79, 82, 125, 127, 128, 129, 170, 172, 174
Gaslight (1944), 71–73
Going Gay, 25
La Grande Illusion, 86
The Great Gay Road, 26

Hatter's Castle, 63
Henry V, 106
The High Command, 17, 30, 31, 39–48, 53, 56, 57, 60, 63, 170
Hill 24 Doesn't Answer, 1, 2, 19, 36, 146–52, 156, 171, 172
His Excellency, 170
The Horse-shoe Nail, 78
Hôtel du Nord, 33, 37, 65, 142
House of Rothschild, 81
Huntingtower, 24

I, Claudius, 57
The Impassive Footman, 28

Java Head, 29, 35
Jew Süss, 81
Joyless Street, 32
Journey's End, 24

Karma, 26

Index of Film Titles

La Kermesse Heroique, 37
Kind Hearts and Coronets, 170

The Last Laugh, 22
The Last Outpost, 42
The Little People, 23
Lloyd of the C.I.D., 26, 54
The Lost Patrol, 47
Love is My Profession, 155
Love of Jeanne Ney, 142
Love Story, 115
Love's Option, 24
Loyalties, 48

Madeleine, 63
Madonna of the Seven Moons, 64
The Malta Story, 146
La Marseillaise, 15
Mayor of Casterbridge, 137–38
The Men in Her Life, 49
Men of Two Worlds, 1, 2, 8, 18, 45, 94, 97–118, 136, 169–72, 174
Michael Strogoff, 23
The Mikado, 52
Miss Grant Goes to the Door, 78
Monsieur Vincent, 15
Mother, 32
Mr. Preedy and the Countess, 22–23

Napoleon, 23
The New Lot, 93
The Next of Kin, 17, 18, 84–93, 102, 110, 135, 139, 169, 171, 172, 174
Night on a Bare Mountain, 28, 32
Nosferatu, 32

October, 32
On the Night of the Fire, 52, 55
One of Our Aircraft Is Missing, 91

Other People's Sins, 25–26
Overture, 154–55

Pacific 231, 32
Perfect Understanding, 44–45, 47
Pink String and Sealing Wax, 63, 170
Les Portes de la Nuit, 139
Power among Men, 153–54, 156
Prelude in C Sharp Minor, 32
The Prime Minister, 17, 79–83
The Private Life of Henry VIII, 18

Le Quai des Brumes, 37
The Queen of Spades, 1, 2, 4, 11, 17, 19, 30, 31, 32, 61, 124–33, 135, 137, 139, 140, 167, 169–70, 172, 174

Raskolnikov, 32
The Red Ground, 146–47, 149
The Red Shoes, 169

Sabotage, 143
Sanders of the River, 45
The School for Scandal, 25
Secret People, 1, 2, 3, 18, 33, 122, 124, 135–46, 155, 171, 172, 174
The Silent Passenger, 29, 39
Sing As We Go, 8, 29–30, 35
So Evil My Love, 63
Spanish ABC, 1, 8, 50–52
The Spanish Gardener, 167
The Sport of Kings, 25
Storm over Asia, 32
The Student of Prague, 131, 133

Then and Now, 122–24, 137
The Thief of Bagdad, 57
Things to Come, 77

Valse Mephistophilis, 32

The Way Ahead, 93, 99
The Way to the Stars, 99
Westward-Ho!—1940, 77
The Wicked Lady, 64
A Window in London, 52

Yesterday is over Your Shoulder, 78

General Index

Ackland, Rodney, 124
Adams, Robert, 108
Addinsell, Richard, 19
Aes, Erik, 23
Ainley, Henry, 28
Alexander, General Sir Harold, 90
Allison, George, 55
Ambler, Eric, 93
Anderson, Lindsay, 15, 138–40, 143, 171, 172, 173
Annabella, 142
Antonioni, Michelangelo, 5, 160
Armes, Roy, 169
Army Kinematograph Service, 93–94, 99–100
Arundell, Dennis, 60
Asquith, Anthony, 32, 34, 76
Asquith, Margot, 34, 69, 76
Association of Ciné-Technicians, 33–35, 48, 76, 167
Atwill, Lionel, 41, 170
Auric, Georges, 19, 127

Baker, Reg, 27, 35
Balchin, Nigel, 142, 146
Balcon, Michael, 10, 83, 89, 138–39, 143
Ball, Sir Joseph, 75–76
Banks, Leslie, 23, 53, 54, 57, 108
Barbour, Joyce, 78
Barry, Joan, 28
Bartlett, Captain Sir Basil, 84–85
Baxter, John, 12–13
Beaverbrook, Lord, 78
Beddington, Jack, 76, 98–100, 104, 110

Ben-Haim, Paul, 19, 148
Bergman, Ingrid, 71–72
Bernstein, Sidney, 31, 70, 92
Bevin, Ernest, 78
Bliss, Sir Arthur, 19, 77, 109, 114
Bokhari, Professor Ahmed, 153
Boland, Bridget, 61
Bond, Ralph, 69
Bower, Dallas, 76
Boyer, Charles, 71–72
Boys, Arthur, 124
Brand, Christianna, 139
Bresson, Robert, 5, 160
Brightwell, Ben, 147
British Film Academy, 10, 161
British Film Institute, 1, 16, 70, 159, 167
Brown, Dr. Felix, 102
Bryan, Julien, 153
Buchan, John, 24, 142
Bull, Donald, 53, 77, 78, 122
Buñuel, Luis, 160

Cahiers du Cinéma, 160
Calvert, Phyllis, 108
Carné, Marcel, 1, 5, 13, 32, 33, 65, 139, 142, 162, 172
Cary, Joyce, 100, 101, 109, 110, 111, 122, 136, 145
Cavalcanti, Alberto, 23
Chaplin, Charlie, 4
Churchill, Winston, 10, 78, 81, 90
The Ciné-Technician, 26 34, 70, 162
Clare, Mary, 87
Clark, Sir Kenneth, 76

General Index

Cloche, Maurice, 9
Cocteau, Jean, 19, 133
Cole, Sidney, 26, 28, 30, 32, 33, 35, 42, 49–51, 61–63, 70, 77, 78, 138, 143, 167, 171
Compton, Fay, 80
Cope, Captain Matthew, 33
Cortesa, Valentina, 139, 142
Cory, Hans, 18, 106, 109
Cotten, Joseph, 71
Cukor, George, 71–73

Dalrymple, Ian, 102
Dane, Clemence, 78
Dateline, 155
Davey, Eric, 105
Day, W. Percy, 106, 114
de Grunwald, Anatole, 124, 126
de la Roche, Catherine, 32, 162
de Sarigny, Peter, 146
Dean, Basil, 27, 28, 29, 39, 42
Deans, Marjorie, 122
del Giudice, Filippo 10, 99, 110, 124
Denham, Reginald, 29
Dennis, John, 109
Dickinson, Beatrice, 22
Dickinson, Charles Henry 22
Dickinson, Desmond, 77–78, 100–101, 105, 107
Dickinson, Joanna, 34, 36 100, 110–11, 147–48, 167
Dickinson, Thorold: Army Kinematograph Service, 83–94; *The Arsenal Stadium Mystery*, 52–58; *The Bright Flame*, 146; death, 167; early years and influences, 22–37; film education, 159–67; *Gaslight*, 60–73; *The High Command*, 39–48; *Hill 24 Doesn't Answer*, 146–52; *Major of Casterbridge*, 137–38; *Men of Two Worlds*, 97–118; Ministry of Information short films, 75–78; *Next of Kin*, 83–93; philosophy of film and method of work, 1–19; *The Prime Minister*, 79–83; *Queen of Spades*, 124–33; *The Red Ground*, 146–147; *Secret People*, 135–45; *Spanish ABC*, 49–52; *Then and Now*, 122–24; United Nations, 152–56
Dighton, John, 84
A Discovery of Cinema, 2, 36, 161
Dixon, Campbell, 114
Dixon, Cecil, 85
Dohnal, Mirek, 165
Donat, Robert, 93
Dovzhenko, Alexander, 34
Drisse, Gus, 127
Dunbar, Rudolph, 108
Durgnat, Raymond, 36, 143, 159–60, 169
Duvivier, Julien, 32

Ealing Studios, 27, 28, 35, 39, 41, 83–84, 138, 143–44
Eisenstein, S. M., 4, 27, 47, 133, 160, 162, 172
Ellis, John, 144–45
Elvey, Maurice, 25
Elvin, George, 33, 76
Emmett, E. V. H., 55
Ericsson, Peter, 138–39
Evans, Edith, 12, 124–25, 132
Evelyn, Judith, 60

Fairchild, William, 146
Farmer, Michael, 26
Fellini, Federico, 5, 160
Feyder, Jacques, 32
Fields, Gracie, 8, 29, 36, 100
A Film Is Made, 15, 162

General Index

The Film Society, 10, 31, 2, 33, 35, 41, 63, 68, 131, 154, 160, 172
Flaherty, Robert, 4
Frangcon-Davies, Gwen, 60
Friedman, Lester, 81
Friend, Philip, 87
Frye, Peter, 147

Galeen, Henrik, 133
Gallone, Carmine, 25
Gardner, Cyril, 27
Geray, Steven, 41
Gerhard, Roberto, 18
Gibbs, Gerald, 147, 150
Gielgud, John, 79–83
Godard, Jean-Luc, 6, 160
Goldner, Charles, 139
Goldwyn, Samuel, 10, 11
Gordon, Leslie Howard, 26
Graham, Arthur, 49–51
Grant, Elspeth, 114
Greene, Graham, 35, 47–48, 57, 101
Gribble, Leonard, 52
Grierson, John, 32, 36, 37
Griffith, D. W., 4, 160, 162
Group 3, 11–12
Guinness, Alec, 125, 146
Gwenn, Edmund, 29

Haddon, Peter, 39
Hall, Stuart, 144
Hamer, Robert, 170
Hamilton, Patrick, 3, 60, 64, 69
Hammid, Alexander, 154
Harareet, Haya, 151
Harcourt-Smith, Simon, 122
Hardwicke, Sir Cedric, 29
Hardy, Thomas, 137–38
Hare, Robertson, 78
Harman, Jympson, 48

Hawkesworth, General John, 83
Hawkins, Jack, 146
Hayman, Alan, 52
Heller, Otto, 17, 42, 126, 127, 174
Hepburn, Audrey, 139
Hess, Dame Myra, 109
Hibbert, Geoffrey, 87, 139
Hill, Sinclair, 25–26
Hiller, Wendy, 108
Hitchcock, Alfred, 68, 143
Hodge, Horace, 78
Hogan, Michael, 79
Honneger, Arthur, 32
Hoover, J. Edgar, 93
Horne, David, 118
House, Jack, 93
Howard, Leslie, 108
Howard, Trevor, 123
Howe, James Wong, 41
Huntley, John, 106, 109
Huntley, Raymond, 93
Hurst, Brian Desmond, 55, 78, 146
Huxley, Gervas, 102–3

Isaacs, Jack, 32

Jenkins, Megs, 139
Johns, Mervyn, 87, 89
Johnson, Nunnally, 92
Jouvet, Louis, 142
Joyce, Eileen, 109

Kauffer, E. McKnight, 28, 31, 32
Kimberley, Paul, 99, 100
Kirwan, Patrick, 53, 58
Knowles, Bernard, 17, 68
Koch, Howard, 14, 15
Kolitz, Zvi, 147
Korda, Alexander, 10, 11, 45, 57–58

Lambert, Gavin, 139, 151
Lauder, Harry, 24
Lawson, Alan, 34, 49, 59
Leacock, Philip, 49
Leahy, James, 145, 164–66
Lean, David, 4, 169
Lee, Rowland V., 26
Lejeune, C. A., 70, 82, 91, 140
Levy, Don, 159
Lewis, Jay, 93
Lindren, Ernest, 122
Loder, John, 29
Lye, Len, 32
Lubitsch, Ernst, 92

Mace, Nigel, 81
Mackenzie, Compton, 10
MacNeice, Louis, 100
MacPhail, Angus, 84, 102
Macrae, Henry, 54
Makumbi, Eseza, 109
Malle, Louis, 6
Mannheim, Lucie, 41
Mansfield, Duncan, 25
Manvell, Roger, 15, 162
Maris, Mona, 23
Martins, Orlando, 108, 118
Marwick, Arthur, 163–64
Mason, James, 41, 170
Mass Observation, 91
Mathieson, Muir, 109
Maugham, W. Somerset, 122
Mendleson, Anthony, 143
Messel, Oliver, 125, 132
Millar, Gavin, 162
Mills, Reginald, 93
Ministry of Information, 12, 36, 70, 75–78, 90, 92, 98–118
Mitchell, Yvonne, 125–32
Montagu, Ivor, 31–33, 35, 49
Morahan, Tom, 18, 85, 100–101, 105, 106, 114

Morgan, Sidney, 25
Motion Picture Association of America, 123
Movie, 165
Mulhare, Edward, 147, 151
Mullally, Frederic, 114
Murnau, F. W., 131
Murray, Stephen, 87

Nesbitt, Cathleen, 118
Newton, Robert, 60
Noble, Peter, 111
Norton, Captain Hon. Richard, 26, 52, 57
Nunn May, R., 103

Oberon, Merle, 57
Olivier, Laurence, 10, 27–28
Ondra, Anny, 68

Pabst, G. W., 142
Padovani, Lea, 139
Palmer, Ernest, 85–86
Pearson, George, 22–25
Pearson, Malcolm, 22
Perier, Francois, 139
Pettingell, Frank, 60
Pickthorn, Kenneth, 10
Pilbeam, Nova, 87
Pitt, Ray, 32, 49, 86
Polidoro, Gian Luigi, 154
Pontecorvo, Lisa, 164
Portman, Eric, 108, 170
Powell, Dilys, 82, 90, 114, 132
Powell, Michael, 4, 114–15, 169–70
Pressburger, Arnold, 123
Pressburger, Emeric, 114
Prévert, Jacques, 13
Price, Vincent, 60
Pudovkin, V. I., 34, 162

General Index

Radford, Basil, 88
Rank, J. Arthur, 111, 124, 146, 159
Ratoff, Gregory, 49
Rawlinson, A. R., 61
Redgrave, Michael, 108
Reed, Carol, 93–94
Reggiani, Serge, 33, 139, 142
Reiniger, Lotte, 32
Reisz, Karel, 15, 139, 162
Renoir, Jean, 4, 9, 32, 86, 142, 160, 172
Resnais, Alain, 7, 160
Richardson, Ralph, 29, 108
Robertson, E. Arnot, 98, 99, 100, 102, 103, 104
Robey, George, 29
Robson, Flora, 146
Rogers, James E., 40
Rosi, Francesco, 5
Rossell, Deac, 171
Rotha, Paul, 69
Ruben, J. Walter, 29

Sabine, Noel, 98, 104
Salt, Barry, 33
Sanders, George, 123
Sarris, Andrew, 72–73
Saville, Victor, 25
Screen, 144–45
Seago, John, 40
Selznick, David O., 69, 79, 92
Sequence, 15, 139
Sight and Sound, 13, 15, 139, 145, 162, 165
Singh, Krishna, 154
Slade Film History Register, 162–64
Solanke, Ladipo, 104
Somlo, Josef, 52, 55
Soviet Cinema, 32, 162
St. John, Earl, 10

Stallich, Jan, 29, 41
Stanmore, Frank, 23
Stead, Peter, 161
Steel, Anthony, 146
Sternberg, Josef von, 57
Stroheim, Eric von, 4, 160
Strueby, Katherine, 40
Sutherland, Duncan, 18, 62, 69
Sutro, John, 100, 108
Swanson, Gloria, 26–27

Tanner, Alain, 155
Tate, Reginald, 87, 139
Taylor, A. J. P., 162
The Technique of Film Editing, 15
Tennant, Pauline, 124
Thompson, Peggy, 48
Thompson, Virgil, 154
Thorpe, Frances, 163–64
Two Cities Films, 10, 93, 94, 99, 104, 122, 124, 136

Ustinov, Peter, 93–94

Veidt, Conrad, 49
Vernon, Richard, 100, 101, 105
Vicas, Victor, 153
Victor, Herbert, 101

Walbrook, Anton, 31, 60, 62–63, 66–69, 72, 124, 131–32, 169
Walton, William, 18, 86
Wavell, Earl, 110
Wayne, Naunton, 28, 88
Wellesley, Gordon, 39–42
West, Rebecca, 10
Whale, James, 129
Whitebait, William, 91, 116
Wilcox, Herbert, 25
Wilhelm, Wolfgang, 137
Wilkinson, Ellen, 32, 70
Wilkinson, Hazel, 126

Williams, Brock, 79
Winnington, Richard, 114
Wood, Sir Henry, 29
Wright, Basil, 32, 48
Wyler, William, 14, 150
Wynyard, Diana, 60, 66, 67, 69, 72

Young, Freddie, 93
Yule, Lady, 60, 70

Zavattini, Cesare, 5

About the Author

Jeffrey Richards is professor of cultural history at Lancaster University. He has published extensively on British cinema. Among his recent works are *Britain Can Take It: British Films and the Second World War* (1994), *Films and British National Identity* (1997), and *The Unknown 1930s* (1997).